Enhanced Test Automation with WebdriverIO

Unlock the superpowers of hybrid testing frameworks

Paul M. Grossman

Larry C. Goddard

BIRMINGHAM—MUMBAI

Enhanced Test Automation with WebdriverIO

Group Product Manager: Kunal Sawant

Book Project Manager: Prajakta Naik

Senior Editor: Kinnari Chohan

Technical Editor: Jubit Pincy

Copy Editor: Safis Editing

Indexer: Rekha Nair

Production Designer: Prashant Ghare

DevRel Marketing Coordinator: Sonia Chauhan

First published: December 2023

Production reference: 2281123

Published by Packt Publishing Ltd.

Grosvenor House

11 St Paul's Square

Birmingham

B3 1RB, UK

ISBN 978-1-83763-018-9

www.packtpub.com

To my wife, Mickey, for her unending love, support, and encouragement in all our crazy endeavors. To my son, Kyle, who always chooses the more challenging road.

– Paul M. Grossman

Dedicated to the memory of my mother, Yvonne, my dad, Kent Cuffy, and my best friends, Raul Cambridge, Randolph Yearwood, and Glen Smart, whose sacrifices and unwavering determination have profoundly shaped me into the person I am today. I extend profound gratitude to my partner, Deniele St. Bernard, for unwaveringly and steadfastly walking by my side throughout our shared life journey. A heartfelt acknowledgment goes to my children—Lee-Ann and Leland "Bobby" Goddard, Leshem "Pumpkin" Stafford, Tyrell John and Sacha Mc Kinnon—the stabilizing influence in my life and the driving force behind my continually expanding technical inquisitiveness.

– Larry C. Goddard

Foreword

In *Enhanced Test Automation with WebdriverIO*, you'll embark on an exciting journey through the lens of a **Software Development Engineer in Test (SDET)** - a role that, quite frankly, is often an unsung hero in software delivery. This book highlights the SDET Superhero in a comic book narrative while sharing the tips and tricks that unlock the superpowers of a successful SDET.

The journey of an SDET is depicted as akin to a superhero's path, full of challenges, learning, and growth. The superhero analogies used are not mere entertainment; they transform abstract concepts into tangible skills and knowledge.

As someone devoted to making complex technical concepts accessible and engaging, I find this book's approach not only refreshing but incredibly effective. It makes the learning process both enjoyable and impactful, adding a layer of relatability to topics that might otherwise seem daunting.

For aspiring and established SDETs, this book serves as an essential collection of armor - filled with tools, insights, and practical strategies. It skillfully guides you from the basics of test environment setup to the complexities of advanced testing techniques. The book's practical application of WebdriverIO in TypeScript offers hands-on experience that is beneficial for readers at all levels.

I invite you to delve into this book with an eagerness to learn. Prepare to navigate the exhilarating path of an SDET, equipped with newfound skills and a deeper understanding of test automation techniques.

Welcome to a journey that promises to be as informative as it is engaging.

-Angie Jones

Vice President of Developer Relations

Contributors

About the authors

Paul M. Grossman, aka @DarkArtsWizard on X and Threads, is a test automation framework architect, project manager, and conference speaker with a love of stage magic. Since 2001, he has worked with numerous toolsets, including WebdriverIO in TypeScript, Selenium in Java, OpenText UFT in VBScript, and WinRunner in C++. He advocates for low-code automation tools for manual testers, including testRigor. He is also the creator of the CandyMapper sandbox website, where he invites novice users to try their hand at automating common challenges. You can find videos of his test automation experiments on his YouTube channel at `https://www.youtube.com/PaulGrossmanTheDarkArtsWizard`.

I extend thanks to my high school coding teacher, Mrs. O'Toole, who awarded exam points for "Syntax Error in Line 20" when I found a misspelled "Print" statement; Rebecca, who took a chance on my automation skills after catching my One-Handed Knotted Rope stunt in the test lab; Mike, who encouraged me to present with fire on stage in Las Vegas; Tarun for his inspiring QTP Unplugged books; and Larry for saving me from the Lone Ranger issues.

Larry C. Goddard, aka "LarryG," is the creator of Klassi-js. He boasts a stellar career as an award-winning test automation framework architect, mentor, career coach, and speaker since 2000. His expertise spans diverse toolsets, including AI, ML, WebdriverIO, JavaScript, TypeScript, and Selenium. With a profound journey across aviation, software testing, and telecommunications sectors, he has also lent his technical prowess to a major fashion house and served as an expert witness for an international law firm. A father of five, an ex-international rugby player for Trinidad and Tobago, ex-military, and a certified physical training instructor, he shares his extensive knowledge via insightful test automation videos on `https://youtube.com/@larryg_01`.

I'm truly grateful to my loving and supportive partner, Deniele, and my children—Lee-Ann, Leland, Leshem, Tyrell, and Sacha—for their unwavering encouragement and support during the book's creation. To my co-author, Paul, for entrusting me with the crucial coding task, a vital component of this book. A special shout-out to my siblings, Gillian, Phillip, Bertrand, Orlando, and Clint, and my beloved niece, Joanna Levine—she knows!!

About the reviewers

Panagiotis Leloudas is a lead quality assurance engineer with more than 10 years of working experience in the industry. He holds several ISTQB certifications and is an expert in testing principles methodologies and techniques. He is also the author of the book *Introduction to Software Testing*.

Ekansh Mehrotra is an analytical, enthusiastic, and innovative consultant with 14+ years of IT experience in management, consulting, implementation, manual and automation testing, and framework designing and development. He has strong experience in the Agile and Waterfall methodologies, Azure DevOps, and automation framework design, development, and testing using various tools. He has good experience in managing critical project deliveries and team projects.

Table of Contents

5

Alter Egos – The ClickAdv Wrapper   81

6

The setValue Wrapper – Entering Text and Dynamic Data Replacement   103

7

The Select Wrapper – Choosing Values in Lists and Comboboxes   119

8

The Assert Wrapper – the Importance of Embedded Details   129

9

The Ancient Spell Book – Building the Page Object Model   141

10

Increased Flexibility – Writing Robust Selectors and Reducing Maintenance   153

11

Echo Location – Skipping the Page Object Model   173

14

The Time-Traveler's Dilemma – State-Driven End to End User Journeys
219

15

The Sentient Cape – Running Tests in a CI/CD Pipeline with Jenkins and LambdaTest
237

Appendix

The Ultimate Guide to TypeScript Error Messages, Causes, and Solutions

Preface

Welcome, and let us embark on an extraordinary journey through the realm of coding with our superhero-themed technical manual! Bid farewell to the mundane as each chapter unfolds like an exciting comic book adventure. Unlike traditional superheroes, you won't need a brush with a radioactive arachnid to unlock your coding powers. Instead, you will arm yourself with the essential tools to forge a formidable framework using WebdriverIO in TypeScript.

For those stepping into the shoes of a **Software Developer Engineer in Test** (**SDET**), the allure of leaping into setting up your JavaScript coding environment, running that inaugural test, and hoping for a victorious pass result might be strong. We've been there, only to discover later that crucial tools were overlooked, tools that could have smoothed the path from the very beginning. That's why the opening chapter dives into system specifications, tools, and configurations, laying the foundation for crafting superior code from day one.

Prepare to be guided by the wisdom of authors who have spent over 20 years in the superhero league of SDETs. Discover tips, tricks, rules of thumb, and advanced techniques tailored to help you not only write more tests but also navigate debugging challenges with finesse. Elevate your testing framework to superhero status—stable, scalable, and requiring minimal code maintenance. Get ready to unleash your coding superpowers and make your mark in the coding superhero universe!

Who this book is for

This book serves as a superhero toolkit for test automation enthusiasts at all levels, from new recruits to seasoned champions in the digital realm. It empowers users with the superpowers of WebdriverIO with Jasmine in TypeScript, offering an arsenal of code examples, advanced strategies in Jenkins, and cloud-based automation tactics. Whether you're just been bitten by the automation bug in the world of test automation or you're a caped veteran looking to upgrade your utility belt gadgets, this book is your secret weapon to mastering the art of test automation.

What this book covers

Chapter 1, *The Utility Belt – Tools Every Superhero SDET Needs*, provides an overview of the initial preparation tools that need to be installed, including Node, Yarn, and the VS Code IDE configurations.

Chapter 2, *Fortress of Solitude – Configuring WebdriverIO*, covers setting up the project workspace folder with an overview of the WDIO install options to run our first test.

Chapter 3, Cybernetic Enhancements – WebdriverIO Config and Debug Tips, provides an in-depth look at the package file and WDIO configuration options for both Mac and Windows with the concept of a function wrapper for enhanced logging.

Chapter 4, Super Speed – Time Travel Paradoxes and Broken Promises, provides an in-depth look at the challenges of multi-threaded execution that are resolved with async and await commands.

Chapter 5, Alter Egos – Why Do We Need Function Wrappers?, introduces the helpers file, the Switchboard object, a smart `click()` wrapper that leverages the `pageSync()` function and resolves speed-related timing issues.

Chapter 6, The setValue Wrapper – Entering Text and Dynamic Data Replacement, introduces the `setValue()` wrapper with dynamic data tags, which provides offset dates in multiple formatting.

Chapter 7, The Select Wrapper – Choosing Values in Lists and Combo Boxes, introduces the `select()` wrapper, which handles multiple types of drop-down elements and advanced scrolling to avoid object overlap errors.

Chapter 8, The Assert Wrapper – The Importance of Embedded Details, introduces a wrapper for soft asserts with custom Allure reporting with screenshots.

Chapter 9, The Ancient Spell Book – Building the Page Object Model, introduces page classes with xPath and CSS locators and atomic actions.

Chapter 10, Increased Flexibility – Writing Robust Selectors and Reducing Maintenance, provides a deep dive into advanced xPath tips and self-healing strategies to reduce maintenance.

Chapter 11, Echo Location – Skipping the Page Object Model, enhances the three basic actions to find elements by text alone with a relative element location.

Chapter 12, Superhero Landing – Setting Up Flexible Navigation Options, introduces concepts for running tests in different test environments where elements may have been removed or do not yet exist without failing.

Chapter 13, The Multiverses – Cross-Browser and Cross-Environment Testing, provides an introduction to the risks and rewards of expanding coverage with horizontal testing of multiple operating systems and browsers.

Chapter 14, The Time Traveler's Dilemma – State-Driven End-to-End User Journeys, discusses advanced concepts to create end-to-end tests that do not rely on any specific page following another with custom decision points and error detection.

Chapter 15, The Sentient Cape – Running Tests in a CI/CD Pipeline with Jenkins and LambdaTest, brings test automation back to the manual testers who can call for complex artifacts to be produced in the cloud with a simple descriptive statement and access video capture replay.

Appendix, The Ultimate Guide to TypeScript Error Messages, Causes, and Solutions, provides an extensive collection of error messages, potential causes, and solutions gathered from years of project development.

To get the most out of this book

Software covered in the book	Operating system requirements
WebdriverIO v.8	Windows, macOS, or Linux
TypeScript v.5.1.6	
Java JDK @latest	
Node v.18	
Yarn @latest	
Git @latest	
GitHub Desktop latest version	GUI frontend for GitHub and GitLab
SelectorsHub 5.0 free edition	Chrome extension
EditThisCookie	Chrome extension
VS Code	
Belarc Advisor Profiler (optional) free, single, personal-use license	Windows only

The authors have attempted to use freely available tools for readers' benefit. There are other paid IDEs available that offer more coding features to make life easier. In addition, the free version of SelectorsHub does an exceptional job, but we recommend the paid Pro version for its advanced Shadow Dom features. Free GitHub accounts are public while paid repos are private.

If you are using the digital version of this book, we advise you to type the code yourself or access the code from the book's GitHub repository (a link is available in the next section). Doing so will help you avoid any potential errors related to the copying and pasting of code.

If you are new to test automation, we advise you to get machines equivalent to, or better than, the specification used by the product development team you will be supporting. There is a common misconception that automation is just "record and playback" and does not require heavy-duty resources. There is one simple fact to keep in mind: parallel browsers and virtual machine testing require more resources.

Download the example code files

You can download the example code files for this book from GitHub at `https://github.com/PacktPublishing/Enhanced-Test-Automation-with-WebdriverIO`. If there's an update to the code, it will be updated in the GitHub repository.

We also have other code bundles from our rich catalog of books and videos available at `https://github.com/PacktPublishing/`. Check them out!

Conventions used

There are a number of text conventions used throughout this book.

`Code in text`: Indicates code words in text, database table names, folder names, filenames, file extensions, pathnames, dummy URLs, user input, and Twitter handles. Here is an example: "We have a `host` command and a `ghost` party. Writing this line of code could potentially take the `host` command from the `ghost` string."

A block of code is set as follows:

```
Set JOURNEY="Attend Ghost"; yarn ch15
if (journey.includes(" host").toLowerCase()) {
// Host path being taken in error.
}
```

Any command-line input or output is written as follows:

```
[0-0] ---> Clicking button[type="submit"] ...
[0-0] ---> button clicked.
[0-0] ---> pageSync() completed in 25 ms
[0-0] ---> Clicking button[type="bogus"] ...
[0-0] ---> button[type="submit"] was not clicked.
[0-0] Error: Can't call click on element with selector
"button[type="bogus"]" because element wasn't found
```

Bold: Indicates a new term, an important word, or words that you see onscreen. For instance, words in menus or dialog boxes appear in **bold**. Here is an example: "In this example, the user does not attend the party and instead clicks the **I'm scared** button."

> **Tips or important notes**
> Appear like this.

Get in touch

Feedback from our readers is always welcome.

General feedback: If you have questions about any aspect of this book, email us at `customercare@packtpub.com` and mention the book title in the subject of your message.

Errata: Although we have taken every care to ensure the accuracy of our content, mistakes do happen. If you have found a mistake in this book, we would be grateful if you would report this to us. Please visit `www.packtpub.com/support/errata` and fill in the form.

Piracy: If you come across any illegal copies of our works in any form on the internet, we would be grateful if you would provide us with the location address or website name. Please contact us at `copyright@packtpub.com` with a link to the material.

If you are interested in becoming an author: If there is a topic that you have expertise in and you are interested in either writing or contributing to a book, please visit `authors.packtpub.com`.

Share Your Thoughts

Once you've read *Enhanced Test Automation with WebdriverIO*, we'd love to hear your thoughts! Scan the QR code below to go straight to the Amazon review page for this book and share your feedback.

https://packt.link/r/1837630186

Your review is important to us and the tech community and will help us make sure we're delivering excellent quality content.

Download a free PDF copy of this book

Thanks for purchasing this book!

Do you like to read on the go but are unable to carry your print books everywhere? Is your eBook purchase not compatible with the device of your choice?

Don't worry, now with every Packt book you get a DRM-free PDF version of that book at no cost.

Read anywhere, any place, on any device. Search, copy, and paste code from your favorite technical books directly into your application.

The perks don't stop there, you can get exclusive access to discounts, newsletters, and great free content in your inbox daily

Follow these simple steps to get the benefits:

1.   Scan the QR code or visit the link below

https://packt.link/free-ebook/978-1-83763-018-9

2.   Submit your proof of purchase
3.   That's it! We'll send your free PDF and other benefits to your email directly

1

The Utility Belt – Tools Every Superhero SDET Needs

This is not your ordinary technical manual, which can be dry and boring. This book is intended to be fun. That's why many of the chapters share a comic book theme. But unlike some superheroes, you won't need to be bitten by a radioactive arachnid to get these powers. We just need some tools to create a great framework using WebdriverIO in TypeScript.

If you are just beginning your journey as a **software developer engineer in test** (**SDET**), you might be tempted to just skip ahead, install the TypeScript coding environment, run your first test, and hopefully see a **Pass** result. I've done that myself, only to realize later there were some tools I missed that could have helped make the journey easier from the start. That is why this first chapter speaks to the system specifications, tools, and configurations that will help us write better code from day one.

Along the way, I'll be providing tips and tricks from more than 20 years as an SDET. There will be rules of thumb and advanced techniques. These are designed to help you write more tests, debug more efficiently, and produce a testing framework that will be stable, scalable, and require far less code maintenance.

The main topics covered in this chapter are:

- The Virgin machine setup
- Installing Visual Studio Code for your operating system
- Writing better code with Prettier, ESLint, and GitLens
- Installing Chrome extensions
- Installing WebdriverIO

Virgin machine setup

Before you can do anything in the world of test automation on a virgin machine, you must install some packages, so you will need admin rights to the machine. So, before going any further, please ensure you have the following packages installed globally with their most stable version:

- NodeJS
- Yarn
- Java JDK
- An **integrated development environment** (IDE) (IntelliJ, VSCode, and so on)
- Git

Here are some extra steps if you are using a Windows machine:

- Set up the PATH environment for your node
- Reboot the machine for all the changes to take effect

Before we get to running our first test, we need to check out system requirements and get our tools. In this chapter, we're going to cover how to install and configure tools that will make our job easier, as follows:

- **Hardware specifications**
- **Node.js**
- **A GitHub account** and **GitHub Desktop** for code change management
- **Microsoft Visual Studio Code**
- **Prettier**, **GitLens**, and **ESLint extensions**
- The **SelectorsHub** and **EditThisCookie** Chrome extensions

Note that to install these tools, you will need local admin rights or know someone in your IT security department who has the rights and can install them for you. Without local admin rights, you won't get far. You should have the same rights as the product development team, whose applications you will be testing.

This brings us to our first rule of thumb.

Rule of thumb – the hardware resources and access rights must match the development team

Throughout this book, I will be bringing up some rules of thumb that I use to keep us on the path and out of the thorn bushes.

Let's talk about why this is important. Upfront, you can assess if your automation project will succeed just by considering if you can install Chrome extensions. If your corporate IT security department prevents the installation of any browser extensions, your automation progress will be severely hindered. We all want to have a successful test automation project. We do not want to start our journey hamstrung. *Test automation is code development; it requires developer tools, and you are a developer.* Do not let anyone tell you differently.

If your employer or client sees your project as just record and playback, you are at risk of having a project that is doomed to fail from the start. The biggest red flag that this is the case is that your computer resources and access do not match that of your developers.

Question: What are the technical spec requirements for my WebdriverIO test automation system?

The answer is a simple *Do* and *Do not*:

Do not use the minimum requirements listed anywhere on the internet. Whatever it is, it is too small.

Do match the CPU speed, the amount of RAM, the drive space, and the number of monitors on desks.

This includes matching the version of the Mac or Windows operating system used by the development team. Windows should be 64-bit and probably the Professional edition.

It also includes the local admin rights of your application developers. This allows you to install browser extensions that will save your team time. This means you might have to propose a business case to meet this requirement.

It is simple, really: without these tools, you will spend time trying to write locators by hand and taking extra steps to clear cookies. The project will go slower, and the company will pay more for fewer tests in the same amount of time. In extreme cases, you may have to walk away from a project and find a new employer who is ready to take QA testing seriously. The only exception is if your application developers are using Eclipse, which is not recommended for professional-level code development.

That said, let's begin by installing the tools for WebdriverIO so that we're heading in the right direction.

We will start by emulating two heroes who have unlimited wealth and brilliant minds. To be effective at fighting crime, one has a utility belt with multiple tools and the other a metal suit with AI intelligence to help bring villains—or, in our case, bugs—to justice faster.

Installing Node.js and npm

Node.js is an open source, cross-platform runtime environment and an asynchronous library that is used for running web applications outside the client's browser. This project was created with Node version 16.13.0 for several reasons. Earlier versions were only required to support synchronous mode, which was deprecated in WebDriverIO 7.0 and removed in version 8.0. While the latest version of Node as of this writing is 19.8.1, it is recommended to use 16.13.0 as it is the most compatible with most other modules and packages.

Make sure you have enough hard drive space for the installation. It will take a minimum of 3 GB to install. By default, these tools are installed on the C: drive. If your drive is nearing capacity, consider installing it on a larger drive partition.

Let's begin by installing Node and npm. The following screenshot shows how you can do this:

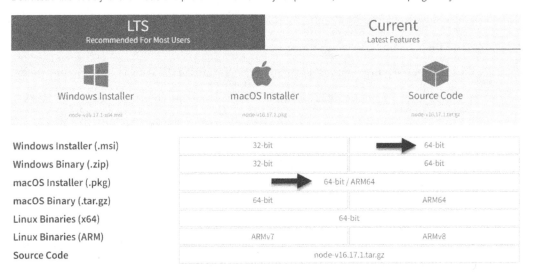

Figure 1.1 – Downloading Node.js from https://nodejs.org/en/download/

For Mac, install the latest .pkg file.

For Windows, download the 64-bit version.

The version of Node.js to install will be **long-term support** (**LTS**), which is version 18.0 as of this writing. Note that WebdriverIO deprecated the @wdio/sync *synchronous mode*, which is supported and stable only through Node.js version 12.0. This book will use asynchronous command execution with the async() and await() commands.

The installation will also install the following:

- **Chocolatey** for Windows or **Brew** for Mac, a package installation tool
- **Python**
- **Node.js**
- **npm**
- **Required system updates**

> Reminder
>
> These all will require admin rights to complete successfully.

Once completed, check whether the Node.js and Chocolatey paths have been added to the system's PATH environment variables, as illustrated in the following screenshot. If not, they must be added manually:

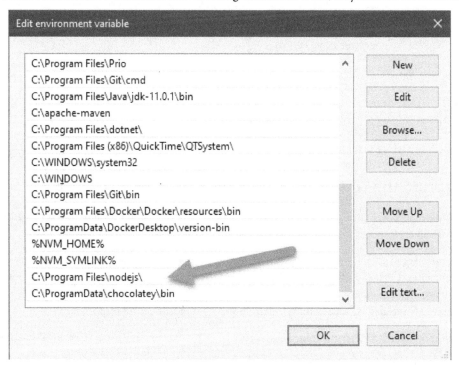

Figure 1.2 – Node.js and Chocolatey paths in the PATH environment variable for Windows

For both Mac and Windows, we will install a version of Node that is at least version 18.0. From the command shell, type these two commands:

```
> nvm install 18
Downloading node.js version 18.17.1 (64-bit)...
> nvm use 18
Now using node v18.17.1 (64-bit)
```

While this completes the Node installation, we need to take note of alternative package managers that offer additional options.

Alternate node package managers – Yarn versus npm

While npm is the default node package manager provided, we recommend using Yarn to both install packages and run programs. One major advantage of Yarn is that it installs packages in parallel. This reduces the build time significantly when initializing or refreshing the package.json file.

Again, from the command shell type the following:

```
> npm install --global yarn
```

After installing Yarn, you can verify the installation by running the following command:

```
> yarn --version
1.19.22
```

With that complete, we will now decide where our project will live.

Configuring the coding environment with GitHub Desktop

In upcoming chapters, we will dive deeper into Git and GitHub for code versioning. But it is good to plan, so we will create a Git folder structure for our projects.

Our wdio project workspace will live in a Git **repository** (**repo**) folder that holds your projects at the root of your largest drive, preferably not the Windows C: drive. The reason is that Node.js projects rely on many supporting packages. These will take up a significant amount of additional space in the node_modules folder. At some point, the drive will be filled, affecting responsiveness.

Let's begin by creating a \repos folder at the root of our drive, or on the desktop on Mac, to hold our projects:

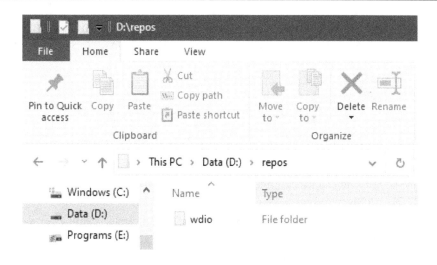

Figure 1.3 – Sample repository and project directory structure

Our project will live inside a local repository named \wdio. This is where we will create a place where our files will be stored. Later, we will use code repositories for version control, such as **GitHub**, **GitLab**, and **Bitbucket**. For this book, we will use GitHub, and GitHub Desktop will be our code-commit tool.

GitHub and the GitHub Desktop tool

One tool all developers require is code version control. It will be a requirement for any team you join, and they will expect you to know Git commands. Learning the syntax and commands can pose a challenge for new coders. Mistakes typed at the Command Prompt can occur at any point, and knowing how to resolve these issues can be a bigger challenge.

However, there is an easier approach that will make life better. Using the **GitHub Desktop** tool for code commits gives a visual insight into code changes. You can examine the Git commands it uses to learn to use the Terminal window with fewer errors.

First, we need a GitHub account.

Getting a GitHub account

Go to www.github.com and click **Sign up**. Enter an email, a password, and a username, and verify your account.

During the account setup process, select the **Automation and CI/CD** option. This configures the project for executions that can be triggered automatically at certain times of the day or week:

Figure 1.4 – Automation and CI/CD configuration

We now have a free public GitHub account to practice commits and version control. Now, go to your GitHub page and create a wdio repository with a README file. Note that free GitHub accounts are public. When working in a professional capacity, it is always best that you or your employer acquire a paid plan to make the repository private:

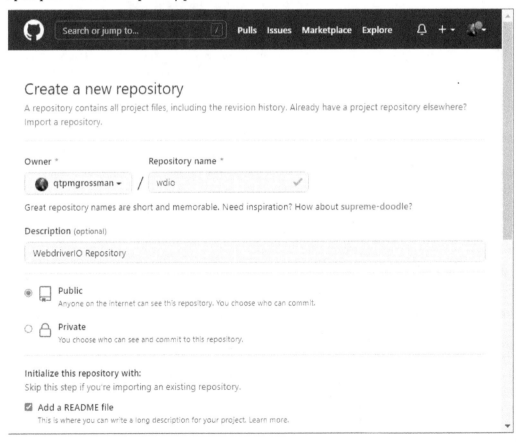

Figure 1.5 – Initializing the wdio project repository with a README file from GitHub

We now have our GitHub account dashboard. It gives suggestions for additional tools to install:

Figure 1.6 – Links in GitHub to install GitHub Desktop and Visual Studio Code

From here, we will add GitHub Desktop and the Visual Studio Code IDE. First, we'll install GitHub Desktop.

Installing GitHub Desktop

Download GitHub Desktop from `https://desktop.github.com/`.

The installation of GitHub Desktop is very straightforward. Simply download the installer for your operating system and launch it. Once the process is complete, GitHub Desktop will launch:

Figure 1.7 – Downloading GitHub Desktop for your operating system

If you have ever seen a beginner's command-line video for Git, learning all the arcane commands may send a shiver down your spine. It might spark fear that the team project could be broken if your changes are committed without pulling changes from other team members first. That is why a GUI for beginners is a better choice over a printed Git cheat sheet – it prevents mistakes while learning Git commands. Here's an example:

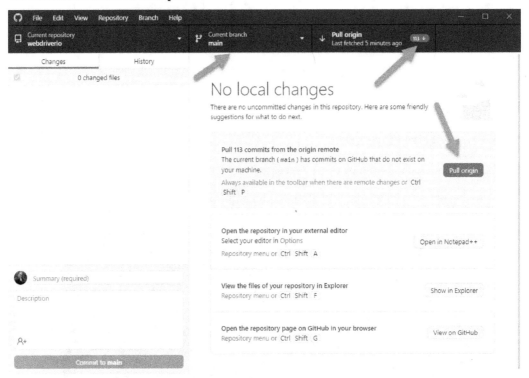

Figure 1.8 – GitHub Desktop showing pending changes that should be pulled before a commit action

A tool with a graphical interface is recommended for both speed and accuracy over the command-line interface. In the preceding example, we know we are in the main branch of the webdriverio repo with changes committed to the project from other team members, and a large blue **Pull origin** button reminds us to pull in the changes other team members have committed first. Skipping this step can revert the code changes, causing trouble.

GitHub Desktop's **History** view supplies descriptions of those recent commits. It tells us which files were changed and the differences between the old and new lines of code:

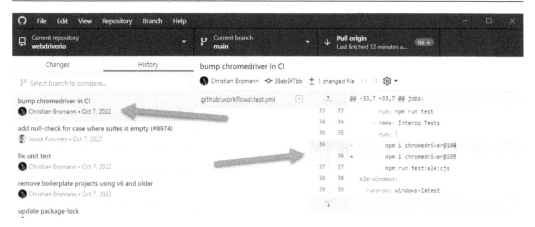

Figure 1.9 – GitHub Desktop's History view showing old and new code changes

Performing a code commit with a single click of a button is faster than typing into a Terminal window. We will link our project shortly. Next, we'll install our coding environment tool.

Choosing your TypeScript development environment – Microsoft Visual Studio Code versus JetBrains Aqua

In this journey of developing a robust framework, we need to make many decisions, and one of those is which IDE will be used to write and run our code. My personal preference would be to use Visual Studio Code because it is easier to code on multiple views.

However, as of this writing, JetBrains Aqua only supports breakpoints when a script is launched from a configuration. It does not pause at breakpoints when a test script is launched from the embedded Terminal window. This is the way we will run our WebdriverIO scripts. Visual Studio Code will be the tool of choice for these projects since it is open source, but I still recommend that you try JetBrains Aqua for its superior code interface design.

Microsoft Visual Studio Code is the free IDE for this book and has a strong company backing it up. However, many free tools lack an income stream to support either a development team or a product support team. Free tools can be years behind paid tools in functionality. Take, for example, Selenium, which introduced relative element location in version 4.0, which was released in May 2019. The same feature was part of most paid toolsets, including Micro Focus **Unified Functional Testing** (UFT), which goes as far back as 2010.

Installing Visual Studio Code for your operating system

Download Visual Studio Code from `https://code.visualstudio.com/download`.

Follow the installation process for your operating system. Again, the recommendation is to have these tools installed on a larger drive above the `\repos` directory.

Now that Visual Studio has been installed, we can check that Node and npm have been installed from the embedded Terminal shell window.

From the main menu, select **Terminal** > **New Terminal** and press *Ctrl + Shift* for Windows and ^ + *Shift* + ` for Mac.

The Terminal shell for launching tests is up to your personal choice. **PowerShell** is recommended for Windows users, **ZSH** is recommended for Mac users, and **Git Bash** is great for command-line Git users. But for debugging, **JavaScript Debug Terminal** is required on both platforms.

From the Terminal window, click the **v** down arrow next to the + button in the lower-right corner, select **JavaScript Debug Terminal**, and type the following:

```
node -v
npm -v
```

The system will respond with the versions of Node and npm you have installed:

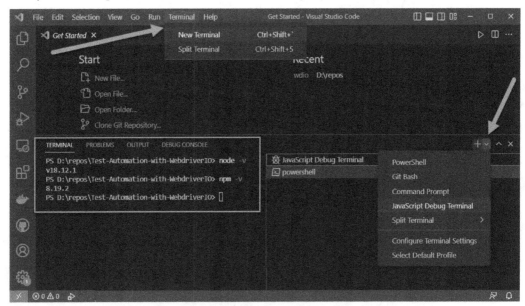

Figure 1.10 – Checking the Node and npm versions you have installed
from the embedded Terminal shell in Visual Studio Code

Note that JavaScript Debug Terminal will run slower than the PowerShell or Bash shells, so it's best to only use it when we need to stop at a breakpoint for debugging. Next, we will initialize our project from Visual Studio Code.

Initializing the Node project

Now that we have installed Visual Studio Code and created our project workspace directory, we can check that Node has been installed and initialize our project. From the Terminal, navigate to the / repos/wdio folder and type the following command:

```
npm init -y
```

This will create a new Node package.json file with default configurations:

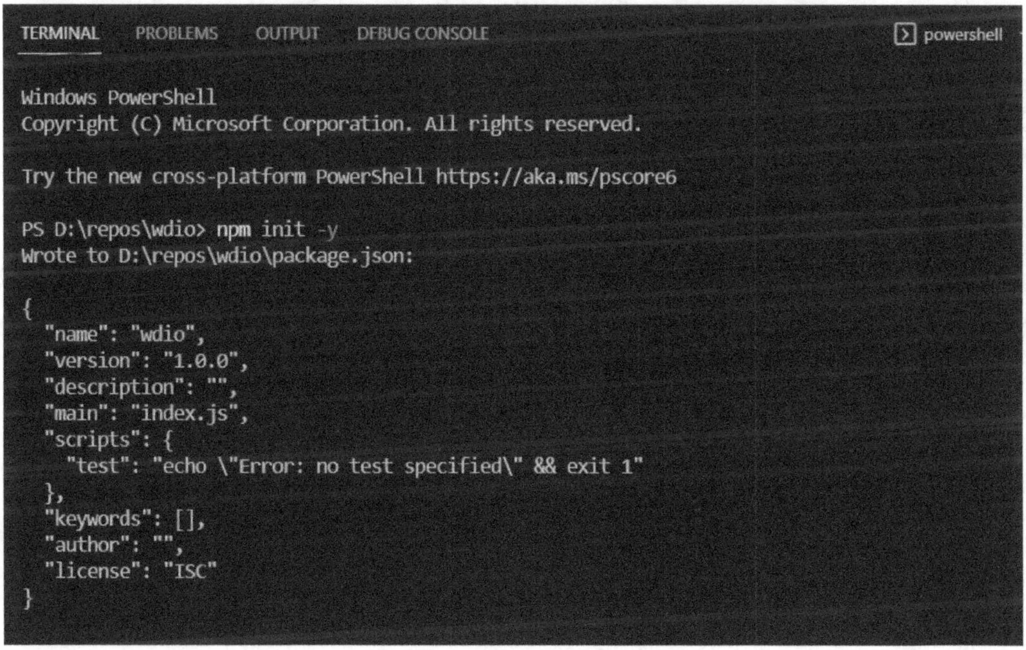

```
TERMINAL     PROBLEMS     OUTPUT     DEBUG CONSOLE                                    [>] powershell

Windows PowerShell
Copyright (C) Microsoft Corporation. All rights reserved.

Try the new cross-platform PowerShell https://aka.ms/pscore6

PS D:\repos\wdio> npm init -y
Wrote to D:\repos\wdio\package.json:

{
  "name": "wdio",
  "version": "1.0.0",
  "description": "",
  "main": "index.js",
  "scripts": {
    "test": "echo \"Error: no test specified\" && exit 1"
  },
  "keywords": [],
  "author": "",
  "license": "ISC"
}
```

Figure 1.11 – Initializing the Node package.json file

This file keeps track of all the supporting Node packages that WebdriverIO uses to build and automate tests.

Now that we have our first project file, next, we will configure our editor settings to make coding less error-prone.

Configuring Visual Studio Code

The first change is when Visual Studio Code will save files. By default, implicit saves do not occur when changing from the code window to the Terminal. Since our tests will be launched from the Terminal, we want to ensure the latest version of the code is executed. Here's how we can configure this:

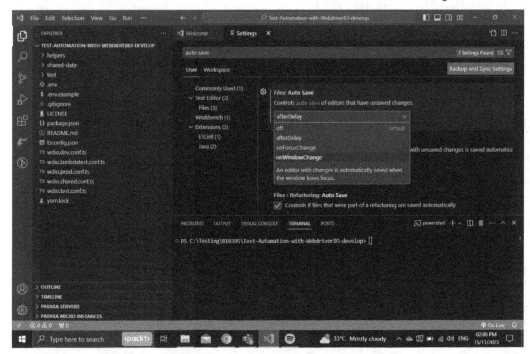

Figure 1.12 – Setting Visual Studio Code to save files when the focus changes to the Terminal window

Go to **File** | **Preferences** | **Settings** and type `auto save`.

Change the setting from **afterDelay** to **onWindowChange**.

This will ensure code is saved when switching from the code console to the Terminal console. This avoids a common issue where the code is updated, but the results that are shown were executed with the unchanged code.

X-ray vision – writing better code with Prettier, ESLint, and GitLens

Developers need coding tools that help them efficiently write code that is formatted correctly, follow good coding practices, and know when team members make code changes. This is where Visual Studio Code extensions such as Prettier, ESLint, and GitLens become invaluable. Let's install these tools.

Installing Visual Studio Code add-ons – Prettier

From the **Extensions** icon, add the **Prettier Code formatter** extension:

Figure 1.13 – Extensions can be accessed by clicking the cubes icon

Prettier will automatically format code without taking extra time to type tabs manually. In this example, the code to the left is unformatted. We can now invoke Prettier by right-clicking the code and selecting **Format Document**:

```
reporters: ['spec']
[['allure', {
outputDir: 'allure-results',
disableWebdriverStepsReporting: true,
disableWebdriverScreenshotsReporting: true,
}]],
```

Rename Symbol	F2
Change All Occurrences	Ctrl+F2
Format Document	Shift+Alt+F
Format Document With...	
Refactor...	Ctrl+Shift+R

Figure 1.14 – Example of unformatted code before Prettier

The code is then reformatted in a structured manner. Note that the square brackets and curly braces are tabbed out, and extra lines are included automatically:

```
reporters: ["spec"][
    [
        "allure",
        {
            outputDir: "allure-results",
            disableWebdriverStepsReporting: true,
            disableWebdriverScreenshotsReporting: true,
        },
    ]
],
```

Figure 1.15 – Tab-indented code formatted by Prettier

The code is now formatted for readability. The next extension will help us when working on a GitHub team.

Installing Visual Studio Code add-ons – GitLens

Among many other features, the GitLens extension will show who last made code changes in our GitHub repository. From **Extensions**, add the **GitLens** extension:

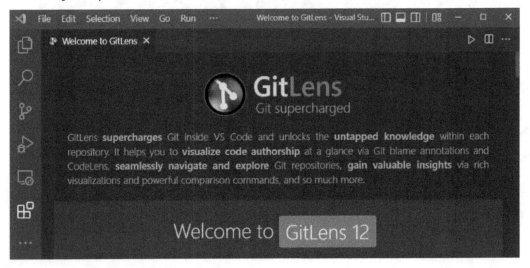

Figure 1.16 – The GitLens extension

Clicking on any line of any tracked document in the project activates GitLens:

```
30     "devDependencies": {
31       "@wdio/cli": "^8.0.0-alpha.249",          Christian Bromann, 2 months ago • add note
32       "@wdio/globals": "^8.0.0-alpha.249",
33       "@wdio/jasmine-framework": "^8.0.0-alpha.249",
34       "@wdio/local-runner": "^8.0.0-alpha.249",
35       "@wdio/sauce-service": "^8.0.0-alpha.249",
36       "@wdio/spec-reporter": "^8.0.0-alpha.249",
37       "eslint": "^8.14.0",
38       "eslint-config-standard": "^17.0.0",
39       "eslint-plugin-import": "^2.26.0",
40       "eslint-plugin-node": "^11.1.0",
41       "eslint-plugin-promise": "^6.0.0",
42       "ts-node": "^10.7.0",
43       "typescript": "^4.6.4",
44       "wdio-chromedriver-service": "^8.0.0-alpha.1",
45       "webdriverio": "^8.0.0-alpha.249"
46     }
47   }
```

Figure 1.17 – GitLens showing the person who last made a code change commit in gray

In the preceding example, we can see that *line 31* was last updated 2 months ago by *Christian Bromann*. This makes it easy to know when a line of code was changed, by whom, and how long ago.

This add-on will help us find code mistakes to improve the reliability of our framework.

Installing Visual Studio Code add-ons – ESLint

A linter is a program that looks for potential problems in our code like dust that gathers in the corner of a room. There are linters for most programming languages, and ESLint is a TypeScript linter. Why ESLint and not JSLint? **ES** stands for **ECMAScript**, which is the code standard for JavaScript that is intended to ensure the interoperability of web pages across different browsers. As of this writing, the current version is ES6. When searching for code samples, pay attention if the code snippet is version ES5 or earlier as new features have been added over the years.

From **Extensions**, add the **ESLint** extension:

Figure 1.18 – The ESLint ECMAScript linter extension

ESLint finds and reports on code patterns found in TypeScript projects. The goal is to make code more consistent and avoid bugs upfront. You can see it in use in the following screenshot:

Figure 1.19 – Example of ESLint reporting 81 potential problems in a TypeScript project

ESLint supplies a new **PROBLEMS** window that lists issues and suggestions for improving our code base as we enhance our framework. It can also be customized with new rules.

What is the difference between ECMAScript, JavaScript, and TypeScript?

ECMAScript is the language definition of JavaScript that's found in modern browsers. ES5 and ES6 are recent descriptions. TypeScript is a superset of JavaScript that adds type declarations to JavaScript, like Java.

Now that we have configured Visual Studio Code, let's add a few tools to our browser for selectors and cookies.

Installing Chrome extensions

Our next two tools are the easiest to install. **SelectorsHub** allows us to create robust locators of elements in Chrome, Edge, and any Chromium-based browser, while **EditThisCookie** allows us to clear the cookie cache from the browser frontend. Later, we will ensure the framework will clear cookies for fresh test execution.

Adding the SelectorsHub Chrome extension

In the top-right corner of your Chrome browser, select the three vertical ellipses. Then, click on **More tools** and then **Extensions**. Click the hamburger icon in the top-left corner. Finally, click **Open Chrome Web Store** in the lower-left corner:

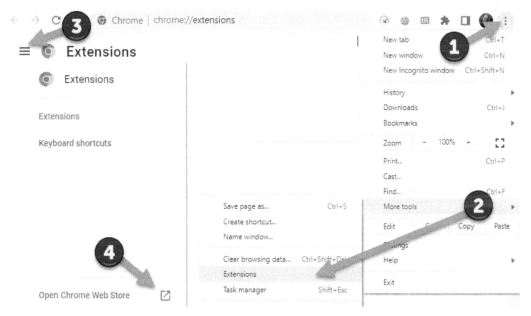

Figure 1.20 – Adding a Chrome extension from Chrome Web Store

In Chrome Web Store, search for and install the **SelectorsHub** extension:

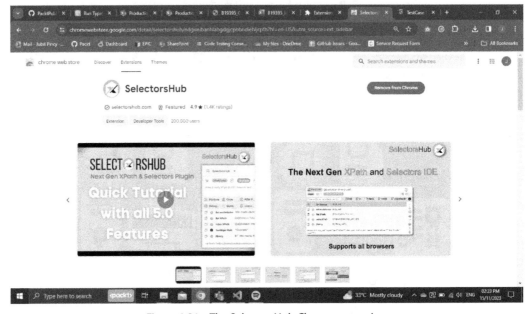

Figure 1.21 – The SelectorsHub Chrome extension

Once the extension has been installed, it should be allowed to interact in **Incognito** mode.

From the **Extensions** page, click the **Details** button for **SelectorsHub** and set the **Allow in Incognito** switch to active:

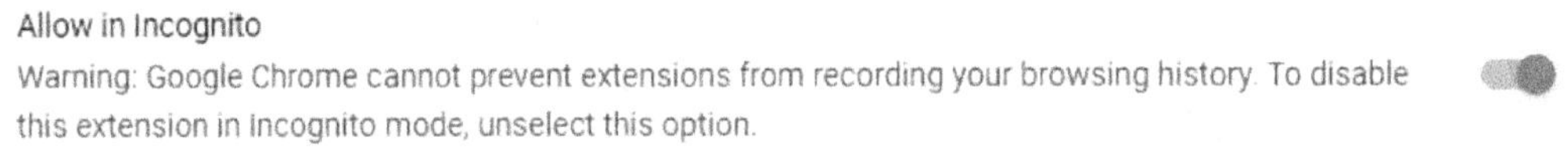

Allow in Incognito
Warning: Google Chrome cannot prevent extensions from recording your browsing history. To disable this extension in Incognito mode, unselect this option.

Figure 1.22 – Allowing the SelectorsHub Chrome extension to appear in Incognito mode

Similarly, we will add an extension that will make clearing our browser cookies faster.

Adding the EditThisCookie Chrome extension

As with the previous extension, search for the **EditThisCookie** extension from Chrome Web Store:

Figure 1.23 – The EditThisCookie Chrome extension

The **EditThisCookie** extension will make it easier to clear cookies in the browser. It takes only two clicks to clear all cookies, and it can clear the cookies of specific applications, such as our application under test.

Next, we will need these extensions to be visible on the Chrome browser for easy access.

Pinning Chrome extensions to the browser title bar

Follow these steps:

1. Click the jigsaw puzzle extensions icon in the top-right corner of the browser.

2. Click the **pushpin** icon next to both extensions.

3. These icons will now appear in the **Extensions** shortcuts area in the top-right corner of the browser for easy access:

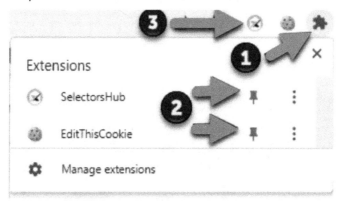

Figure 1.24 – Pinning an extension to the browser bar

Our utility belt is now complete. We have the coding environment, source code editor, and a few troubleshooting tools to help us leap tall projects in a single bound. Next, we'll install WebdriverIO.

Installing WebdriverIO

There are two options to use and install WebdriverIO

- Using WDIO TestRunner in async mode

- Using WedbriverIO in standalone mode

In the next chapter and throughout this book, we will be using the first option. Despite this, take a closer look at both options:

Option 1: Using WebdriverIO with its built-in WDIO TestRunner is the default mode and most common use case. The test runner efficiently addresses numerous challenges often encountered when utilizing basic automation libraries. First, it streamlines the management of your test executions by organizing and distributing test specifications to maximize concurrent testing. Additionally, it adeptly manages session operations and offers an array of features designed to aid in troubleshooting and error identification within your test suite.

Option 2: When using WebdriverIO in standalone mode, you not only retain access to all protocol commands but also gain a valuable set of supplementary commands that facilitate a more advanced interaction with the web browser. This feature empowers you to seamlessly incorporate this automation tool into your projects, particularly for the development of custom automation libraries. Well-known instances of such integration are found in tools such as klassi-js, Spectron, and CodeceptJS. This mode's usage is outside the scope of this book but you can check out the `klassi-js` repo (https://github.com/klassijs/klassi-js) at your leisure. There is also a project template that you can clone (`https://github.com/klassijs/klassi-example-test-suite`) so that you have a running project in seconds.

The following is a sample script written as a test spec and executed by WDIO:

```
import { browser, $ } from '@wdio/globals'

describe('DuckDuckGo search', () => {
    it('Searches for WebdriverIO', async () => {
        await browser.url('https://duckduckgo.com/')

        await $('#search_form_input_homepage').setValue('WebdriverIO')
        await $('#search_button_homepage').click()

        const title = await browser.getTitle()
        expect(title).toBe('WebdriverIO at DuckDuckGo')
        // or just
        await expect(browser).toHaveTitle('WebdriverIO at DuckDuckGo')
    })
})
```

> **Note**
> All WebdriverIO commands are asynchronous and need to be properly handled using `async/await`.

Summary

In this chapter, we installed many of the tools required to begin coding a robust test automation framework. We enhanced our browser with two extensions to ease element-locator creation and handle cookies. The Node.js environment was installed with npm and a code repository folder was created. The Visual Studio Code IDE was installed with tools for static code analysis and code formatting, and we provided detailed information about when the code was modified and by whom.

In the next chapter, we will install WebdriverIO and begin to explore the folder structure of the WebdriverIO TypeScript framework project.

2
Fortress of Solitude – Configuring WebdriverIO

In this chapter, we will install WebdriverIO and its dependencies. There are two approaches, and we will discuss the advantages of each. It is also important to keep the versions of the dependencies up to date. To help with this, we will use Yarn to keep our package.json and yarn.lock files up to date.

The setup instructions for WDIO can be found in the **Getting Started** section on the official website (`https://webdriver.io/docs/gettingstarted`):

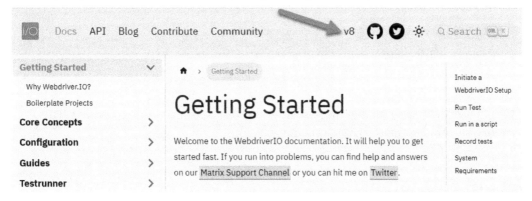

Figure 2.1 – Getting Started

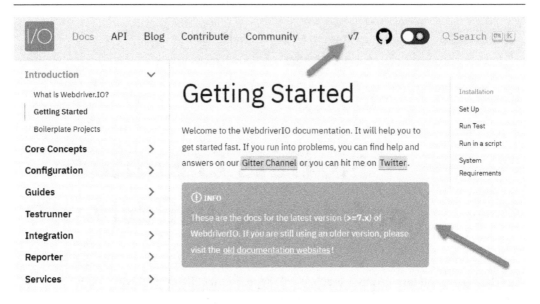

Figure 2.2 – Current documentation indicators for version 7.x

In this section, we'll cover the following main topics:

- WebdriverIO setup
- Building and installing the project dependencies
- Making out first commit

> **Tip**
>
> Be sure you are viewing the latest version of WDIO 8.0. Googling questions about WDIO features can lead to support pages of prior versions.

WebdriverIO setup

The WDIO team works hard to make everything easy to install, as described in the documentation. WDIO can be set up in two ways:

- Custom configuration while answering a series of questions
- Cloned from an existing project on GitHub

For this project, we will show the questions and the selected answers. The second option, cloning the boilerplate project approach, is described in the following section.

Option 1 – required steps to start installing WebdriverIO 8.0 for TypeScript

Navigate from the **TERMINAL** window to the `\repos\wdio` folder. The quickest way to set up a WDIO project quickly from Yarn is to type `yarn create wdio`, ending with a dot (.):

```
> yarn create wdio .
```

The WDIO robot will appear, and a list of configuration questions will be presented:

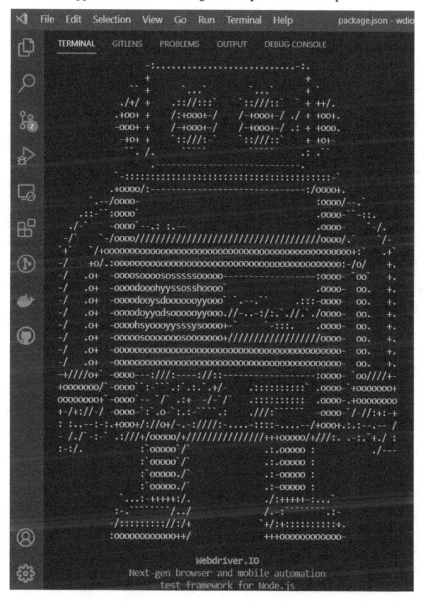

Figure 2.3 – WDIO initialization from the code TERMINAL window

The initialization will ask how to configure WDIO from scratch. Here is the list of settings for WebDriver 8.0. There are several options, and many will use the default. Each item with a star (*) shows the choice selected at setup:

> **Note**
>
> WebdriverIO is always being updated. These questions themselves should be similar for both Mac and Windows users. However, the order, phrasing, and selection details do change slightly as new features are added.

```
===============================
🌀 WDIO Configuration Wizard 🧪
===============================

? What type of testing would you like to do? E2E Testing – of Web or Mobile Applications
? Where is your automation backend located? On my local machine
? Which environment you would like to automate? Web – web applications in the browser
? With which browser should we start? Chrome
? Which framework do you want to use? Jasmine (https://jasmine.github.io/)
? Do you want to use a compiler? TypeScript (https://www.typescriptlang.org/)
? Do you want WebdriverIO to autogenerate some test files? Yes
? What should be the location of your spec files? C:\stuff\test\specs\**\*.ts
? Do you want to use page objects (https://martinfowler.com/bliki/PageObject.html)? Yes
? Where are your page objects located? C:\stuff\test\pageobjects\**\*.ts
? Which reporter do you want to use? spec, allure
? Do you want to add a plugin to your test setup?
? Do you want to add a service to your test setup?
? What is the base url? http://localhost
? Do you want me to run `npm install` (Y/n) Yes
```

Figure 2.4 – Settings

? What type of testing would you like to do? (Use arrow keys)

- > (*) E2E Testing - of Web or Mobile Applications
- ( ) Component or Unit Testing - in the browser
- > https://webdriver.io/docs/component-testing
- ( ) Desktop Testing - of Electron Applications
- > https://webdriver.io/docs/desktop-testing/electron
- ( ) Desktop Testing - of MacOS Applications
- > https://webdriver.io/docs/desktop-testing/macos

? Where is your automation backend located? (Use arrow keys)

- > (*) On my local machine (default)
- ( ) In the cloud using Experitest
- ( ) In the cloud using Sauce Labs
- ( ) In the cloud using Browserstack or Testingbot or LambdaTest or a different service
- ( ) I have my own Selenium cloud

Today, there are many cloud options, including `Experitest`, `Sauce Labs`, `BrowserStack`, `Testingbot`, and `LambdaTest`. For this book, we will install the automation backend on our local Mac or Windows machine.

Next is the environment type. For these purposes, we will use `Web`:

? Which environment would you like to automate? (Use arrow keys)

- (*) Web - web applications in the browser
- ( ) Mobile - native, hybrid, and mobile web apps, on Android or iOS

Then, select the browser(s) we will be using. Select the default of Chrome. Note that we can add others later:

? With which browser should we start? (Press <space> to select, <a> to toggle all, <i> to invert selection, and <enter> to proceed)

- (*) Chrome
- ( ) Firefox
- ( ) Safari
- ( ) Microsoft Edge

Next is the reporting framework type. For this book, we will be using Jasmine. However, much of the code that's supplied will apply to all listed frameworks:

? Which framework do you want to use? (Use arrow keys)

- ( ) Mocha (https://mochajs.org/)
- ( ) Mocha with Serenity/JS (https://serenity-js.org/)
- (*) Jasmine (https://jasmine.github.io/)
- ( ) Jasmine with Serenity/JS (https://serenity-js.org/)
- ( ) Cucumber (https://cucumber.io/)
- ( ) Cucumber with Serenity/JS (https://serenity-js.org/)

Out of the box, WebdriverIO uses Mocha by default. However, it also supports Jasmine and can be combined with Chai for advanced assertions. Cucumber is an extra layer of abstraction framework that hides the core code. This allows fewer technical resources to create tests from Feature files. Cucumber is outside the scope of this book, but the techniques described can be implemented in a Cucumber WDIO project. Next, we will tell WDIO this is a Typescript project:

? Do you want to use a compiler? (Use arrow keys

- ( ) Babel (https://babeljs.io/)
- (*) TypeScript (https://www.typescriptlang.org/)
- ( ) No!

Question: What is Babel and is it needed?

Babel (`https://babeljs.io/`) is a JavaScript transpiler. Because JavaScript is implemented differently in different browsers, a transpiler is used to transform our code to an older JavaScript version. Some features are not implemented in certain browsers, such as async/await, depending on what browser version we are testing against. So, a transpiler allows us to have our framework be backward compatible. Although this is a TypeScript project, we do not need the TypeScript transpiler.

Question: How to know what features are available in different browsers and versions?

The `caniuse.com` website provides descriptive tables of the different ECMAScript features that are supported:

We will be creating our tests in TypeScript, which is a superset of JavaScript. The Typescript transpiler will be used. Now to get a quick startup sample script.

? Do you want WebdriverIO to autogenerate some test files?

(Y/n) Yes

This will automatically set up a sample test to run to ensure WebdriverIO is working. It is also where we will build a framework unit test to check features are working. Oh yes, we are developers, and our automation project has its own unit and integration tests.

The following is the default path for the TypeScript sample test cases and should not be changed:

? Where should be the location of your specs files?

./test/specs/**/*.ts

Tests can be organized into feature sub-folders and smoke tests under the specs folder. Notice that because we selected TypeScript in the prior question, the test extensions (.js) replaced with .ts.

? Do you want to use page objects (`https://martinfowler.com/bliki/PageObject.html`)**?**

Yes

This sets up a Page Object Model folder structure for our project.

? Where are your page objects located? ./test/pageobjects/**/*.ts

Now, we want to configure our reporters.

Which reporter do you want to use?

- (*) spec
- ( ) dot
- ( ) junit
- (*) allure
- ( ) video
- ( ) mochawesome
- ( ) slack

WebdriverIO supports a wide variety of reporters. For this small sample, we will start with the spec and allure reporters. Note that WDIO even supports a **Video** option. You may notice that Slack is included. In the final chapter of this book, we will be using Jenkins to send update messages to a Slack channel.

? Do you want to add a plugin to your test setup?

- ( ) wait-for: utilities that provide functionalities to wait for certain conditions till a defined task is complete.
- > https://www.npmjs.com/package/wdio-wait-for
- ( ) angular-component-harnesses: support for Angular component test harnesses
- > https://www.npmjs.com/package/@badisi/wdio-harness
- ( ) Testing Library: utilities that encourage good testing practices laid down by dom-testing-library.
- > https://testing-library.com/docs/webdriverio-testing-library/intro

In our framework, we will have an advanced approach for waiting for page synchronization. This option will be left as-is.

If the application under test (AUT) is an Angular project, it is recommended to use the Angular Component Harnesses configuration.

? Do you want to add a service to your test setup?

- ( ) vscode
- ( ) eslinter-service

- ( ) lambdatest
- ( ) crossbrowsertesting
- ( ) vscode
- ( ) docker
- ( ) slack

> **Note**
> 34 additional services are integrated into WDIO, including Slack, Cross Browser Testing (Selenium Standalone), and ES-Linter. Covering them all is beyond the scope of this book.

The WebdriverIO **Visual Studio Code (VS Code)** service allows us to seamlessly test extensions from end to end in the VS Code Desktop ID. By providing a path to your extension, the service does the rest, as follows:

- Installs VS Code (either stable, insiders, or a specified version).
- Download Chromedriver specific to the given VS Code version.
- Enables you to access the VS Code API from your tests.
- Starts VS Code with custom user settings (including support for VS Code on Ubuntu, macOS, and Windows).
- Serves VS Code from a server to be accessed by any browser for testing web extensions.
- Bootstraps page objects with locators that match your VS Code version.

The next question asks you to enter the landing page for the application under test. For this, we will use the default provided as the sample tests use this to navigate internally to a website for testing.

? What is the base URL?

`http://localhost`

This is the base landing page that our tests will launch.

A base landing page ensures we do not repeatedly add code to navigate to the same landing page. Later in this book, we will see how to customize this value. For the moment, we will use the internet sandbox for testing.

The final installation step is to have npm download and install all the packages. While this part can be performed by the installer, we need to make one modification. Choose No for the final question.

? Do you want me to run `npm install` (Y/n)

No

We will be using Yarn rather than npm as our package manager due to its speed. This completes the setup for installing and configuring WebdriverIO from the wizard. Another option is to clone an existing project, which will be covered next. Skip to the *Installing and configuring WebdriverIO* section if you do not plan to clone from an existing project.

Because we are using Yarn as our package manager instead of npm, we will need to remove the package-lock.json file and run the yarn install command to build the equivalent yarn.lock file.

```
> yarn install
```

Option 1 – cloning WebdriverIO from a boilerplate project

An alternate way to set up WDIO is to use a preconfigured WDIO boilerplate project from the WDIO GitHub repo. This means that less troubleshooting might be needed. We can choose from many preconfigured boilerplate projects with all the necessary components.

For this project, we will fork the `Jasmine TypeScript Boilerplate` project from GitHub:

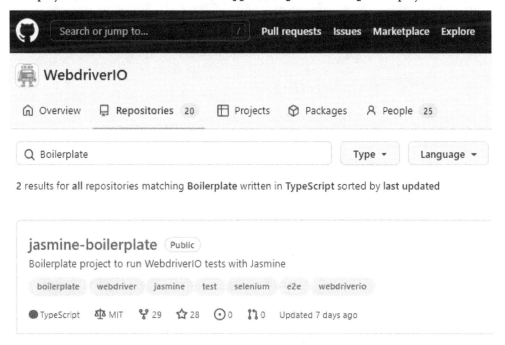

Figure 2.5 – The Jasmine TypeScript boilerplate project on GitHub

Click the **jasmine-boilerplate** link. This will allow us to create our own version via the **Code** button:

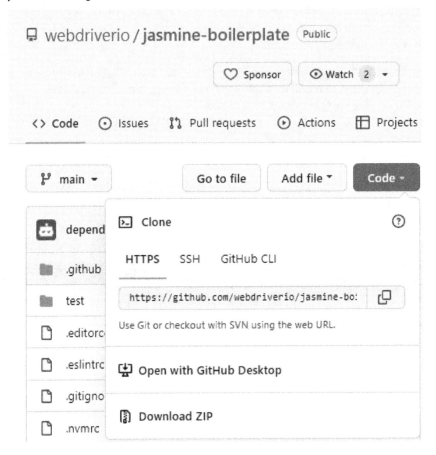

Figure 2.6 – Copying the project URL from GitHub

Click **Code**. Multiple choices for cloning the project will be displayed. Select **Open with GitHub Desktop**:

Clone a repository   ✕

GitHub.com	GitHub Enterprise	URL

Repository URL or GitHub username and repository
(hubot/cool-repo)

https://github.com/webdriverio/jasmine-boilerplate

Local path

D:\git\github\jasmine-boilerplate   Choose...

Clone   Cancel

Figure 2.7 – Cloning from the source path to the local destination

Click **Clone**; the project will be put in the `repos` path.

Next, we will change the **Local path** directory so that it points to where our project lives. We can do this by clicking **Choose...**, changing the directory to `repo\wdio`, and clicking **Clone**:

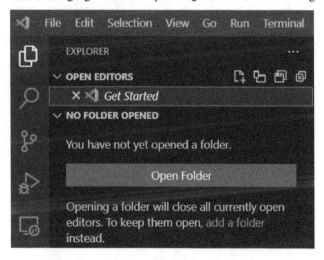

Figure 2.8 – The project's Explorer icon in VS Code

Click the **Explorer** icon in the top-left corner of VS Code and open the WDIO folder.

Then, click **Open Folder**, navigate to the repo\wdio folder, and click **Open**:

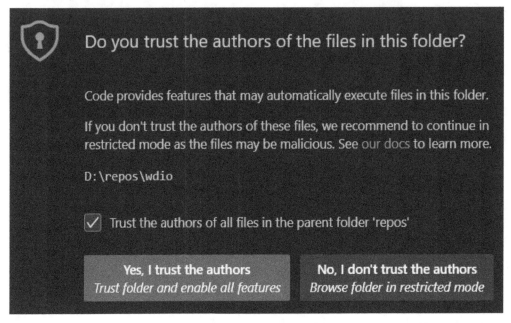

Figure 2.9 – Trusting the authors of a project

If this dialogue appears, check the **Trust the authors of all files in the parent folder 'repos'** option and click **Yes, I trust the authors**.

With that, we have covered the clone installation approach. Next, we will install everything.

Building and installing the project dependencies

If you installed WebdriverIO from an existing project, this is where we continue. We need to build the project before we can run our first test. From the Terminal, type the following:

```
> yarn install
```

This will bring in all the associated packages to run the project. Sometime in the future, vulnerabilities may occur and we will have to update our packages. We can use Yarn to check which packages are current and which are outdated:

```
> yarn outdated
```

The output can be seen in the following screenshot:

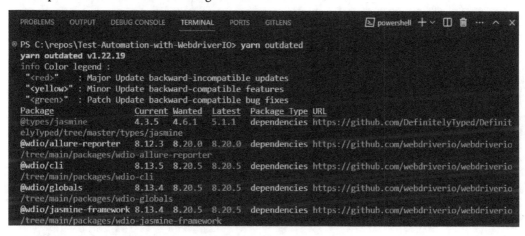

Figure 2.10 – Displaying the outdated package

Incompatibility could occur if we upgrade all packages blindly. Fortunately, there is the yarn upgrade command, which allows the packages to be upgraded individually:

```
> yarn upgrade-interactive
```

We will see the following output:

```
PROBLEMS    OUTPUT    DEBUG CONSOLE    TERMINAL    PORTS    GITLENS

PS C:\repos\Test-Automation-with-WebdriverIO>  yarn upgrade-interactive
yarn upgrade-interactive v1.22.19
info Color legend :
 "<red>"    : Major Update backward-incompatible updates
 "<yellow>" : Minor Update backward-compatible features
 "<green>"  : Patch Update backward-compatible bug fixes
? Choose which packages to update. (Press <space> to select, <a> to toggle all,
 dependencies
   name                        range      from         to       url
>( ) @types/jasmine            ^4.3.5     4.3.5    >  4.6.1    https://github.com/Def
  ( ) @wdio/allure-reporter    ^8.12.2    8.12.3   >  8.20.0   https://github.com/web
  ( ) @wdio/cli                ^8.12.2    8.13.5   >  8.20.5   https://github.com/web
  ( ) @wdio/globals            ^8.12.1    8.13.4   >  8.20.5   https://github.com/web
  ( ) @wdio/jasmine-framework  ^8.12.1    8.13.4   >  8.20.5   https://github.com/web
  ( ) @wdio/local-runner       ^8.12.1    8.13.4   >  8.20.5   https://github.com/web
  ( ) @wdio/spec-reporter      ^8.12.2    8.12.2   >  8.20.0   https://github.com/web
  ( ) allure-commandline       ^2.23.0    2.23.0   >  2.24.1   https://github.com/all
  ( ) expect-webdriverio       ^4.2.7     4.2.7    >  4.4.1    https://webdriver.io
  ( ) geckodriver              ^4.0.5     4.0.5    >  4.2.1    https://github.com/web
  ( ) typescript               ^5.1.6     5.1.6    >  5.2.2    https://www.typescript
```

Figure 2.11 – Interactive package list for upgrading

This gives us the most flexibility when we're keeping our project packages up to date.

> **Quick tip**
>
> If you want to clear the Terminal, use cls in Windows or Ctrl + K or clear on Mac.

After the installation, the yarn.lock file will be updated and the node_modules folder will have all the supporting dependencies downloaded. This contains the expanded list of packages, which has been included to support the packages in package.json. The `yarn.lock` file will never need to be edited.

At this point, we should point out that the WebdriverIO setup assumes that a novice user may not know what to do to bring in all the supporting packages:

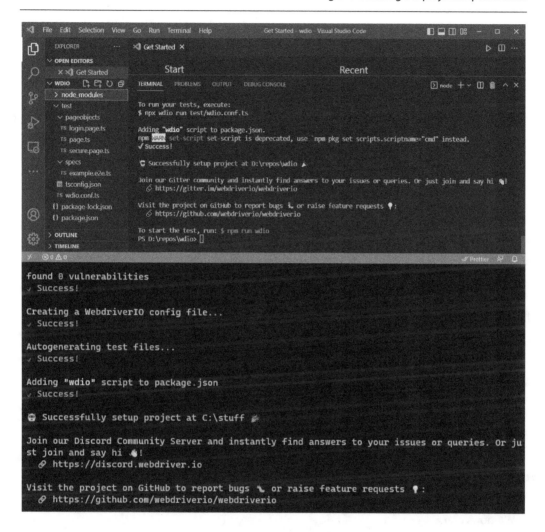

Figure 2.12 – WebdriverIO with TypeScript successfully installed

Lastly, we can confirm the version of WebdriverIO that is installed with the version flag.

For Windows users:

```
> npx wdio --version
```

For Mac users:

```
> wdio --version
```

We made it! All the supported features have been added to the package.json file. WDIO even gives us a hint to try out our first test – `npm run wdio`:

TERMINAL
PROBLEMS
OUTPUT
DEBUG CONSOLE
To start the test, run: $ npm run wdio
PS D:\repos\wdio>

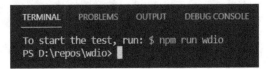

Figure 2.13 – WebdriverIO gives us a hint on how to run the first test

This has set up WebdriverIO and created a sample test that can be executed with the following yarn command:

```
> yarn wdio
```

This results in the following output:

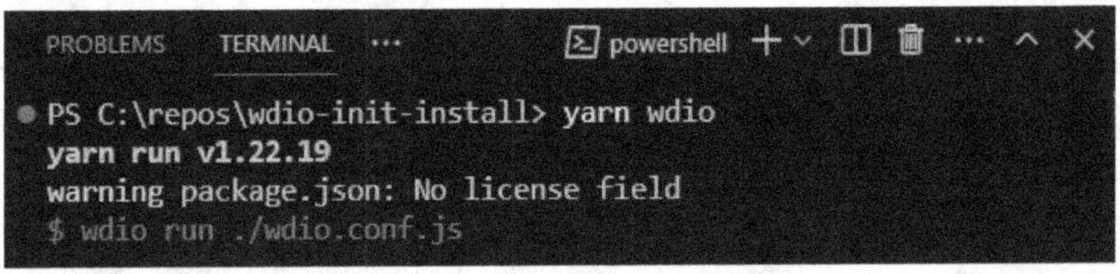

PROBLEMS
TERMINAL
powershell
PS C:\repos\wdio-init-install> yarn wdio
yarn run v1.22.19
warning package.json: No license field
$ wdio run ./wdio.conf.js

Figure 2.14 – Output of yard command

Tests can also be executed by running a command. Let's take a look at the options for both Windows and Mac:

For Windows users:

```
> npx wdio run test/wdio.conf.ts
```

For Mac users:

```
> wdio run test/wdio.conf.ts
```

All the test examples can be found in this book's GitHub repository: `https://github.com/PacktPublishing/Enhanced-Test-Automation-with-WebdriverIO`.

This runs the sample tests with basic output detail to the Terminal window from the **spec Reporter** window:

```
"spec" Reporter:
------------------------------------------------------------
[chrome 107.0.5304.88 windows #0-0] Running: chrome (v107.0.5304.88) on windows
[chrome 107.0.5304.88 windows #0-0] Session ID: 85b0c7f5e91f05ffbb18b09998d2aa2c
[chrome 107.0.5304.88 windows #0-0]
[chrome 107.0.5304.88 windows #0-0] » \test\specs\example.e2e.js
[chrome 107.0.5304.88 windows #0-0] My Login application
[chrome 107.0.5304.88 windows #0-0]    √ should login with valid credentials
[chrome 107.0.5304.88 windows #0-0]
[chrome 107.0.5304.88 windows #0-0] 1 passing (2s)


Spec Files:      1 passed, 1 total (100% completed) in 00:00:05

2022-11-06T22:08:27.978Z INFO @wdio/local-runner: Shutting down spawned worker
2022-11-06T22:08:28.231Z INFO @wdio/local-runner: Waiting for 0 to shut down gracefully
2022-11-06T22:08:28.232Z INFO @wdio/local-runner: shutting down
PS D:\repos\wdio>
```

Figure 2.15 – Pass results shown in the spec report from the sample WDIO test

Now that we have set up our project, either by answering the initial configuration questions or cloning an existing project, we are ready to look at the configurations and file settings of our new WDIO automation project:

```
test > specs > TS test.e2e.ts > ...
 1  import { expect } from '@wdio/globals'
 2  import LoginPage from '../pageobjects/login.page.js'
 3  import SecurePage from '../pageobjects/secure.page.js'
 4
 5  describe('My Login application', () => {
 6      it('should login with valid credentials', async () => {
 7          await LoginPage.open()
 8
 9          await LoginPage.login('tomsmith', 'SuperSecretPassword!')
10          await expect(SecurePage.flashAlert).toBeExisting()
11          await expect(SecurePage.flashAlert).toHaveTextContaining(
12              'You logged into a secure area!')
13      })
14  })
15
16
```

Figure 2.16 – All project files

This will display all the files and folders in the project. There are quite a lot of them, so we will cover the important ones here. Open the README.md file first.

For any project, the README file is the best place to start. It gives us critical information about how the project is configured, its features, and, most importantly, how to quick-start a sample test.

Next, open the package.json file.

This is where much of the Node.js configuration occurs:

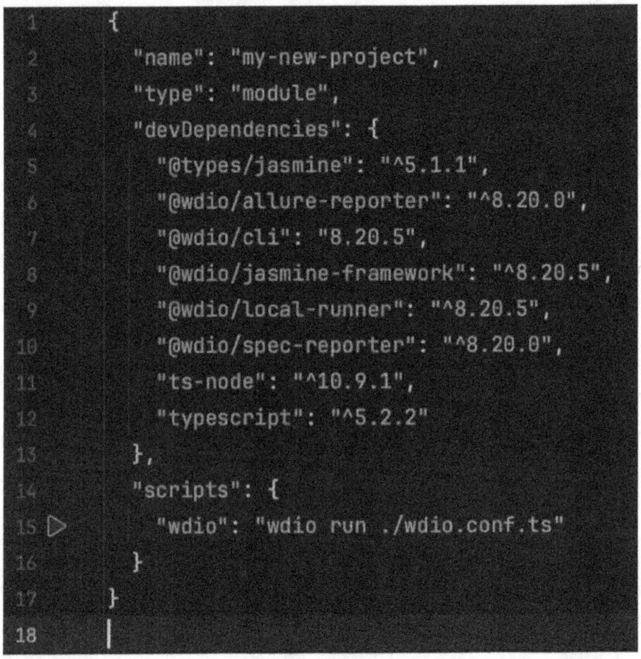

```
 1    {
 2        "name": "my-new-project",
 3        "type": "module",
 4        "devDependencies": {
 5          "@types/jasmine": "^5.1.1",
 6          "@wdio/allure-reporter": "^8.20.0",
 7          "@wdio/cli": "8.20.5",
 8          "@wdio/jasmine-framework": "^8.20.5",
 9          "@wdio/local-runner": "^8.20.5",
10          "@wdio/spec-reporter": "^8.20.0",
11          "ts-node": "^10.9.1",
12          "typescript": "^5.2.2"
13        },
14        "scripts": {
15          "wdio": "wdio run ./wdio.conf.ts"
16        }
17    }
18
```

Figure 2.17 – All devDependancies in the wdio project

What is the yarn.lock file?

The yarn.lock file contains the full list of required project packages, including ones that support other packages in package.json. It is massive, but don't worry – you will never have to change it. Yarn Package Manager handles all of this. Whew!

Let's run Yarn Package Manager with the `install` command to get everything loaded and up to date:

```
> yarn install
```

This can be seen in the following screenshot:

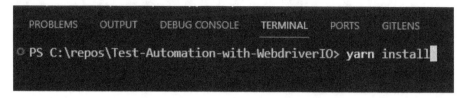

Figure 2.18 – Building the project using Yarn Package Manager

Making our first commit

Now that we have our first test running, it is time to bring it all to our fortress of solitude – by committing it to our local repo and then to the GitHub repository.

Ignoring files in the Git repository

Before we make our first commit to the Git repo, we need to ignore some files. Once we have set up our WDIO project, VS Code might suggest that the `node_modules` folder should be included in the `gitignore` file:

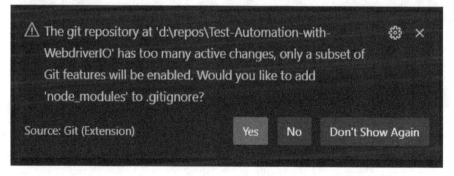

Figure 2.19 – VS Code detects that the node_modules folder can be ignored

We never want to commit this folder to our Git repo as it gets updated constantly by npm. Having npm create the folder contents on the fly with the most up-to-date versions is better:

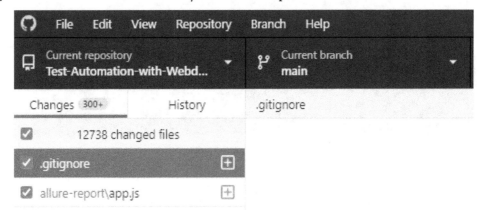

Figure 2.20 – GitHub Desktop indicates over 12,000 files to be committed to the new repo

This is far more files than we need.

To tell Git to ignore this project folder, simply create a `.gitignore` file in the root of the project and enter the `node_modules` folder name:

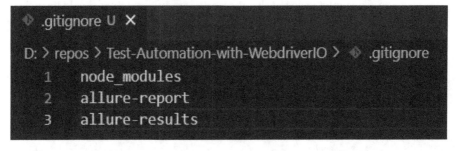

Figure 2.21 – A .gitignore file contains files and folders that should not be committed

The same goes for our Allure report and results folders. These files will be rebuilt repeatedly after each test and will not need to be under version control. Once these tests are run from Jenkins, prior runs can be preserved there temporarily or permanently.

By simply adding and saving the `.gitignore` file, the list of files changes dramatically:

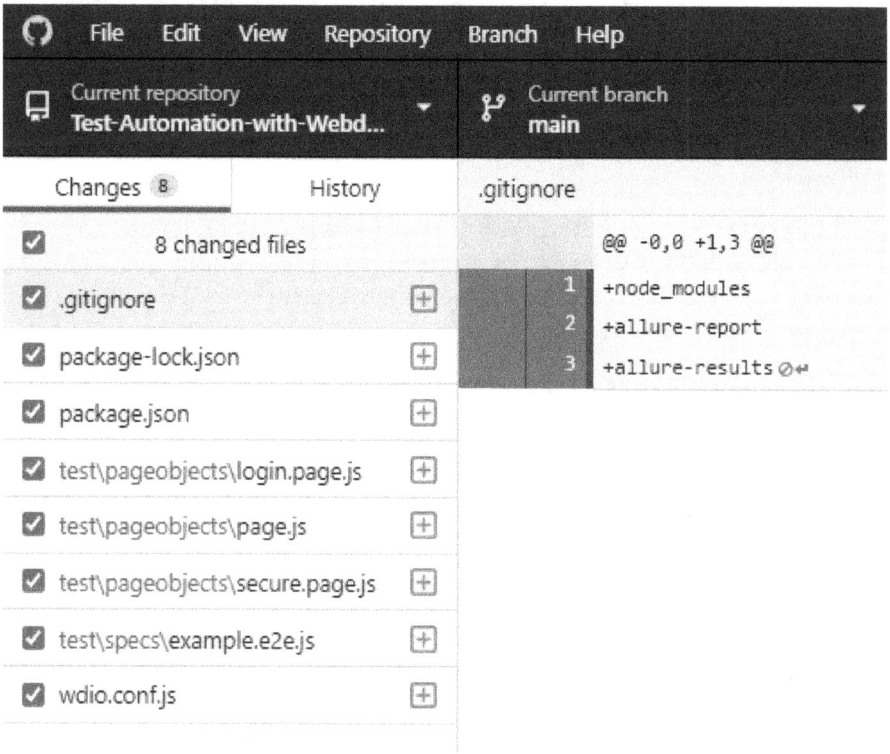

Figure 2.22 – The repo now only stores the files

Once this `.gitignore` file is saved, we will see the changes reflected in GitHub Desktop with a manageable size of just eight files.

> **Tip**
>
> Never store passwords in the repo. A password should be provided by a secure data provider service such as Vault or AWS Secrets. If no such option exists, then a password file could be referenced in the folder above the project. Otherwise, storing such a credential file in the project requires adding it to the `.gitignore` file for security.

One of the first bugs I found in my career was related to passwords. Here, the user had the option to reset their password with a random string of characters. This page would occasionally crash. The reason was that the requirement had the password generated from all 128 ASCII characters. This included BELL, unprintable characters, as well as ones that were difficult to type on the keyboard. The real problem was that this set included angle brackets (< and >). The page would only crash when a new password was generated with one of those two characters, as they were interpreted as opening or closing HTML tags on the page.

There are tools that IT security uses to detect passwords in repos, but they often only check the `main` or `master` repos and ignore the later `feature` branches. This, too, is a security risk. Always clean up old branches, as this can be considered a **security operations center (SOC)** II compliance violation, even if the passwords have long since expired.

We can now add a summary description and optional details. Simply click **Commit to main** – all our new files will be committed to our local main branch:

Figure 2.23 – Adding a comment and details to a local commit

However, this is just staged on our local Git repo. The final step is to click **Push origin**, which will push it up to GitHub for our team to pull down:

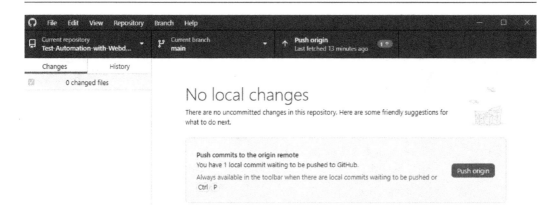

Figure 2.24 – GitHub Desktop shows that all changes have been
committed and suggests pushing any new changes

Congratulations! You have made your first commit to your Git repo. Your team members can now pull your changes to be sure all their tests are running smoothly.

But what if you need to add new functionality that will take a few days to complete?

Branching out

To be a part of an automation team, you may be asked to add new and complex functionality. If this takes a few days, we might consider feature branching. A new branch is created from main. Your changes will be committed to your branch, and changes from main will be brought in periodically:

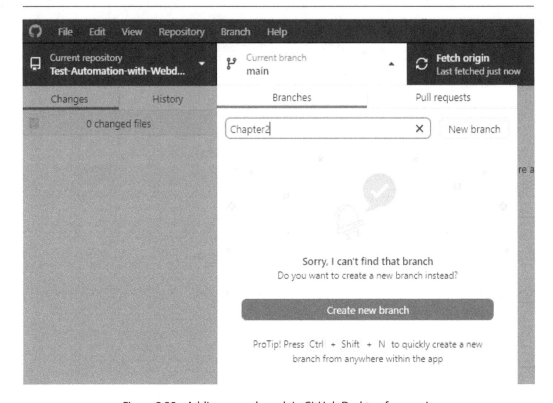

Figure 2.25 – Adding a new branch in GitHub Desktop from main

When your changes are complete, a pull request will be made to pull your changes into the `main` branch, and the `feature` branch may be deleted.

For this book, the final state of the framework will be in a branch named after this chapter. The `main` branch will contain the final project.

Summary

In this chapter, we installed WebdriverIO with several options added to a set of configuration questions. We also showed how Yarn can keep dependencies current. Lastly, we showed how to make a commit to the repo from GitHub Desktop.

If you run into issues, check the *Appendix* at the end of this book. There, you will find a detailed list of common and arcane issues with causes, explanations, and resolutions. It also includes a node command cheatsheet for many of these initial processes.

In the next chapter, we will explore the files and connections in the `wdio` config file and look at different ways to debug our code.

3

Cybernetic Enhancements – WebdriverIO Config and Debug Tips

In this chapter, we are going to cover the techniques for creating and debugging a custom WebdriverIO framework. This will take us through the services that help keep the project up to date. A lot of files get used and interact with each other in the project. Helpers and other features will be added to help enhance the framework as well as make debugging easier. We will cover the node files of the framework and demonstrate the differences between launching tests on Mac and Windows operating systems. We will also create our first hook customization for debugging on a single monitor. Lastly, we will write our first log wrapper to take more control over the output in the console window to improve debugging efficiency by customizing logging.

Specifically, these are our main topics for this chapter:

- Main files of WebdriverIO node project
- Letting Yarn help keep files up to date
- Dynamic configuration
- The `global.log()` method
- Rules to enforce the coding standard

The three main files of a WebdriverIO node project

A lot of files are added while following the WDIO configuration. This is a good time to walk through the project roadmap to get familiar with the features of and relationships between these files, beginning with these three:

- `package.json`
- `yarn.lock`
- `wdio.config.ts`

Let's look at each one in order of execution.

The package.json file

The first configuration file we will discuss is the `package.json` file. It helps manage the project's dependencies and provides a way to run scripts and access other information about the project. This file serves several purposes:

- It can specify scripts that can be run from the command line. For example, a WebdriverIO project might include a `wdio` script that starts the Webdriver server and a `wdio-docker` script configured specifically to run on a Docker container instance.

- It specifies the project's dependencies, which are packages that the project needs to function properly. For example, a Webdriver project will depend on the `expect-wdio` package for validations. We won't have to worry about dependency conflicts of all these packages. Yarn provides an interactive upgrade mode when you use the upgrade command with the --interactive or -i flag. The interactive upgrade mode allows you to select which packages to upgrade. When running >yarn upgrade-interactive, Yarn will display a list of outdated packages and prompt to choose which ones to upgrade. Yarn respects the version ranges specified in your package. json file when determining the versions to be upgraded.

- It can specify `devDependencies`, which are packages that are needed for developers, but not necessarily for execution. For example, a WebdriverIO project will depend on the `@wdio/ cli` package. Again, the `node-check-version` utility will keep the versions in sync.

- It can include metadata about the project, such as the project's name, version, and authors:

```
"scripts": {
  "test": "echo \"Error: no test specified\" && exit 1",
  "wdio": "wdio run test/wdio.conf.ts",
  "debug": "cross-env set DEBUG=true && wdio run test/wdio.
conf.ts",
  "report": "cross-env DEBUG=false wdio run test/wdio.conf.
ts && allure generate report allure-results --clean && allure
open",
```

```
        "wdio-docker": "DEBUG=false wdio run test/wdio.conf.ts &&
    allure generate report allure-results --clean"
      },

      "devDependencies": {
        "@types/jasmine": "^4.3.0",
        "@wdio/allure-reporter": "^7.26.0",
        "@wdio/cli": "^7.27.0",
        "@wdio/jasmine-framework": "^7.26.0",
        "@wdio/local-runner": "^7.27.0",
        "@wdio/mocha-framework": "^7.26.0",
        "@wdio/spec-reporter": "^7.26.0",
        "ts-node": "^10.9.1",
        "typescript": "^4.9.3",
      },

      "dependencies": {
        "expect-webdriverio": "^3.0.0"
      }
    }
```

The `package.json` file also contains the `"scripts"` schema. This is where we can create custom-run configuration shortcuts. For example, to run a test at the command prompt, we can use **Node Package Executor** (npx) with the **WebdriverIO** (wdio) package and provide the path to the WebdriverIO configuration file:

```
>npx wdio run ./wdio.conf.js
```

At installation, WebdriverIO includes a wdio run configuration in the scripts package schema:

```
    "scripts": {
        "wdio": "wdio wdio.conf.ts"
    }
```

We can implicitly run the node executor from the package manager with the wdio shortcut:

```
yarn wdio
```

We can now add a shortcut for running the Allure report from the previous chapter:

```
    "scripts": {
        "wdio": "wdio wdio.conf.ts"
    "report": "allure generate --clean allure-results && allure open"
    }
```

The command line to run the test and generate the report is now reduced to the following:

```
yarn wdio
yarn report
```

In *Chapter 13*, this will come into play again as we run tests on multiple browsers. For now, let's take a look brief look at all the different packages.

The yarn.lock file

This file tracks all the external supporting packages brought in by the `package.json` file that are stored in the `node_modules` folder. If the same version of a package has already been detected as downloaded, the node will skip it for efficiency. This file is extensive and since it is rebuilt each time `yarn add` is executed, it never needs to be modified manually.

Next, we'll cover the heart of WebdriverIO.

The wdio.conf.ts file and webhooks

This file is where all the WDIO package features are configured. It includes webhooks – code that executes automatically at certain points of the framework. This saves us from rewriting code repeatedly. This code can be injected before or after every session, suite, test, WebdriverIO command, or even every hook. All the default features are documented inside each hook, ready to be modified. Let's take, for example, the `beforeTest` code:

```
/**
 * Function to be executed before a test (in Mocha/Jasmine) starts.
 */
// beforeTest: function (test, context) {
// },
```

By uncommenting the `beforeTest` hook function, we can customize the functionality of WebdriverIO. This is just for running on the local machine where there is limited space on a small monitor. For example, we can maximize the browser's full screen before each test:

```
beforeTest: function (test, context) {

    browser.maximizeWindow();
},
```

Rule of thumb – match your developer's hardware

Here is a good reason to request a second monitor. We just expanded our browser at runtime to full screen. If we only have a single monitor, this will completely block our **Visual Studio Code** (**VS Code**) window from view. To be efficient, we need to see the Terminal window in VS Code on an external monitor while the test executes in full screen mode on the primary monitor.

But if you only have a single monitor, this is a simple trick you can implement in the webhooks of the `wdio.config.ts` file: set the browser height to three-quarters of the display resolution. First, get the current display's height and width by going to **Settings** and then **Display** on Windows:

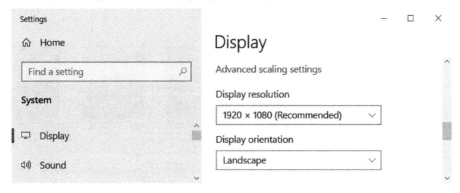

Figure 3.1 – Primary display resolution on Windows

On Mac, go to the **Apple** menu and select **About this Mac** > **Displays**:

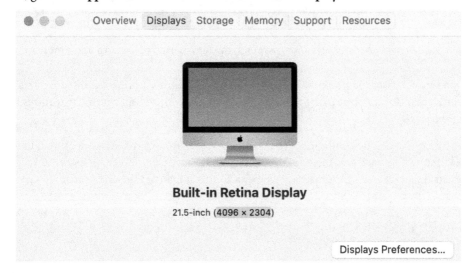

Figure 3.2 – Primary display resolution on Mac

Multiply the height of the display by 0.75. In the `wdio.conf.ts` file, uncomment the `beforeTest()` method. Enter the width and reduced height values (in this example, `970`) in the `browser.setWindow` method, as follows:

```
beforeTest: function (test, context) {
    // VS Code Terminal visible on the bottom of the screen
    browser.setWindowSize(1920, 970)
},
```

This way, you can have the best of both worlds on a single monitor, as shown in the following screenshot:

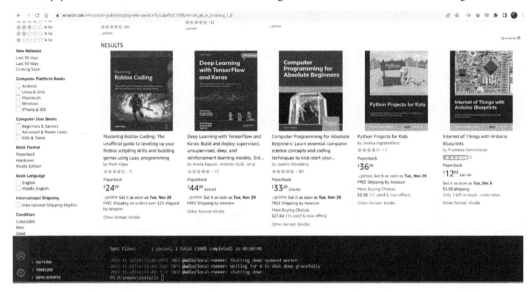

Figure 3.3 – Running a custom-sized browser with the Terminal log below on a single monitor

You can read more about the hooks of WebdriverIO in the online documentation at `https://webdriver.io/docs/options/#hooks`. Since this is a TypeScript project, it requires some configuration as well.

The `tsconfig.json` file configures TypeScript compiler options for the node. It includes the framework that will be used and includes the WebdriverIO `expect` library for assertions. This is where we can change the ECMAScript target version so that it matches the node version:

```
{
    "compilerOptions": {
        "moduleResolution": "node",
        "types": [
            "node",
            "webdriverio/async",
```

```
            "@wdio/jasmine-framework",
            "expect-webdriverio"
        ],
        "target": "es2022"
    }
}
```

The es2022 target is ECMAScript version 10. The correlation of ECMAScript version names and features can be found at https://en.wikipedia.org/wiki/ECMAScript and the correlation of node to ECMAScript versions is found at https://node.green/.

The test/spec folder is the location of the test scripts to execute. Subfolders can help divide tests into categories. It is recommended not to get too deep with these folder structures as it makes relative paths difficult to keep track of.

The test/pageObjects folder holds the page object module that's used to find and populate elements.

Finally, the node_modules folder keeps all the supporting packages that are downloaded to support the node project.

The Chrome browser is always getting updated. Next, we need to ensure the project resources stay current. WebdriverIO has a service to do just that.

Letting Yarn help keep files up to date

Just as the Yarn upgrade-interactive tool has to keep all the supporting packages current, WebdriverIO provides the ChromeDriver service to keep up with constant Chrome updates. We can install the service from the console by running this command:

```
yarn add wdio-chromedriver-service
```

Then, it must be configured in the wdio.config.ts file. To do so, find the following:

```
    services: ['chromedriver'],
```

Replace it with this:

```
    outputDir: 'all-logs',
    services: [
        ['chromedriver', {
            args: ['--silent']
        }]
    ],
```

Finally, the `all-logs` folder should be added to the `.gitignore` file. Now, let's cover some debugging tips.

Configuring debugging with VS Code

VS Code supplies four command prompt shells to launch scripts. Which one you use depends on your operating system. For Windows, there is PowerShell, Git Bash, Command Prompt, and the JavaScript debug terminal. Mac includes the ZSH shell:

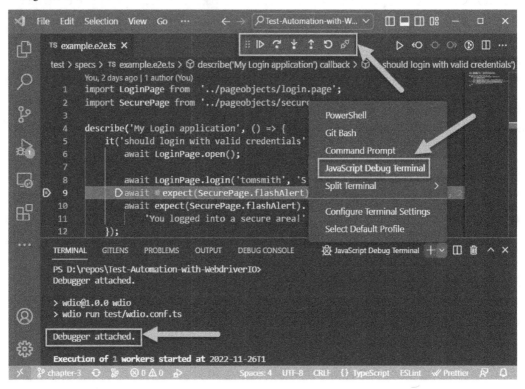

Figure 3.4 – VS Code debugging controls and shell terminals on Windows

Here's how it looks on Mac:

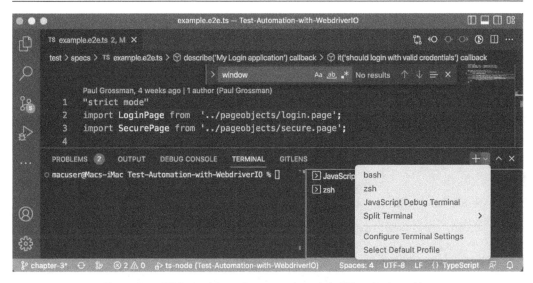

Figure 3.5 – VS Code debugging controls and shell Terminals on Mac

Script execution stops when a breakpoint is entered in the code by clicking in the gutter to the left of a line number, as seen on line 9. This will attach a debugger and a control panel. From the panel, the code execution can continue, step over a method call, step into the method, step out back up to the calling code, or restart or disconnect the debugging session.

The JavaScript debug terminal always attaches the debugger. Debug mode slows the execution. So, for Mac, a practical choice would be to have two shells open: the JavaScript debug terminal and ZSH for faster non-debug execution. Any shell can have debugging activated with auto attach:

> **Temporarily disable auto attach in this session**
>
> **Always** Auto attach to every Node.js process launched in the terminal
>
> **Smart** Auto attach when running scripts that aren't in a node_modules folder
>
> **Only With Flag** Only auto attach when the `--inspect` flag is given
>
> **Disabled** Auto attach is disabled and not shown in status bar

Figure 3.6 – Command palette options to auto attach the debugger

PowerShell, Git Bash, ZSH, and Command Prompt must have the debugging configuration enabled by setting **Auto Attach** to **Always** from the Command Palette. It can be disabled temporarily from the VS Code status bar:

Figure 3.7 – Auto Attach mode can be temporarily disabled from the status bar at the bottom of VS Code

At this point, we can further customize our framework by passing **environment variables**. In Mac, this is easy with any Terminal:

```
> DEBUG=true yarn wdio
```

Windows makes this tricky. To add a variable such as DEBUG, each shell has a separate syntax for multiple-line execution. Here's the list:

- Git Bash:

```
> set DEBUG=false && yarn wdio
```

- PowerShell and JavaScript debug terminal:

```
> set DEBUG=false; yarn wdio
```

- Command Prompt and ZSH (Mac):

```
> DEBUG=true yarn wdio
```

Furthermore, the syntax for this is different in package shortcuts:

- Mac:

```
"debug": "DEBUG=true wdio run test/wdio.conf.ts",
```

- Windows:

```
"debug": "set DEBUG=true && wdio run test/wdio.conf.ts",
```

If you have a mix of Mac and Windows team members, the situation may look dire. But superheroes have sidekicks and Node is no exception.

Rule of thumb – the cross-env node package

To resolve all this, we will install the cross-env package:

```
yarn add cross-env
```

By adding the cross-env package, we now can create a new debug shortcut that runs with a common syntax on both Mac and Windows:

```
debug: cross-env DEBUG=true wdio wdio.conf.ts
```

---

browser.debug()

Another way to debug our code is to add the `browser.debug()` statement:

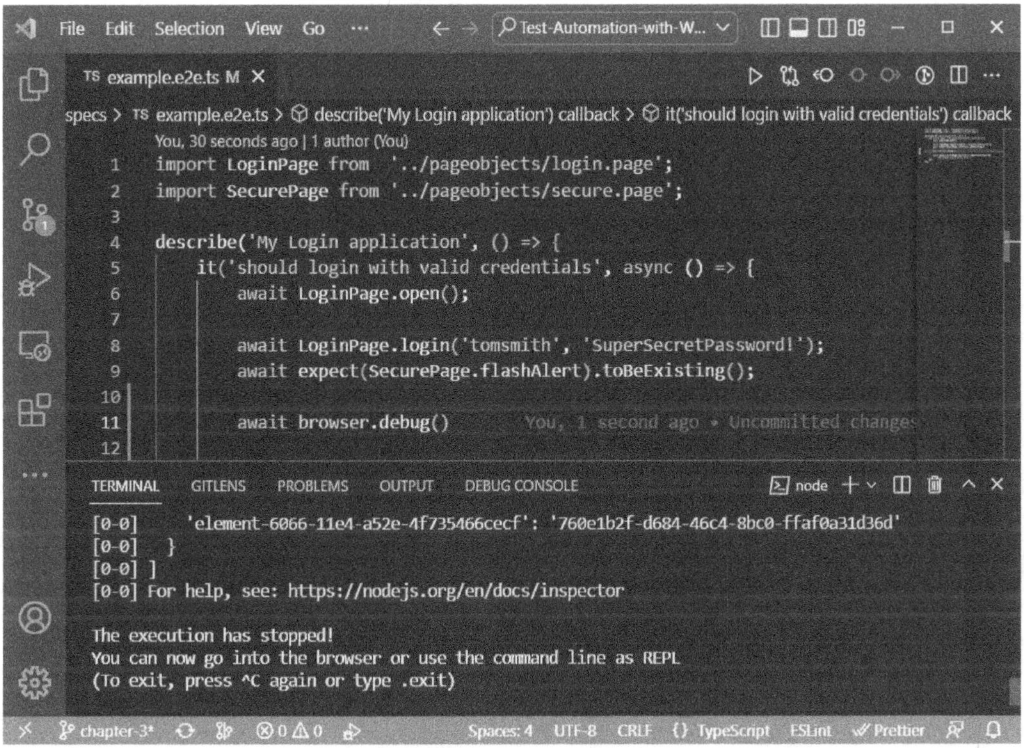

Figure 3.8 – Pausing execution in VS Code with browser.debug()

By default, WebdriverIO will pause the execution, but it is limited by the default timeout interval of our framework. For Jasmine, the default is about 1 minute. However, we need more time for debugging when an error occurs. By setting `defaultTimeoutInterval` to 15,000,000 milliseconds (about 4 hours), the script will have more time to debug any issues:

```
jasmineOpts: {
  defaultTimeoutInterval: 15_000_000,
```

Of course, we do not want to change this value back and forth manually, particularly if we're running in a cloud environment. This can be handled with our next superpower.

Dynamic configuration

Dynamic configuration means we can change the way the framework behaves by assigning system variables and passing them to our framework. These variables follow the ALL_CAPS naming convention of a constant. Let's begin by assigning a timeout based on the value of a DEBUG environment variable. At the top of the config file, we will capture the value of the DEBUG environment variable:

```
const DEBUG = (process.env.DEBUG === undefined) ? false : (process.
env.DEBUG === `true`)
```

This sets a default of false if DEBUG is not explicitly defined. Now, we can have a variable that extends the framework timeout when we explicitly execute a debug shortcut:

```
let timeout = DEBUG ? 10_000 : 16_000_000
```

> **Rule of thumb**
>
> Make your code readable with numeric separators. TypeScript supports underscores in place of commas with both integer and floating-point numbers. This makes 16_000_000 a valid integer while making the code more readable to humans.

We can find the timeout under jasmineOpts. Let's reference this new timeout variable. Find the following code:

```
jasmineOpts: {
defaultTimeoutInterval: 10000,
```

Change it to the following:

```
jasmineOpts: {
defaultTimeoutInterval: timeout,
```

You may consider setting the DEBUG default to True when it's omitted in a shortcut, then explicitly turning it off when run in a CI/CD environment such as Docker from Jenkins:

```
const DEBUG = (process.env.DEBUG === undefined) ? true : (process.env.
DEBUG === `true`)
```

The reason is that we spend most of our time writing and debugging our code is spent running the test. This means we spend less time typing this over and over to launch a test:

```
DEBUG=true yarn wdio
```

This just extend timeouts when run locally:

```
yarn wdio
```

Then, we can have the `debug` switch implicit in the shortcut and explicit for CI/CD:

```
"scripts": {
    "wdio": "wdio wdio.conf.ts"
    "debug": "DEBUG=true wdio wdio.conf.ts"
    "wdio-docker": "DEBUG=false wdio wdio.conf.ts"
}
```

In future chapters, we will execute tests in Docker. In those cases, we do not want our tests to wait several hours while we debug an error. In this script, we will change `DEBUG` to `false`; the test will use a short timeout specifically with that in mind:

```
yarn wdio-docker
```

Question: who is the customer of the automation framework? You might think it is the stakeholders, but not really. The stakeholders are the beneficiaries with pretty alluring graphs. Your team is the one who works with the framework every day. This means you are the customer. Prioritize your framework features with standards that help you to be efficient in your day-to-day work, not the whims of your benefactors.

You can read more about dynamic configurations here: `https://webdriver.io/docs/debugging/#dynamic-configuration`.

While we are looking at the Jasmine options, we might consider automatically adding screen captures to the results if the test fails. These can be added to the following code:

```
expectationResultHandler
expectationResultHandler: function(passed, assertion) {
  /**
   * only take screenshot if assertion failed
   */
  if(passed) {
      return
  }
  browser.saveScreenshot(`assertionError_${assertion.error.message}.
png`)
  }
```

This will create a screen capture at the root of our project. Screen captures do not need to take up space in the Git repo. So, we will add them inside the `.gitIgnore *.png` file.

A note about template strings

You may have noticed that template `'strings'` with accent marks are being extensively used in these code examples. While TypeScript supports `'single'` quotes and `"double"` quotes for strings, template strings make more sense in a test automation project.

Let's say, for example, we wish to write this string to our console log:

```
Meet Dwane "The Rock" Johnson at Moe's tavern
```

If we use quotes, we need to double escape the quotes in the string:

```
console.log("Meet ""Dwayne The Rock"" Johnson at Moe's  tavern")
```

If we used single quotes, the apostrophe would need to be escaped with a backslash:

```
console.log('Meet Dwyane "The Rock" Johnson at Moe\'s  tavern')
```

But with an accent template string, no escape is necessary:

```
console.log(`Meet Dwayne "The Rock" Johnson at Moe's tavern today`)
```

Templated strings can also pass `${variables}` to make reporting far more flexible and descriptive:

```
let guest = `Dwayne "The Rock" Johnson`
let location = `Moe's tavern`
```

Now, we can output a templated string to the console that is much easier to read than one with single or double quotes:

```
console.log(`Meet ${guest} at ${location} today`)
```

Much of the purpose of custom reporting functions is to reduce noise during debugging.

Reducing the signal-to-noise ratio

Now, we need to do some negative testing. Change the `ch3.ts` script so that it generates an error by adding `.not` to the expect validation chain:

```
await expect(SecurePage.flashAlert).not.toBeExisting();
```

Now, when we run the code, we'll get a lot of message details:

```
[0-0] 2022-11-28T09:14:03.160Z INFO webdriver: COMMAND
findElements("css selector", "#flash")
[0-0] 2022-11-28T09:14:03.160Z INFO webdriver: [POST] http://
localhost:9515/session/2e35b72bb526b5f0e346ba1379e4f5d9/elements
```

```
[0-0] 2022-11-28T09:14:03.161Z INFO webdriver: DATA { using: 'css
selector', value: '#flash' }
[0-0] 2022-11-28T09:14:03.174Z INFO webdriver: RESULT [
[0-0]    {
[0-0]       'element-6066-11e4-a52e-4f735466cecf': 'd6b5d426-fbbb-4871-
b190-94de4ef331cd'
[0-0]    }
```

A lot of information is produced that is not all that insightful. Inside the `wdio.config.ts` file, we can control how much detail is displayed in the console with `logLevel` settings:

```
// Level of logging verbosity: trace | debug | info | warn | error |
silent
    logLevel: 'info',
```

The order of options is listed in order of verbosity. The default of `'info'` can be overwhelming. Reducing it to `'warn'` is more adequate for our purposes.

Our final debugging technique is to enhance the `console.log()` command with a wrapper.

Our first custom wrapper method – global.log()

Question: what is a wrapper?

A wrapper is a bespoke method or function that is almost identical in signature to an intrinsic method but with added functionality. In our first example, we will create a global wrapper for `console.log()`.

While the `console.log()` method is good for outputting information to the console window, it can be enhanced and shortened. Let's build our first `log()` wrapper at the end of the `wdio.config.ts` file:

```
/**
 * log wrapper
 * @param text to be output to the console window
 */
global.log = async (text: any) => {
    console.log(`---> ${text}`)
}
```

This `global.log()` wrapper is almost identical to `console.log` except it has some text formatting that stands out. Let's look at this by adding some examples to the test:

```
console.log (`Entering password`)
[0-0] Entering password
await global.log (`Entering password`)
[0-0] ---> Entering password
```

This way, we can separate the custom messages being added to the framework from what is being generated by the Jasmine and node reporting output.

> **Rule of thumb**
>
> Even when a function has only one line, use curly brackets. There are two reasons for this. First, it makes logic branch issues easier to spot. Second, when adding brackets, there is a good chance you will soon add more lines of code.

Let's say we want to ignore empty strings and nulls passed to the log. When written as a single line of code, the intention is not very clear:

```
global.log = async (text: any) => {
    if (text) console.log(`---> ${text}`)
}
```

But with the brackets in place, the logic looks much clearer:

```
global.log = async (text: any) => {
    if (text) {
        console.log(`---> ${text}`)
    }
}
```

This follows the lines of the second reason we mentioned in the *Rule of thumb* box – you will soon add more lines of code. The preceding code would be better if we knew when an unresolved promise was passed to the log and what line had the issue. So, we will add an exception for `Promise` objects and display the console trace to show the line:

```
global.log = async (text: any) => {
    if (text) //truthy value check
    {
        if (text===Promise){
            console.log(`--->        WARN: Log was passed a Promise
object`)
            console.trace()
        }else{
            console.log(`---> ${text}`)
        }
    }
}
```

Question: why is the text assigned a type of `any` and not `string`?

In most cases, we will declare the type of the argument in TypeScript. That's the whole point of using it over JavaScript. But in this case, we want to have our debugging be a little more robust. We will add six log examples to the ch3.ts script:

```
describe(' Ch3: Cybernetic Enhancements', () => {
    it(should give detailed report and resize browser', async () => {
        await LoginPage.open();

        console.log (`Entering password`) // Intrinsic Log
        await global.log (`Entering password`) // Custom
        await global.log (``) // Does not print
        await global.log (null) // Does not print
        await global.log (Promise) // Adds trace
        await LoginPage.login('tomsmith', 'SuperSecretPassword!');

        await expect(SecurePage.flashAlert).toBeExisting();
        await expect(SecurePage.flashAlert).toHaveTextContaining(
            'You logged into a secure area!');
    });
});
```

With that, we have added our own level of detail that stands out. It skips empty and null strings. It also gives line numbers of where issues such as unresolved Promise originated:

```
[0-0] Entering password
[0-0] ---> Entering password
[0-0] --->      WARN: Log was passed a Promise object
[0-0] Trace
[0-0]      at global.log (D:\repos\Test-Automation-with-WebdriverIO\
test\wdio.conf.ts:379:21)
[0-0]      at UserContext.<anonymous> (D:\repos\wdio\test\specs\ch3.
ts:13:22)
...
[0-0] PASSED in chrome - D:\repos\wdio\test\specs\ch3.ts
```

Running this code gives us more flexibility in logging what our framework is doing. We have one last topic to discuss to ensure we write good code.

Rules to enforce coding standards

Every coding project should have a document that states what coding rules will be enforced during a code review. Tools called "linters" are good at detecting these rules. They need to be activated at the start of a project to ensure everyone is on the same page. Several rules can be activated in a TypeScript project. The first is called **strict mode**.

Strict mode

JavaScript has a strict mode feature. Adding `"use strict"` as the first line of a JavaScript source file enables extra rules to ensure good coding practices are followed that avoid subtle code errors.

This includes forcing variables to be explicitly declared with a `let`, `var`, or `const` keyword. TypeScript has a similar strict mode that can further force all variables to be assigned a type, such as `string`, `number`, or `boolean`. This is to avoid implicitly assigning a variable to the `any` type, which can lead to type coercion issues:

```
363        // onReload: fun  (parameter) text: any
364        // }
365    }                     to be output to the console window
366
367    /**                   @param text — to be output to the console window
368     * log wrapper
369     * @param text to be   Parameter 'text' implicitly has an 'any' type, but a better type may be
370     */                    inferred from usage. ts(7044)
371  global.log = async (text) =>   Quick Fix... (Ctrl+.)
372  {        You, 3 days ago • Added custom logging and screen captures …
373
```

Figure 3.9 – A strict mode warning where text is implicitly declared to be of the any type

In the preceding example, the `text` variable is implicitly assumed to be of the `any` type because no type assignment was provided for the `text` variable:

```
global.log = async (text) =>
```

With strict mode enabled, three dots appear under the `text` argument. Hovering the mouse over these dots reveals the issue description. It also includes the possibility for VS Code to suggest a quick fix that will infer the parameter type from usage:

```
global.log = async (text: any) =>
```

In a new TypeScript project, strict rules should be enabled from the start. These rules are enabled by adding them under the `"compiler options"` section of the `tsconfig.json` file. This rule enables all subset rules listed:

```
"compiler options": {
"strict": true,
. . .
```

However, turning on all rules in an existing project will likely create so much code to refactor that it causes significant delays in test creation. In that case, subsets of strict rules can be enabled and refactored over time.

Turning on individual TypeScript subset rule checks

Here is a list of the rules that can be enabled or disabled under the strict mode coding standards umbrella.

"noImplicitAny": true

This rule raises an error on expressions and declarations with an implied any type. In the following example, the x and y variables are implicitly set to the any type. Thus, if a string is passed, the code will coerce the number into a string and concatenate values rather than adding them:

```
function add(x, y) {
   return x + y;
}
const result = add(10, '20');
console.log(result); // '1020'
```

The following code resolves this issue by explicitly assigning the type of x and y to a number type. The only types of variables to be passed now are numbers, not strings:

```
function add(x: number, y: number) {
   return x + y;
}
const result = add(10, 20);
console.log(result); // 30
```

"strictNullChecks": true

This rule raises an error when variables are implicitly assigned a null value. This can cause issues when an empty string is a valid variable but a Null value is passed, throwing an error.

"strictFunctionTypes": true

This rule will enable strict checking of function parameter types. Take this code as an example:

```
const multiply = function(x: number, y: number) { return x * y; };
```

To fix this error, you would need to annotate the type of the multiply function:

```
const multiply: (x: number, y: number) => number = function(x, y) {
   return x * y;
};
```

"strictBindCallApply": true

This rule forces strict `bind`, `call`, and `apply` methods on functions. This is beyond the scope of the techniques that will be covered in this book.

bind()

The `bind()` function creates a new function with a specific value for this. It takes the value you want to use for this as the first argument; any additional arguments are passed to the original function when it is called. Here's an example:

```
class MyClass {
  public myProperty: string = 'hello';

  public someMethod() {
    setTimeout(function() {
      console.log(this.myProperty); // 'this' is not properly bound to
                                    // an object
    }, 1000);
  }
}
```

In the preceding example, the `someMethod()` method contains an anonymous function that uses the `this` keyword to access a property on the current object. However, the `this` keyword is not properly bound to the object:

```
class MyClass {
  public myProperty: string = 'hello';

  public someMethod() {
    setTimeout(function() {
      console.log(this.myProperty);
    }.bind(this), 1000);
  }
}
```

In the preceding code, the error has been resolved by binding the `this` keyword to the current object using the `bind()` function.

call()

The `call()` function is similar to `bind()`, but it calls the original function immediately, rather than creating a new function. It takes the value you want to use for `this` as the first argument; any additional arguments are passed to the original function when it is called:

```
class MyClass {
  public myProperty: string = 'hello';

  public someMethod() {
    const greeting = 'Hello';
    console.log(greeting.call(this, greeting)); // error: 'call' is
                                                // not a function
  }
}
```

In this example, the `someMethod()` method calls the `call()` function on a string value (greeting). However, the `call()` function can only be called on functions, so this will cause an error when the code is executed.

If you have the `strictBindCallApply` rule enabled, ESLint will catch this error and alert you to the issue. To fix the error, call the `call()` function on a function, rather than a string:

```
public greet(greeting: string) {
  console.log(`${greeting}, ${this.name}`);
}

public someMethod() {
  const greeting = 'Hello';
  this.greet.call(this, greeting); // calls the greet() method with
                                   // a specific value for 'this'
}
}
```

apply()

The `apply()` function is similar to `call()`, but it takes the arguments to pass to the original function as an array rather than a list of separate arguments. It takes the value you want to use for `this` as the first argument, and the array of arguments as the second argument:

```
class MyClass {
  public myProperty: string = 'hello';

  public someMethod() {
    const greeting = 'Hello';
    console.log(greeting.apply(this, greeting));
```

```
// error: 'apply' is not a function
  }
}
```

In the preceding example, the someMethod() method calls the apply() function on a (`greeting`) string value. However, the apply() function can only be called on functions, so this will cause an error when the code is executed:

```
class MyClass {
  public myProperty: string = 'hello';

  public greet(greeting: string) {
    console.log(`${greeting}, ${this.name}`);
  }

  public someMethod() {
    const greeting = 'Hello';
    this.greet.apply(this, [greeting]);
// calls the greet() method with a specific value for 'this'
  }
}
```

The preceding code shows how to fix the error by calling the apply() function on a function, rather than a string:

```
"strictPropertyInitialization": true,
```

This ESLint rule checks for properties that are declared in classes but are not initialized in the constructor. This rule can be used to enforce that all properties in a class are properly initialized before they are used:

```
class MyClass {
  public myProperty: string;

  constructor() {
    // myProperty is not initialized in the constructor
  }

  public someMethod() {
    console.log(this.myProperty.toUpperCase());
  }
}
```

ESLint will throw an error when you try to lint the code because `myProperty` is not initialized in the constructor. To resolve this, assign `myProperty` to a string:

```
public myProperty: string = "";
```

"noImplicitThis": true

This raises an error on expressions with an implied `any` type. In TypeScript, the `this` keyword refers to the current instance of a class, and it is often used inside class methods to access properties or methods on the current object:

```
class MyClass { public myProperty: string = 'hello';
  public someMethod() {
    setTimeout(function() {
      console.log(this.myProperty);
      // 'this' is not properly bound to an object
    }, 1000);
  }
}
```

ESLint will throw an error because the `this` keyword inside the anonymous function is not properly bound to an object. To fix this error, use an arrow function to bind the function to an object:

```
setTimeout(() => { console.log(this.myProperty);
// 'this' is now properly bound to the current object
```

"alwaysStrict": true

This final rule ensures the TypeScript files add `use strict` to the first line. In truth, this instructs the compiler to create TypeScript in strict mode, even if the command is missing from the TypeScript file.

@ts-ignore directive

At the end of the day, you may need to tell the compiler to ignore a warning. For example, the custom `log()` function intentionally has the message assigned to the `any` type instead of `string`. This is to ignore null strings and catch unwrapped promises that are passed that can be traced back to a specific line of code:

```
// @ts-ignore
global.log = async (text: any) => {
    console.log(`---> ${text}`)
}
```

It's important to note that the `@ts-ignore` directive is only meant to be used as a temporary measure to help get past an error or warning while you're working on your code. It's not a good idea to use this directive to suppress errors or warnings extensively as it can lead to unsafe or unreliable code.

The next question is, when will we ever have the time to refactor and document our framework when we are spending all our time writing test scripts?

> **Tip – "get it done" Friday**
>
> The best way is to plan for refactoring as part of sprint activities. Agile projects have a daily standup meeting. Some teams choose to eliminate the Friday standup and specifically dedicate additional time to code cleanup, refactoring, and documentation. The idea is that our weekends should be our own with our families and not dedicated to working.

> **Leverage artificial intelligence**
>
> **GitHub Copilot**: Developed by GitHub and OpenAI, it provides AI-powered code suggestions right in the editor. It's like a pair programmer that helps you write code faster and learn new APIs and languages along the way.
>
> **Tabnine**: An AI code-completion tool that works with popular IDEs. It predicts and suggests the next chunk of code you might write and supports multiple programming languages.
>
> **CodeGPT**: A powerful and innovative AI-driven coding assistant developed by OpenAI. It builds upon the foundation of GPT-3, a state-of-the-art language model, and is specifically tailored to assist developers and programmers in their coding tasks.

CodeGPT

CodeGPT is a revolutionary AI-powered code generation tool developed by OpenAI. It leverages the GPT-3.5 architecture to assist developers in creating code snippets, functions, and even entire programs in various programming languages, including TypeScript. This technology is a game-changer for developers as it can accelerate the coding process, enhance code quality, and help with debugging and problem-solving. With CodeGPT, you can quickly generate code examples, write unit tests, or even get suggestions on how to implement specific features, making it an invaluable addition to any developer's toolkit.

Here's an example of how CodeGPT can assist with TypeScript code generation. Suppose you want to create a TypeScript function that calculates the factorial of a number. With CodeGPT, you can request a code snippet like this:

```typescript
function factorial(n: number): number {
  if (n <= 1) {
    return 1;
```

```
    }
    return n * factorial(n - 1);
}
```

CodeGPT generates the TypeScript code for the factorial function, which takes an input number, n, and recursively calculates its factorial. This is just one example of how CodeGPT can simplify coding tasks by providing accurate and efficient code snippets.

Here is a real-life example that I encountered while writing this book. We asked for an advanced function that parses values from a string in the key=value format that could be transposed into a dictionary object with some examples. GitHub Copilot already knew of the SwitchboardFactory SBF object and came up with this function with a header:

```
/**
 * Parses a string of key-value pairs and updates the SwitchBoard
state with those values.
 * Each pair within the testData string should be separated by spaces,
and
 * keys/values should be separated by an '=' character.
 *
 * For example, a string "guests=2 zipcode=12345" will result in SBF
having
 * "guests" set to 2 and "zipcode" set to 12345.
 * @param {string} testData - The string containing key-value pairs to
be parsed.
 */
export function parseToSBF(testData: string) {
  let parts = testData.split(" ");
  parts.forEach(part => {
    if (part.includes('=')) {
      let [key, value] = part.split("=");
      SBF.set(key, parseInt(value));
    }
  });
}
```

Artificial intelligence is the way of the future. We are at a point in time similar to when sledgehammers were used to break up concrete at the moment that Charles Brady King invented the jackhammer. This is our jackhammer!

Summary

In this chapter, we reviewed the node files of the Webdriver node framework. We showed you how to make launching tests common between Mac and Windows team members. We also showed you how to set up the environment to enable debugging and writing better code in TypeScript. Finally, we wrote our first custom log wrapper, which optimized the output to the console window.

By taking control of logging, we can make our debugging process more productive by deciding how it's formatted and what is sent to the Allure report. In upcoming chapters, we will even add color for visibility and apply this same wrapper concept to the most common WebdriverIO browser methods to make supercharged robust tests.

But we do not want to get ahead of ourselves, Doc! Next, we will talk about the effects of time travel because TypeScript is a bit of a speedster!

4

Super Speed – Time-Travel Paradoxes and Broken Promises

In this chapter, we will discuss how we deal with issues that arise with multithreaded execution in an event loop of a test framework. Then, we'll look at a way to keep the switches in a framework in a consistent location when we begin to add more complex functionality.

JavaScript is an insanely fast programming language. Because its primary goal is to build website pages as fast as possible, it executes lines of code in an event loop with multiple threads. This is an advantage in building web pages as fast as possible, but it can be a hindrance in test automation that needs events executed in a particular order.

In fact, this speedster is so fast it can time travel. Let us take a look at an example in the next section.

Before we do that, here's a list of the topics we'll cover in this chapter:

- The time-travel dilemma
- Schrödinger and the quantum mechanics of test automation
- Callbacks, promises, and async/await
- The death of fibers and synchronous mode

Technical requirements

All test examples can be found at this GitHub repository: `https://github.com/PacktPublishing/Enhanced-Test-Automation-with-WebdriverIO`.

The time-travel dilemma

Let's begin with the most basic script – login. Open `login.page.ts` in the `\pageobjects` folder. Note there is an `async` command in the `login()` function:

```
public async login (username: string, password: string)
    await this.inputUsername.setValue(username);
    await this.inputPassword.setValue(password);
    await this.btnSubmit.click();
}
```

The `async` keyword forces the function to always be asynchronous, returning a `Promise` object representing the completion or failure of the function. There is also an `await` keyword preceding the `.setValue` and `.click` commands, which pauses the function until the `Promise` object is resolved or rejected. What would happen if the `await` command were removed?

```
public async login (username: string, password: string) {
    //Removed await keyword
    this.inputUsername.setValue(username);
    this.inputPassword.setValue(password);
    this.btnSubmit.click();
}
```

From the Visual Studio Code shell, run the `wdio` test:

```
> yarn wdio
```

When the test is executed, it fails! It indicates that the username provided was invalid in the following results, which leads us down a rabbit hole because the password is in fact perfectly valid:

```
» \test\specs\ch2.ts
 My Login application
    x should login with valid credentials
 1 failing (12.2s)
 1) My Login application should login with valid credentials
 Expect $(`#flash`) to have text containing
- Expected  - 1
+ Received  + 2
- You logged into a secure area!
+ Your username is invalid!
```

So, what changed? The execution order of the lines of code! Without the await keyword, Node.js will execute all the JavaScript commands simultaneously. So, the **Submit** button could get clicked before the credentials are populated. This fails the final validation in the main script checking for the text You are logged into a secure area!. It fails because the **Login** button was clicked before the Username field was completely populated. It instead reports Your username is invalid because the username was still blank when the **Submit** button was clicked.

Of course, the best superhero detectives need more evidence. No one thought to take a picture at the scene of the crime. So, let's add some debugging output and try the test again:

```
global.log (`Logging in with '${username}' and '${password}'`)
this.inputUsername.setValue(username);
global.log (`Entered '${username}'`)
this.inputPassword.setValue(password);
global.log (`Entered '${password}' and clicking Submit`)
this.btnSubmit.click();
global.log ("Submit clicked!")
```

This time, the results show the test passed. However, we have now encountered a stale element:

```
[0-0] ---> Logging in with 'tomsmith' and 'SuperSecretPassword!'
[0-0] ---> Entered 'tomsmith'
[0-0] ---> Entered 'SuperSecretPassword!' and clicking Submit
[0-0] ---> Submit clicked!
[0-0] 2022-12-03T18:07:52.839Z WARN webdriver: Request encountered a
stale element - terminating request
[0-0] PASSED in chrome - D:\repos\wdio\test\specs\ch2.ts
```

Which element was stale? In order to find out, we need to change the logLevel back to info in wdio.conf.ts:

```
    logLevel: 'info',
```

Now, when we rerun the test, we get a completely different error buried in a lot of information:

```
[0-0]    error: 'no such element',
[0-0]    message: 'no such element: Unable to locate element:
{"method":"css selector","selector":"#flash"}\n' +
[0-0]    ' (Session info: chrome=107.0.5304.122)',
```

It looks like things have gotten out of hand. If we try to add more debug statements, we'll get differing results that might not be repeatable. Would you believe this exact phenomenon is described in a book far more advanced than this one?

Schrödinger and the quantum mechanics of test automation

This issue is similar to what is known as the *measurement problem* in quantum mechanics. Putting it simply, measuring the outcome of an event at the quantum level can change the outcome of the event. Imagine testing the temperature of cold water with a warm thermometer. Over time, the measuring equipment warms the cold water slightly and the equipment itself cools from the cold water. Thus, readings over time become inconclusive.

In this case, sending details to the console window puts a little more overhead on the system. The speed of execution of the statements changes slightly, and so does the completion order, giving different results each time. This has a lot to do with the prioritization of statement execution in the JavaScript event Loop, as shown next:

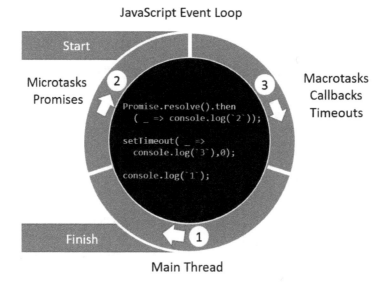

Figure 4.1 – A visualization of the execution order of promises and callbacks in the JavaScript Event loop

JavaScript has an Event Loop with the main thread, with macro tasks and micro tasks. The latter, which are promises, execute after the main thread statements. `MacroTasks`, which include callbacks and the timeout statement, *can* execute prior to the Main thread but after promises. When these tasks are completed in an unexpected order, you can waste hours of time trying to isolate the issue during debugging.

`MacroTasks` are usually related to I/O operations or UI rendering. Examples of `MacroTasks` include `setTimeout`, `setInterval`, `setImmediate`, and I/O operations. These tasks are executed by the event loop, and they can run before or after `MicroTasks`.

`MicroTasks` are usually related to promises. They can also include mutation observers. Developers use these in various scenarios, such as tracking changes to attributes, detecting additions or removals of child elements, or even observing changes to character data within an element. `MicroTasks` are executed after the main thread statements and before the execution of the next `macroTask`. They are used to handle callbacks and resolve promises.

When tasks complete in an unexpected order, it can lead to debugging challenges. This is because the order of execution impacts the overall behavior of the test. This is fine for optimizing the time spent building a web page on multiple threads, but it causes havoc for SDETs trying to run script steps in a sequential order.

Callbacks, promises, and async/await

To resolve these issues, we need to force JavaScript to execute code in a linear order. JavaScript provides three solutions – callbacks, promises, and `async/await` keywords. JavaScript promises and callbacks are two ways of knowing when the asynchronous call has a result. Callbacks allow you to execute a function once a response is received. Promises do the same and allow you to specify an easily readable order for multiple operations, as well as handle error cases. However, did you know there was an even easier way to deal with promises called synchronous mode?

The death of fibers and synchronous mode

Promises were added to JavaScript to make asynchronous callbacks to functions easier to implement. Functions were passed without parenthesis, making them visibly similar to variables and objects. Then, the **async** and **await** keywords were also added as syntactic sugar to make promises and callbacks easier. However, way back in 2014, there was the `node-fibers` package project, which implicitly wrapped statements as callbacks in the background.

Up until version 7.0, WebdriverIO leveraged the `node-fibers` package as part of the `@wdio/sync` feature. This meant all browser methods would execute synchronously without callbacks, promises, or **await**. This was a brilliant trade-off for WebdriverIO framework architects! It avoided the time travel issues while making the code less complex.

Unfortunately, the `node-fibers` project was discontinued in 2021. WebdriverIO was forced to notify users of two solutions – they could lock Node to the last supported version that was compatible with `node-fibers`, missing out on new features as JavaScript added more functionality defined by the evolving ECMAScript standard. Alternatively, they could refactor the code base to include `async` in functions and `await` in browser methods. Most chose the latter and faced a large amount of time refactoring code.

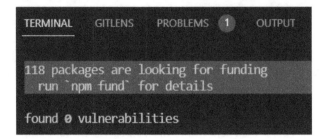

Figure 4.2 – Packages looking for funding

That said, let us look at how we solve this time crisis. In our previous chapter, we simulated an error by passing a `promise` object:

```
await global.log (Promise) // Adds trace
```

What happens if we remove the `await` keyword?

```
global.log (Promise) // Adds trace with WARN out of order
[0-0] Trace
[0-0]     at global.log (D:\repos\Test-Automation-with-WebdriverIO\
test\wdio.conf.ts:379:21)
[0-0]     at UserContext.<anonymous> (D:\repos\wdio\test\specs\
example.e2e.ts:13:22)
[0-0] --->     WARN: Log was passed a Promise object
```

Note that when `await` is missing from the code, all that happens is the custom WARN message appears after the error detail, instead of before it. This relates to JavaScript executing in multiple threads. We have proof of the effect of events executing out of sequence.

Keep it simple with async and await

Every custom method in this book will execute asynchronously. In theory, we might think it would be clever to populate fields and drop-down lists concurrently for speed. However, often choosing a value from a list will kick off an `Ajax` method that will update the web page. This would then have fields generating errors if the elements do not yet exist because the code executed while the page was built anew.

Summary

In this chapter, we learned about the impact synchronous code execution can have on our framework. While callbacks and promises are ways to keep code running in sequential order, it is best to use async and await to keep it consistent. We also upgraded global values to a single `switchboard` object that can be viewed during debugging sessions.

In the next chapter, we will combine everything so far to enhance our first method wrapper function.

Alter Egos – The ClickAdv Wrapper

In this and the next few chapters, we will introduce the concept of adding wrappers for the `.click()`, `.select()`, and `.setValue()` intrinsic methods. These wrappers allow us to add more functionality to these methods to make the framework more robust and less likely to fail during a test.

Wrappers are the easiest way to extend functionality throughout the test suite, eliminating the need to repeatedly add code in the form of multiple test scripts. Sometimes when testing, the page loads slowly and our elements take longer to load. Sometimes, the page is updated due to **Asynchronous JavaScript and XML (AJAX)** and the element we found is now stale and must be found again. Our results, shown in both the console window and Allure, should be detailed enough to indicate what is occurring. Wrappers allow us to start handling all that information efficiently, including scrolling an element into view for screen captures, looking for similar replacement objects to reduce maintenance, and burning time during page builds so that elements have time to appear without resorting to slower hardcoded wait methods.

There are three ways that we will explore for injecting superpowers into our framework:

- Helper commands
- Browser commands
- Element commands

We will first start adding a `helpers` file along with its prerequisites.

Adding a helpers file

We begin by preparing our helper commands, which require the `utility-types` package in order to support optional parameters in TypeScript. This package is installed with the following command:

```
> yarn add utility-types
```

We will next add a \helpers folder that contains a helpers.ts file module. This contains several methods for resolving issues in the framework. This is where we will store the majority of our custom supporting code for the framework.

To create a helpers file in a WebdriverIO project written in TypeScript, we need to do the following:

1. Create a new directory in our project to store our helper functions. This directory will be called helpers, located within our src directory.

2. Within the helpers directory, create a new TypeScript file for our helper functions. Let's call this file helpers.ts.

3. At the top of the helpers.ts file, we need to import the necessary types and functions to support file paths, global objects, and Allure reports. Some of these will come into play in future chapters:

    ```
    import * from as fs from "fs"
    import * as path from "path";
    import { ASB } from "./globalObjects.ts";
    import allure from "@wdio/allure-reporter";
    ```

4. Within the helpers.ts file, we need to define our helper functions. The structure of the file will include the public method wrappers such as click(), pageSync(), and assert(). It will also contain private supporting methods for finding and replacing data tokens, and getElementType() to determine how to handle errors by class:

    ```
    export const clickElement = async (driver: WebDriver, element:
    WebDriver.Element) => {p
      try {p
        await driver.click(element)p
      } catch (error) {p
        throw new WebDriverError(`Unable to click element: ${error.
    message}`)p
      }p
    }
    ```

5. In the files where we want to use the helper functions, we import the functions from the helpers.ts file as follows:

    ```
    import { clickAdv } from './helpers/helpers'p

    We can then use the clickAdv function in our test code like
    this:
    await clickAdv(driver, element)
    ```

This is just one example of how we can create and use helper functions in a WebdriverIO project written in TypeScript. We can define as many helper functions as we need in the helpers.ts file and import them into our test code as and when required.

Before we get to the `click()` method, let's begin with a wrapper of `console.log` so we can customize the detail. If we happen to call it with a string such as `is blank` or `empty`, or a `null` variable, it does not need to print anything. But if anything other than a string or number is passed, such as a promise or an object, it should output a warning without failing:

```
p
/**
 * Console.log wrapper
 *     - Does not print if string is empty / null
 *     - Prints trace if not passed string or number
 * @param message
 */
export async function log(message: any): Promise<void> {
  try {
    if (typeof message === "string" || typeof message === "number") {
      if (message) {
        console.log(`---> ${message}`);
      }
    } else {
      console.log(`--->   helpers.console() received: ${message}`);
      console.trace();
    }
  } catch (error: any) {
    console.log(`--->   helpers.console(): ${error.message}`);
  }
}
```

Notice there is some extra spacing when the error is output to the console. This is intentional. We will be making our output visually helpful with spacing and color later.

To utilize the helpers, we add the following import line to our test files:

```
import * as helpers from '../../helpers/helpers.ts';
```

To call the method, we use this statement:

```
helpers.log (`Hello, World!`)
> [0-0] ---> Hello, World!
```

If the method is called with a null string, it does not output anything to the console:

```
helpers.log (``)
```

If anything other than a string or number is passed then the object and a trace is output, something like the following commonly occurs, where a promise object is returned instead of a string due to a missing `await` keyword:

```
helpers.log (Promise)
> [0-0] --->   helpers.console() received: function Promise() {
[native code] }
> [0-0] Trace
> [0-0]     at Module.log (file:///D:/repos/Test-Automation-with-
WebdriverIO/helpers/helpers.ts:14:15)
> [0-0]     at UserContext.<anonymous> (file:///D:/repos/Test-
Automation-with-WebdriverIO/test/specs/example.e2e.ts:10:17)
```

When a problematic element is passed to the `helper.log` wrapper, the second line of code, `UserContext`, will identify where the actual error occurred. Our debugging is now starting to look a little bit better.

Let's next identify and resolve a potential problem in the `.click` method of the `login.page.ts` file.

The "Hello, World!" of test automation

The test-automation equivalent of `Hello, World!` is usually a test that checks for the presence of a simple element on a web page, such as a heading or a paragraph of text. This can involve writing a test that does the following:

- Navigates to a web page
- Locates an element on the page using an XPath or CSS selector method
- Verifies that the element is present and displayed on the page

In our first example, we have the following five simple steps to perform a login:

1. Navigate to a simulated login screen.
2. Enter the username.
3. Enter the password credentials.
4. Click the login button.
5. Validate that a message appears, indicating the login was successful.

An example can be found in the `pageObjects\login.page.ts` file:

```
await this.inputUsername.setValue(username);
await this.inputPassword.setValue(password);
await this.btnSubmit.click();
```

We have already resolved errors that can arise from lines of code executing out of order by using the `await` statement. However, element locators may become stale over time as developers change the pages we are automating. For example, imagine the class of the login button was initially a `button` class:

```
<button class="radius" type="submit" fdprocessedid="ra4xrd">p
    <i class="fa fa-2x fa-sign-in"> Login</i>p
</button>
```

But in the next release, it was changed to an anchor link class:

```
<a class="radius" type="submit" fdprocessedid="ra4xrd">p
    <i class="fa fa-2x fa-sign-in"> Login</i>p
</a>p
```

Then the `.click` method will throw the following error:

```
[0-0] Error: Can't call click on element with selector
"button[type="submit"]" because element wasn't found
```

We could surround the click with a `try/catch` method to capture exceptions and get more detail about what exactly caused an error to be thrown. In this example, if the click method was successful, we output the successful event. However, if the element did not exist, was covered by another element, or otherwise could not be clicked, we output the `captured` error detail and send it to our console:

```
try{
    await this.btnSubmit.click();
    helpers.log(` Clicked button`);
} catch (err)
    helpers.log(`    Click failed because\n${err}`);
}
```

We would like to have this for every element, but we do not want to have to add this code repeatedly in all of our test scripts. Fortunately, with wrappers, there is a better way.

ES6 helper modules versus overriding intrinsic methods

There are multiple ways to achieve this goal. One way to do this would be to completely override the intrinsic actions of the `click()` method in every call. Alternatively, we could create our own custom method with its own unique naming convention. Lastly, we can create our own function that takes the object as a parameter and performs additional functionality. Here is what those three approaches might look like:

We could override all intrinsic `click()` methods:

```
btnLogin.click() // Customized with overWriteCommand
```

We could add a custom method:

```
btnLogin.clickAdv()
```

Or create a custom function in our `Helpers` file:

```
clickAdv(btnLogin)
```

The approach you use is up to you. But the key is to pick one and stick with it consistently, rather than having a mishmash of different approaches. Each one has its own advantages worth considering. Let us look at the pros and cons of the first two approaches.

Overriding intrinsic element methods

One way we could enhance the `click()` method is to completely override the intrinsic element methods from the `ts.config.json` file, as follows:

```
browser.overwriteCommand('click', async(origClick, element)= {
    let success = true;
    try{ p           element = await getValidElement(element,
"button");
        await element.click(); // Instrinsic click
        console.log(' Clicked ${element.selector}');
    } catch (err)
        success = false;
        console.log(`$   {element.selector}click failed\n ${err)`);
  }
    return success;
})
```

This command will encapsulate features such as checking the object validity, setting the frame, setting the framework to somewhere, and skipping additional methods if called when the element does not exist. The way we do this is with sanity testing. For example, we will attempt to click on a nonexistent button called `btnBogus` and see how the rest of the script executes. Here is an object description of the bogus button:

```
await this.btnBogus.click();
```

With this approach, the signature stays the same and all our test scripts are enhanced:

```
await this.btnSubmit.click();
```

The custom `click()` method can add more detail as to what is happening:

```
[0-0] ---> Clicking button[type="submit"] ...
[0-0] --->   button clicked.
```

This approach efficiently adds enhanced functionality to the `click()` method of every element in the entire suite of tests. But this is also a drawback – an error in this method could break everywhere the `click()` method is used. There is no easy way to revert a specific line in a test script to the original intrinsic method to see whether the error caused the overridden code. We can only turn it all on or turn it all off.

There must be another way!

Adding a custom element method

We can add a custom element command to the browser object. In this case, let us call it `clickAdv()`. It can be implemented by changing the first and last lines of the preceding code to the following:

```
browser.addCommand("clickAdv", async function (){
...
}, true);
```

The call to the method becomes this:

```
await this.btnSubmit.clickAdv();
```

The custom `clickAdv()` method has the same detail as the overridden version:

```
[0-0] ---> Clicking button[type="submit"]
[0-0] --->    button clicked.;
```

> **Quick tip**
>
> Avoid "magic" values. These are values known only to the developer and may not be easily found in the documentation. In this preceding example, the last line overrides the implicit `false` with `true`. The meaning is that the custom method is to be added to an element rather than the browser.

Now we have the flexibility of a `clickAdv()` custom method that can be reverted to an intrinsic version by removing `Adv` at an atomic level:

```
await this.btnAddToCart.clickAdv();
```

This is done by removing `Adv` from the method:

```
await this.btnAddToCart.click();
```

This seems perfect! All we need now is to do a little negative testing with a bogus element and see whether the output indicates the click failed.

Who tests the SDET's code? Sanity testing of the automation framework

Unit testing is an important part of any development project. Since it is expected that developers will write unit tests for the functionality of the application, so too it would be reasonable that the SDETs write unit tests for the framework code base itself. However, the terms "unit testing" and "integration testing" often cause confusion when applied to the automation framework itself. Let us refer to this aspect as "sanity testing of the automation framework", although it is really unit testing of discreet framework functionality and the integration of those features. These are scripts written to intentionally test the viability of the features in the framework. Like the previous "Hello, World" example, test automation has a version of sanity testing that exercises each of our advanced methods. Since automation is a development project, we should have a short test that intentionally exercises the capabilities of the framework. This may include finding elements with stale XPath or CSS locators, dynamically changing embedded data tags to the current date, or writing detailed logging from the wrapper methods. It might include a negative test on a non-existent element that intentionally fails as its expected result.

As we add more functionality, we should also add sanity testing to our scripts. We will add a non-existent button called `btnBogus` that will force the method to fail:

```
public get btnBogus () {
    return $('button[type="bogus"]');
}
```

To sanity test, we will click the `btnBogus` button followed by the `submit` button in our `login fail` method in the `login page` class:

```
await this.btnBogus.clickAdv();
```

And our results are not what we expected:

```
Error: Can't call clickAdv on element with selector
"button[type="bogus"]" because element wasn't found
```

WebdriverIO validates the element before it executes the custom method. The same occurs if the method was overridden. The problem here is that it prevents us from implementing self-healing objects in our framework or replacing a stale element with a viable one.

There must be another way.

Extending our ES module helper file with a custom click method

There are two ways to write error-free programs; only the third one works.

– Allen J. Perlis

Our third option is to create a `click()` method in the `helpers` file. While it changes our signature, it allows us more control to recover from issues with elements:

```
await helpers.clickAdv(this.btnSubmit);
await helpers.clickAdv(this.btnBogus);
```

The output now looks like this:

```
[0-0] ---> Clicking button[type="submit"] ...
[0-0] --->    button clicked.
[0-0] --->    pageSync() completed in 25 ms
[0-0] ---> Clicking button[type="bogus"] ...
[0-0] --->    button[type="submit"] was not clicked.
[0-0] Error: Can't call click on element with selector
"button[type="bogus"]" because element wasn't found
```

> **Quick tip**
>
> Unlike many coding conventions, there is no common approach for naming wrapper methods. Some teams may use a trailing underscore (_) while others might append the word `Wrapper`. The important takeaway here is that teams should agree on an identifiable naming convention that is documented in a Coding Standards document and followed in code reviews.

Now that we are checking that our button can be clicked, let's look at what happens afterward.

Why are waits difficult to implement correctly?

All automation tools have ways to determine what to do when an element does not exist. The most common solution is to wait until the object exists. WebdriverIO has an option to adjust the timeout for elements in the `wdio.config.json` file:

```
// Default timeout for all waitFor* commands.
waitforTimeout: 10_000,
```

The default is 10 seconds. For years, the most common choice was to wait 30 seconds. The problem was, depending on our tool, if our script navigated to the wrong page, that timeout might happen on every element. That is a long time to wait for the script to finally end if a lot of elements do not exist.

Back in 2000s, the founder of WorkSoft, Linda Hayes, noted that there is a way to calculate a good wait timeout for our framework. Take the average time for our slowest page to render and triple it. This means we will anticipate a load will be added to our application under test and can be flexible enough to handle it.

Different tools have many ways to wait for elements to appear. Tools such as Selenium, for example, have three: implicit, explicit, and fluent waits. Implicit waits tell Selenium to wait a certain amount of time before throwing an exception if an element is not found on the page. Explicit waits wait for a specific condition to be met before continuing, such as `enabled` or `clickable`. Fluent waits allow customization of the maximum wait time, the frequency with which the condition should be checked, and the types of exceptions that should be ignored.

But what is the next most common reason that an element does not exist? It is because the page is still building. We could just add a hardcoded wait for an element to appear.

The problem is when these waits are mixed together that the actual wait time of a Selenium script can add up to several minutes and become difficult to debug.

Similarly, WebdriverIO provides several types of waits to handle dynamic elements on a web page. These include commands such as `waitUntil()`, `waitForExist()`, `waitForDisplayed()`, `waitForEnabled()`, and `waitForSelected()`, which allow waiting for specific conditions to be met before continuing with test execution.

Note that the `waitForExist()` command rarely has a use in test automation. It merely means the element exists in the DOM, not that it appears on the page. `waitForDisplayed()` provides the same check and makes it more likely the element can be interacted with by the user.

Again, Linda Hayes noted that to make a framework more robust, each element should be checked to make sure that it exists and is enabled. This provides the breaks for our high-speed car as we make our way down the curvy mountain road at night.

What if, instead of waiting for every element to appear and be enabled, we could wait for the page build to complete after each click? Then it would be more likely that every element on the page is viable. This would eliminate the need to check whether the element exists every time. Only if the element is not found then the framework can get creative about finding it before throwing an error.

"I don't always use Pause(), but when I do, It's less than 1000 milliseconds"

Yes, there will be times when we need to perform a wait but we want to be smarter about it. For example, the `pageSync()` wrapper method needs a quarter-second wait as it counts how many elements are on the page. This is the code for the custom `pause(ms)` method that will tell us when a hardcoded wait of half a second occurs:

```
/**
 * Wrapper for browser.pause
```

```
 * @param ms reports if wait is more than 1/2 second
 */
export async function pause(ms: number) {
  if (ms > 500){
  log(`  Waiting ${ms} ms...`); // Custom log
  }

  const start = Date.now();
  let now = start;
  while (now - start < ms) {
    now = Date.now();
  }
}
```

The method will write to the console if the delay is more than half a second. This is to remind us to be aware of how much delay is in the framework. `wait` is like adding salt to a soup: a little is okay, but too much spoils it for everyone. We could also count how much time is wasted in total.

Highlighting elements

Next, we will add a way to highlight an element to make sure we can see what is occurring when we are debugging. These highlights are also a handy way to check whether an element is visible. This code will highlight an element in green, although we can override that color. It also has a check to see whether the element we are highlighting has gone stale. If that is the case, the element is saved to the automation switchboard and a stale element switch is set to `true`. This allows us to update the element in the calling routines to eliminate the chance of stale elements slowing our test execution. Lastly, the function returns whether the element was visible or not:

```
export async function highlightOn(
  element: WebdriverIO.Element,
  color: string = "green"
): Promise<boolean> {
  let elementSelector:any
  let visible: boolean = true;
  try {
    elementSelector = await element.selector;
    try {
      await browser.execute(`arguments[0].style.border = '5px solid
${color}';`, element);
      visible = await isElementVisible(element)
    } catch (error: any) {
      // Handle stale element
      const newElement = await browser.$(elementSelector)
      ASB.set("element", newElement)
      ASB.set("staleElement", true)
```

```
        await browser.execute(`arguments[0].style.border = '5px solid
${color}';`, newElement);
        //log (` highlightOn ${elementSelector} refresh success`)
      }

  } catch (error) {
    // Element no longer exists
    visible = false
  }
  return visible;
}
```

Since we have the highlight functionality turned on, we should add something that turns the highlight off, for which we will use a spinner detection method:

```
export async function highlightOff(element: WebdriverIO.Element):
Promise<boolean> {
  let visible: boolean = true;
  try {
      await browser.execute(`arguments[0].style.border = "0px";`,
element);
  } catch (error) {
      // Element no longer exists
      visible = false;
  }
  return visible;
}
```

This method simply tells us whether the element was visible or not when removing the highlight.

Next, let us implement a spinner detection method that waits until a spinner no longer appears on the page:

Note that this element locator will be different from project to project. In some projects, we look for spinners and loaders:

```
export async function waitForSpinner(): Promise<boolean> {
  let spinnerDetected: boolean = false;
  // This spinner locator is unique to each project
  const spinnerLocator: string = `//img[contains(@src,'loader')]`;
  await pause(100); // Let browser begin building spinner on page
  let spinner = await browser.$(spinnerLocator);
  let found = await highlightOn(spinner);
```

```
let timeout = ASB.get("spinnerTimeoutInSeconds")
const start = Date.now();
if (found) {
  const startTime = performance.now();
  spinnerDetected = true;
  try {
    while (found) {
      found = await highlightOn(spinner);
      if (!found) break;
      await pause(100);
      found = await highlightOff(spinner);
      if (!found) break;
      await pause(100);
      if (Date.now() - start > timeout * 1000) {
        log (`ERROR: Spinner did not close after ${timeout}
        seconds`)
        break;
      }
    }
  } catch (error) {
    // Spinner no longer exists
  }
  log(`  Spinner Elapsed time: ${Math.floor(performance.now() -
  startTime)} ms`);
}
return spinnerDetected;
}
```

The method utilizes the highlightOn() and the highlightOff() methods to flash the spinner or **loading...** element when it is detected. It will log a message if the spinner did not disappear within the timeout. And finally, it returns a Boolean value if a spinner was detected. This helps us optimize our framework, as we would need to perform a page sync if a spinner appeared.

Now we can proceed to expand the click() wrapper. It will require a dynamic method to wait for the page to build.

Expanding the click method wrapper

Let's extend the clickAdv() method to make it more robust and less likely to fail. First, we will add a pageSync() function to the helper class. This function is an alternative way to determine when the page build has settled. After each click, we will perform the following actions:

1. Count the number of visible / span elements on the page.
2. Wait 1/4 of a second.

3. Repeat until either of the following occur:

    - The count of /span elements is stable 3 times

    - The timeout is reached

4. Report service-level-agreement metrics on how long it took to complete.

5. Add the option to customize the length of the wait time.

The page sync method will dynamically wait for the page to build. It is optimized to spend a minimum of 0.75 seconds detecting when the page is completed. This reduces the chance of throwing an error if our element does not exist as the page is building. But it also gives us the flexibility to wait longer, up to 30 seconds for the page if there is a significant load put on the system slowing everything down.

It is rather large, so let us break it down:

```
/**
 * pageSync - Dynamic wait for the page to stabilize.
 * Use after click
 * ms = default time wait between loops 125 = 1/8 sec
 *      Minimum 25 for speed / stability balance
 */
let LAST_URL: String = "";
export async function pageSync(
  ms: number = 25,
  waitOnSamePage: boolean = false
): Promise<boolean> {
  await waitForSpinner();
```

We begin by waiting for any spinner or **loading...** elements to appear. Then we optimize by executing only when the URL has changed:

```
let result = false;
  let skipToEnd = false;
  let thisUrl = await browser.getUrl();
  if (waitOnSamePage === false) {
    if (thisUrl === LAST_URL) {
      //skip rest of function
      result = true;
      skipToEnd = true;
    }
  }
```

If the URL has not changed, it is more likely that a spinner simply appeared because a list option was selected, changing the elements on the page. If the URL is new then we begin by getting the first count of elements. This is a dynamic loop that executes no less than three times:

```
if (skipToEnd === false) {
  LAST_URL = thisUrl;
  const waitforTimeout = browser.options.waitforTimeout;
  let visibleSpans: String = `span:not([style*="visibility:
hidden"])`;
  let elements: any = await $$(visibleSpans);
  let exit: boolean = false;
  let count: number = elements.length;
  let lastCount: number = 0;
  let retries: number = 3;
  let retry: number = retries;
  let timeout: number = 20; // 5 second timeout
  const startTime: number = Date.now();
  while (retry > 0) {
    if ((lastCount != count) || (count < 20)) {
      retry = retries; // Reset the count of attempts
    }
    // Exit after 3 stable element counts
    if (retry == 0) {
      break;
    }
    if (timeout-- === 0) {
      log("Page never settled");
      exit = true;
      break;
    }
    lastCount = count;
```

After each element count, we let the page continue building for a brief moment. Then we count the elements again until the count is the same for three consecutive attempts. In addition, we keep checking whether the page count is greater than 20 elements. Often, this is the threshold below which lies a blank page without a spinner or **loading…** element.

It is important to note that we only count Span elements. This could be div elements, but we should not count all elements with a star wildcard, the reason being that counting every element on the page itself can take longer than a quarter-second:

```
// wait 1/4 sec before next count check
await pause(ms);
try {
  elements = await $$(visibleSpans);
} catch (error: any) {
```

```
      exit = true;
      switch (error.name) {
        case "TimeoutError":
          log(`ERROR: Timed out while trying to find visible
          spans.`);
          break;
        case "NoSuchElementError":
          log(`ERROR: Could not find any visible spans.`);
          break;
        default:
          if (error.message === `Couldn't find page handle`) {
            log(`WARN: Browser closed. (Possibly missing await)`);
          }
      }
      // Error thrown: Exit loop
      break;
    }
    count = await elements.length;
    retry--;
  }
```

The count of elements could throw errors. The function could time out. The page could have no span elements or the call might have been performed without an `await` keyword. In any case, the function exits:

```
  // Metric: Report if the page took more than 3 seconds to build
  const endTime = Date.now();
  const duration = endTime - startTime;
  if (duration > waitforTimeout) {
    log(`  WARN: pageSync() completed in ${duration / 1000}
    sec  (${duration} ms) `);
  }
}
return result;
}
```

This method takes two optional arguments. The first is the amount of milliseconds to wait for between counts of the page elements. The default value can be as low as 25 milliseconds but should not be more than 250. This gives us an optimal amount of time for the page to complete building after a click. If the page has not changed when the click was executed, the synchronization is skipped for speed, and it will exit early if no span element exists. This generally occurs when the page is blank. It will exit if the page did not settle within a few seconds and report this to the console.

It also gives us a warning if the wait time exceeded the expected timeout for the framework. This means that the page is taking longer to load than a user might be willing to wait. We could call our DBA and check for SQL queries with excessive record retrieval times.

For greater efficiency, `pageSync` will only execute if the page URL has changed. This is a speed optimization. The second parameter is a switch to force a page sync check even if the page URL remains the same.

Lastly, it will indicate whether the browser no longer exists. This can occur if an await statement is missing in the calling method and the test ends early.

Supercharged scroll before a click event

It is a good practice to check whether an element is on screen before performing a click. This method returns `true` if the element is in the viewport:

```
export async function isElementInViewport(element: WebdriverIO.
Element): Promise<boolean> {
  let isInViewport = await element.isDisplayedInViewport();
  return isInViewport;
}
```

Using this method, we can optimize our code to scroll an element only if it is off-screen before performing the click event. However, there is a caveat: if an element is moving while WebdriverIO is attempting to click it, it may click the wrong element! So, we need another function to tell us when the element stops moving:

```
export async function waitForElementToStopMoving(element: WebdriverIO.
Element, timeout: number = 1500): Promise<boolean> {
  let rect = await element.getRect();
  pause (100);
  let isMoving = (rect !== await element.getRect())
  let startTime = Date.now();

  // Keep checking the element's position until it stops moving or the
timeout is reached
  while (isMoving) {
    // If the element's position hasn't changed, it is not moving
    if (rect === await element.getRect()) {
      // Element is static
      isMoving = false;
    }else{
      // Element is moving...
      pause (100)
    }
    // If the timeout has been reached, stop the loop
```

```
      if (Date.now() - startTime > timeout) {
        break;
      }
      // Wait for a short amount of time before checking the element's
   position again
      await pause(100);
    }
    return !isMoving;
}
```

This method checks to see whether the element location has changed horizontally or vertically. To optimize speed, this will only be called if it was detected that the element was off-screen.

Let's now tie all this together into a `clickAdv()` method to make it less likely to fail.

> **Quick tip: accuracy over speed**
>
> Running a test faster delivers no advantage if the test can't reach a successful conclusion. The wait between element counts in `pageSync()` can be reduced to 0 milliseconds, but it increases the risk of executing too soon. You can tweak this value for optimal performance, but be careful that the framework doesn't run *too* fast.

Expanding the click method wrapper

We are now ready to add our `clickAdv()` wrapper method. We will have a `pageSync()` method execute after every click to build in the flexible timing while we wait for the page to complete:

```
export async function clickAdv(
  element: ChainablePromiseElement<WebdriverIO.Element>) {
  let success: boolean = false;
  const SELECTOR = await element.selector;
  log(`Clicking ${SELECTOR}`);
  try {
    //await element.waitForDisplayed();

    if (!await isElementInViewport(element)){
      await element.scrollIntoView({ block: "center", inline: "center"
});
      await waitForElementToStopMoving(element)
    }
    await highlightOn(element);
    await element.click({ block: "center" });
    await pageSync();
    success = true;
  } catch (error: any) {
```

```
    log(`   ERROR: ${SELECTOR} was not clicked.\n
    ${error.message}`);
    expect(`to be clickable`).toEqual(SELECTOR);
    // Throw the error to stop the test
    await element.click({ block: "center" });
  }
  return success;
}
```

In this code, we get the name of the selector from the element. We use a try/catch around the click method. Then, we end the test by forcing a failure with our own custom error message indicating the element could not be clicked. In the automation switchboard, we set the value already failed to true to ensure the execution of the additional methods in the framework is skipped because the click failed. Finally, we return a Boolean value of true or false for success.

Now when we run the test with a bad element, we get more detail on the underlying issue:

```
[0-0] ---> Clicking button[type="bogus"]
[0-0] --->    ERROR: button[type="bogus"] was not clicked. [0-0] Error:
element ("button[type="bogus"]") still not displayed after 30000ms
```

Notice that we get an error that the element could not be found after 30 seconds. However, our page was built 28 seconds ago. So, let us change our timeout to be more efficient. This can be done by modifying the waitforTimeout value in the wdio.conf.ts file as follows:

```
waitforTimeout: 3000,
```

Now when the test runs, no more than three seconds will be used before the test fails, but the test will wait longer for the page to build:

```
public get btnBogus() {
   return $('//button[type="bogus"]');
}

await helpers.clickAdv(this.btnBogus);
```

Again, this time-out value will differ from project to project. Next, we need implement functionality to track some information about our execution.

The importance of metrics

These methods report how much time they take to execute. ClickAdv() also reports a warning if the time taken to build the page was longer than the default timeout of the framework. With this, we can begin to get insights into how much our changes impact the application responsiveness over time, as well as how much the framework itself affects the speed of execution.

For example, using a baseline execution time for a given test, we can see whether framework enhancements are impacting total time positively, or inadvertently slowing down execution. A good page stabilization method will often continue execution sooner than a hardcoded wait. Tracking to total amount of time added by `Pause()` methods are added to the total execution time.

Self-healing elements

With custom method wrappers, we can now start to work to reduce the required maintenance in our framework with self-healing elements. These are elements in a user interface that automatically recover from issues without the need for updating the page object model. This can include link elements that have become invalid because the class has changed since the last release. Self-healing elements are designed to improve the testing experience by reducing the need for manual input and allowing the test a better chance to run to completion.

For example, let's say the `Login` button in the last release was a link:

```
public get lnkSubmit() {
    return $('//a[text()="submit"]');
}
```

After this, we call the button that is no longer valid:

```
// Class switching
await helpers.clickAdv(this.lnkSubmit);
```

Normally, if this element were clicked, it would throw an error. But if we inject a function that gets a valid element based on the locator, we have a chance of getting through this step even if the underlying class has changed:

```
element = await getValidElement(element);
const SELECTOR = await element.selector;
await log(`Clicking ${SELECTOR}`);
```

In the following code, we will extract the class tag name and the text from the link and generate a button element locator on the fly. While unlikely, the code also covers the reverse case, where the button class has become a link:

```
export async function getValidElement(
    element: WebdriverIO.Element
): Promise<WebdriverIO.Element> {
    let selector: any = await element.selector;
    // Get a collection of matching elements
    let found: boolean = true;
    let newSelector: string = ""
    let newElement: any = element;
```

```
let elements: WebdriverIO.Element[];
let elementType:string = ""
let elementText:string = ""
try {
  elements = await $$(selector);
  if (elements.length === 0) {
    let index: number = selector.indexOf("[");
    elementType = selector.substring(0, index);
```

At this point, we have found no elements matching the locator. So we need to get creative based on the element that has gone missing since the last release. In the following code, we will look at a potential change of class from a link anchor to a button or vice versa:

```
switch (elementType) {
  case "//a":
    elementText = selector.match(/=".*"/)[0].slice(2, -1);
    newSelector = `//button[contains(@type,'${elementText}')]`

    break;
  case "//button":
    elementText = selector.match(/=".*"/)[0].slice(2, -1);
    newSelector =`//a[contains(text(),'${elementText}'])`

    break;
```

In the following code, we will add similar class-switching code to handle lists and Input elements:

```
  default:
    found = false;
    newElement = element;
    break;
  }
  newElement = await $(newSelector);
  found = await isElementVisible (newElement)
}
} catch (error) {
  found = false;
}
// Successful class switch
if (found) {
  await log(
    ` WARNING: Replaced ${selector}\n with ${newSelector}`
  );
} else {
```

```
    await log(`  ERROR: Unable to find ${selector}`);
  }
  return newElement;
}
```

Keep in mind that `getValidElement()` will not solve all of our maintenance issues. The goal is to reduce our maintenance by a significant amount by having a framework that is smart enough to recover from multiple stale elements and still get to a given endpoint. The code for replacement locators will be unique to each project, but it may be surprising how robust your tests will remain. There is some overhead with extra code and console logging, but it is minor compared to the amount of time required for updating element locators when a new release is pushed to the staging environment.

Stubbing out methods with the "alreadyFailed" switchboard key

A framework with a single point of exit can use the switchboard to track the number of pass, fail, and skipped steps. By embedding the `alreadyFailed` switch in the ASB switchboard, methods can be written to be stubbed out, reporting only what the action had been intended to do:

```
  ASB.set(`alreadyFailed`, !found)
  if (ASB.get(`alreadyFailed`) === true)) {
     allure.addStep(`Click '${selector}'`, undefined, 'skipped');
     ASB.set(`skipped`, ASB.get(`skipped`)++)
     return;
  }
```

This skips all page sync time and delays while incrementing a counter for the number of steps needed to get the test to its destination.

Summary

In this chapter, we added a `helpers` library with several methods to enhance our `click` method. We then addressed bringing elements on screen if they are outside the viewport and using page synchronization to wait for flexible amounts of time for the page to build to ensure that our elements do not throw an error when testing. We added highlights as well as a spinner detector. We introduced the concept of class switching to try finding, and also included some details of execution speed.

Now that we have most of our supporting framework in place for the `click()` method, let us do the same thing with `setValue()`. This includes validating our input elements and using the quickest way to populate a field via the clipboard. Next, we'll see how to enter text and replace dynamic data.

6

The setValue Wrapper – Entering Text and Dynamic Data Replacement

In this chapter, we're going to adapt the functionality from the `click()` method in the earlier chapter and extend it to the `setValue()` method. In addition, the wrapper method introduces multiple approaches to clear the field before entering the data. This chapter shows you how to implement a dynamic data tag replacement as an enhancement. This is the focal point where data can be prevented from becoming stale. For example, a test might require a future or past date. Lastly, we will look at detecting a password field and masking it with the `setPassword()` function.

In this chapter, we will cover the following topics:

- Creating a `setValue` Wrapper
- Normalizing the element class description from plain English
- Alternative ways to clear a field and enter data
- Dynamically replacing `<Today>` tags with a date
- Masking sensitive credential data

First, some housekeeping is in order. In the last chapter, we introduced class switching for our button. We will do the same thing for our input fields and upcoming lists and text elements. While we can deduce the type of element being passed to the `getValidElement()` method, we can just as easily pass the type directly from the wrapper:

```
inputField = await getValidElement(inputField, "field");
```

This means we can optimize the code for speed by skipping the code that extracts the `element` class, by explicitly stating the element type:

```
// Extract the element type if not provided
if (elementType === "") {
let index: number = selector.indexOf("[");
elementType = selector.substring(0, index);
}else{
elementText = normalizeElementType(elementType);
}
```

However, the explicit `field` string will not match the implicit string type of `//input`. To resolve this, we will add a method that will change generic descriptors such as `field` or `item` to a suitable class string such as `//input` and "`//li`".

Normalizing the element type

This is where we will write a method to normalize all the explicit strings. Here, `link` becomes `//a`, `button` becomes `//button`, and so on. Your framework can continue to expand with many other element types as needed. The following function, `normalizeElementType()`, will take a plain English description of the element and translate it into a common xPath equivalent. Note that `field` and `input` become the same class, while an empty class description becomes a locator for all elements:

```
function normalizeElementType(elementType: string)
{
  // Pessimistic: return all matches if the type is unknown
  let elementText = "//*"

  switch (elementType)
  {
    case "link":
      elementText = "//a";
      break;
    case "button":
      elementText = "//button";
      break;
    // Support different terms of the same field type
    case "field": // plain English reference to a type input field
    case "input": // type input
      elementText = "//input";
      break;
    case "list":
      elementText = "//select";
      break;
```

```
  case "text":
    elementText = "//p";
    break;
  default:
    log (`WARNING: Unable to normalize element type ${elementType}`)
}
return elementText;
}
```

There are a couple of items of note in this function. The first is the pessimistic nature of the function, which assumes the locator string passed was empty or `null`. `elementText` is initialized to `//*` to return all the elements in the first line. This means we assume at some point that a value might get passed a string that is yet to be implemented – for example, `list`. For documentation, we output the name of the unknown string as a warning to the console log.

Second, we change the element to match all values rather than stopping the test. We want the framework to try its best to get to the endpoint without incurring more maintenance time. However, it does give a warning that we should be as descriptive as possible.

Because we are now supporting unknown element types, we will add a generic locator to the `getValidElement()` function:

```
case "//*":
elementText = selector.match(/=".*"/)[0].slice(2, -1);
newSelector = `//*[contains(text(), '${elementText}'])`;
found = await isElementVisible(await $(newSelector));
break;
```

When we normalize text, we take common English descriptors and replace them with `xpath` element or CSS string locator equivalents. However, that's not just applicable in the class. This same concept is leveraged in many attributes as well. Let's take a moment to look at a link before we move on to input fields.

Normalizing text can be seen in XPath locators to allow us to find elements that have embedded carriage returns and extraneous transient white space. In this example, the "Embedded Carriage Return" web page element has extra spaces and a carriage return:

```
 <!DOCTYPE html>
<html>
<head>
    <title>Dynamic Loading Example</title>
    <script>
        function embeddedCarriageReturn() {
```

```
                var paragraph = document.getElementById("change-me");
                paragraph.innerHTML = "You clicked the Embedded Carriage
                Return link!";
            }
        </script>
    </head>
    <body>
        <h1>Weblink Challenge!</h1>
        <p>Can you framework click the link below</p>
        <a href="#" onclick="embeddedCarriageReturn()">Embedded <br>
            Carriage   Return</a>
        <p id="change-me"></p>
    </body>
    </html>
```

Weblink Challenge!

Can your framework click the link below

Embedded
Carriage Return

This means that this xPath won't work to recognize the link:

```
public get btnEmbeddedCarriageReturn() {
    return $("//a[text()='Embedded Carriage Return']");
}
```

html	body

//a[text()='Embedded Carriage Return']	0 of 0 ∧ ∨

However, we can normalize the text with the normalize-space() node to remove carriage return <br> breaks and even stray white space:

```
public get btnEmbeddedCarriageReturn () {
    return $("//a[contains(normalize-space(),'Embedded Carriage
    Return')] ");
}
```

```
···    ▼<a href="#" onclick="embeddedCarriageReturn()"> == $0
         "Embedded "
         <br>
         " Carriage Return"
      </a>
```

html   body   a

//a[contains(normalize-space(),'Embedded Carriage Return')]   1 of 1 ∧ ∨

Now that we have yet another tool in our utility belt, we can write locators that can find elements with extra spaces and line breaks, reducing the maintenance time should these be cleaned up by the developers. Let's take this to the next level with input elements and the setValue method.

Adding the setValue() method wrapper

We begin by adding a new wrapper to our helpers file that we will extend with several checks, before performing the intrinsic setValue() method:

```
export async function setValueAdv(
   inputField: ChainablePromiseElement<WebdriverIO.Element>,
   text: string) {
//Custom setValue wrapper code here
await element.setValue(newValue);
}
```

Now, we are ready to begin to enhance the data population aspect of our framework.

Is this trip really necessary?

The first thing to do is to check whether any of the following code must be executed at all. There is no reason to find and replace a state element with a valid one if we don't have any text to enter. So, we will first check whether any data has been passed to be entered:

```
//Custom setValue wrapper code here
try{
    if (text.length === 0) {
        log (`        Warning: Attempted to enter "" into ${element.
selector}`)
    return true;
}
}catch (error){
    log (`        Warning: Attempted to enter NULL into ${element.
selector}`)
```

```
    log (`      Check if there was a query column to a missing column
in a data file `)
    return false;
}
```

This function has three actions:

- If the text is not null and not empty, the code continues to execute the rest of the method.

- If the text was an empty string it returns `true`, meaning the test can continue. This is useful, as we might be populating an entire page, but not every field takes a value. We could be searching by any combination of last name, zip code, and state. This allows for a page method design that has every input field but only interacts with the elements that receive some data.

- A null value is a special situation. It's a clue that something is amiss. As superheroes, we always want to collect clues to identify the usual suspect who is committing the crime. If the clue is in the form of a riddle, we might check with the local asylum to see whether the cell adorned with question marks still holds an inmate.

- In this case, a NULL value usually shows that the value was returned from a query that found nothing. We send a warning to the console and return `false` as the status. Just like with an empty value, it skips the rest of the function.

With the input data confirmed, we will take a second step and add the ability to keep our data fresh.

Coal into diamonds – replacing dynamic data tags

A very common task in test automation is to populate a field with the current date. Now, we don't want to be changing the date every single day manually, so we want something dynamic that provides us with that functionality. If we're clever, that functionality can return the current, past, or future date. Even the date format could be modified. This is where the techniques of embedded dynamic data tags come into play.

Dynamic data tags are a way to keep data that changes at a regular cadence fresh. It might be the current day of the week, a unique order number that was created by a batch job that needs completion, or a future business date excluding weekends and holidays.

There are many applications that will be unique to each individual project. In this case, we will provide a simple example of the most common data replacement – replacing a tag name, `"Today is: <today>"`, with the current date (i.e., `"Today is 6/21/2023`).

However, we won't stop there. We will also offset the date by any amount of days for a future date:

```
"Tomorrow is: <today+1>"
"Tomorrow is: 6/22/2023"
```

Alternatively, we can do it for a past date:

```
"Last week was: <today-7>"
"Last week was: 6/14/2023"
```

Finally, we want to have the ability to change the formatting:

```
"Yesterday in European format: <today-1 dd/mm/yyyy>"
"Yesterday in European format: 20/6/2023"
```

The basic format of this `<today>` tag gets replaced with a past or future date, with the custom `replaceTags()` function. Next, we add the function that detects these tags in every string passed through `setValueAdv()`. This will handle all sorts of tags:

```
function replaceTags(text: string) {
  //check if the passed tag is in the format of "<someTag>"
  let newText: string = text;
  // Capture anything that is not a space
  let match = newText.match(/\<(.*?)\>/);
```

We use a bit of dark magic called a regular expression, which identifies strings encased in square brackets and extracts them:

- `/`: This is the start delimiter for the regular expression.

- `\<`: This matches the opening angle bracket, `<`, in the text.

- `(.*?)`: This is a capturing group that matches any character (represented by the dot, `.`) zero or more times (represented by `*?`) until it encounters the next character in the regular expression (in this case, the closing angle bracket `>`). `?` makes the `*` quantifier lazy, meaning it will match as few characters as possible to satisfy the regex pattern.

- `\>`: This matches the closing angle bracket, `>`, in the text.

- `/`: This is the end delimiter for the regular expression.

It is possible that multiple tags might need to be replaced in the string. So, we will loop through all of them. Tag identification is case-insensitive, meaning `<today>` and `<TODAY>` are equivalent:

```
while (match) {
  let tag = match[0].toLowerCase();
  let tagType = match[1].toLowerCase();
```

This `switch` statement matches the first part of the tag extension to multiple tags in the future. In this case, our first match will be a tag that starts with `<today` and splits out + or - with the following value to offset the date:

```
switch (true) {
  case tag.includes("<today"):
```

We have the `tag` string. Now, we split the date format, if it exists, to transform the date at the end of the function:

```
    let format: string = tagType.split(" ")[1] ? tagType.split("
")[1] : "";


    let days: number = 0;
    const match = tag.match(/[+-](\d+)/);
```

Another regular expression here extracts the days to offset the date:

- `/` : This is the start delimiter for the regular expression.

- `[+-]` : This matches either the + or - character in the text. The square brackets denote a character class, which means that the regular expression will match any one of the characters inside the brackets.

- `(\d+)` : This is a capturing group that matches one or more digits (represented by `\d`) in the text). The parentheses surrounding `\d+` capture the matched digits as a group. The + quantifier means that the regular expression will match one or more digits.

- `/`: This is the end delimiter for the regular expression.

The next action is to determine whether there is an offset by a number of days to a past or future date:

```
    if (match) {
      const days = parseInt(match[0]);
    }
```

Here, we replace the tag in the string with a function that gets the current date offset and custom format:

```
    newText = newText.replace(tag, getToday(days, format));
    break;

  default:
    log(`ERROR: Unknown tag <${tag}>`);
    break;
}
```

```
    match = newText.match(/\<(.*?)\>/);
  }
```

This loop continues until all the tags have been replaced. If any tags are discovered and replaced, the new text is output to the console for logging:

```
if (newText !== text) {
  log(`    Replaced tags in '${text}' with '${newText}'`);
}
return newText;
}
```

Now that we have the ability to extract dynamic date tags, we need to process the offset date and formatting with the getToday() function. The default, today's date, is empty, and the date format is MM-dd-yyyy if the format argument is blank.

```
export function getToday(offset: number = 0, format: string = "MM-dd-yyyy") {
  const currentDate = new Date();
  currentDate.setDate(currentDate.getDate() + offset);
```

Here is our super-secret serum. This code will produce the date based on the format passed in. Why write loads of code to support all date formats, from 2-digit or 4-digit years and 0 leading dates to a European format, when Date.toLocalDateString can do it all for us in just these few lines of code?

```
return currentDate.toLocaleDateString(undefined, {
  year: format.includes("yyyy") ? "numeric" : undefined,
  month: format.includes("MM")
    ? "2-digit"
    : format.includes("M")
    ? "numeric"
    : undefined,
  day: format.includes("dd")
    ? "2-digit"
    : format.includes("d")
    ? "numeric"
    : undefined,
});
}
```

Our dynamic date tag extractor and formatter are complete! The next trick is to populate it in a field. And, as you might guess, there is more than one way to do this – the slow way and the fast way.

Injecting versus typing text into a field

We may want to override the intrinsic `setValue()` command to populate a field:

```
await inputField.setValue(newValue);
```

The reason is that injecting a value into an element may not necessarily kick off any additional JavaScript code behind the element. This might also skip some formatting that the developers added when we inject the data. Alternatively, we could use `addValue()`:

```
await inputField.addValue(newValue);
```

Now, we might be appending text into a field that already has text. What we want is a function that will first clear the field, if populated, and then type just as a user would – letter by letter followed by the *Tab* key to move out of the field.

This can be accomplished in our framework in two ways.

First, we set the focus on the element and sending keystrokes through the `browser.keys()` method. Second, we send keys to the element directly with its `AddValue()` method. This would be a backup approach being slightly slower. Regardless of the tool used, sometimes an element just does not receive the text correctly when entered at a high typing speed. So, the `AddValue` approach would be a backup to ensure fields get populated accurately.

Let's begin with the first approach, using the `browser.keys` method to send text to the element, with a focus on speed. This is carried out by setting focus on the element with a click:

```
await highlightOn(inputField);
await inputField.click();
```

The element now has focus, and thanks to the highlight, we can see which element will take the input. We should check whether the field needs to be cleared.

Checking whether the field is pre-populated for speed

Next, we will clear the field if it has any pre-existing text. The basic way to do this is with the `clear()` method:

```
if (await inputField.getAttribute('value') !== '') {
await inputField.clear();
}
```

An alternative way to clear the field can also be done by issuing a `Meta-a` command to select all the text. The selected text is cleared by sending the backspace ASCII key code from the browser:

```
await browser.keys(['Meta', 'a']);
await browser.keys(['\ue003']);
```

Now, we will type the text passed to the wrapper into the field from the browser:

```
await browser.keys(text);
```

Faster is not always better. If you find the speed of WebdriverIO typing text is causing issues, you can control how quickly text is typed with this alternative code:

```
// type text letter by letter
for (let letter = 0; letter < text.length; letter++){
await pause(10); // control the typing speed
await inputField.addValue(text[letter]);
}
```

Once the text is entered, the field can be activated by typing the *Tab* key:

```
await browser.keys(['tab']);
```

While the *Tab* key is universal to activate an element, sometimes the *Enter* key is needed instead:

```
await browser.keys(['\ue007']);
```

However, are we about to send our password to the console for everyone to see? It's a bad day in the city when a supervillain is able to take the hero's supercharged crime-fighting vehicle for a joyride. Let's make that less likely to happen.

Behind the mask – SetValuePassword() to keep data secure

Superheroes wear a mask to protect family and friends. In test automation, we need to protect our sensitive data such as passwords. In this method, we take the extra step to be sure our passwords are not displayed in the console and report output by replacing most of the string with asterisks (`Password"` = `"Pa****rd`). However, if the root cause of our issues is that a password expired, we might want to have a small clue. So, we need to mask just a part of our credentials:

```
function maskString(str: string): string {
   let maskedStr = '';
```

```
  for (let charIndex = 0; charIndex < str.length; charIndex++) {
    if (charIndex > 1 && charIndex < str.length - 2) {
      maskedStr += '*';
    } else {
      maskedStr += str[charIndex];
    }
  }
  return maskedStr;
}
```

Here is an example of the original password and the value returned:

```
let originalString = "SuperSecretPassword!";
let maskedString = maskString(originalString);


console.log(originalString); // Output: 'SuperSecretPassword! '
console.log(maskedString); // Output: 'se***********ation'
```

Detecting and masking passwords in your output

The next step is to detect a field that might be a password and then scrub the data that's being passed to it. We'll send the password to the field but output a scrubbed version of the data to our results. First, let's get a scrubbed version of the text:

```
scrubbedtext = maskString (text)
```

Next, we will get the field element name and check whether it includes the ssword string pattern. This makes it likely that we will scrub any field that has the password or Password string. This is provided by a custom getFieldName() helper method:

```
/**
* Returns the first non-null property from the prioritized list:
'name', 'id', 'type', and 'class'. Can be amended to add other
attributes such as "aria-label"
* @param {WebdriverIO.Element} element - The WebdriverIO element to
get the name of the field
* @returns {string | null} The field name, or null if no properties
have a value
*/


async function getFieldName(element: WebdriverIO.Element) {

// Add any custom properties here, e.g.:
// const customPropertyName = await element.getAttribute("aria-
label");
```

```
// if (customPropertyName) return custom;

// Get the 'name' property of the element
  const name = await element.getAttribute("name");
  if (name) return name;

  // Get the 'id' property of the element
  const id = await element.getAttribute("id");
  if (id) return id;

  // Get the 'type' property of the element
  const type = await element.getAttribute("type");
  if (type) return type;

  // Get the 'class' property of the element if others are null
  const className = await element.getAttribute("class");
  return className;
}
```

You might be wondering, why not create a generic method called getElementName() to return the name of any element? The reason is that the properties and prioritizations can be different, depending on whether we are seeking an input field, a button, a list, or other elements. This allows us to optimize the code execution based on the element type.

Putting it all together

Now that we've got all the custom-made parts, let's put together our superpowered method. These methods will return a success value of true or false. We ensure that we have a valid element from the earlier chapter. We will replace tags such as the date with a future or past offset. We will detect whether the field is a password and mask our value output accordingly:

```
export async function setValueAdv(
  inputField: WebdriverIO.Element,
  text: string
) {
  let success: boolean = false;
  inputField = await getValidElement(inputField, "field");
  const SELECTOR = await inputField.selector;

  let newValue: string = replaceTags(text);
  let scrubbedValue: string = newValue
  let fieldName: string = await getFieldName(inputField)
```

```
//Mask Passwords in output
if (fieldName.includes("ssword") ){
  scrubbedValue = maskValue(scrubbedValue)
}
await log(`Entering '${scrubbedValue}' into ${SELECTOR}`);

try {
  // await element.waitForDisplayed();
  if (!(await isElementInViewport(inputField))) {
    await scrollIntoView(inputField);
    await waitForElementToStopMoving(inputField);
  }
  await highlightOn(inputField);
  //Check if text was entered
  // Clear input field
  await inputField.click();

  // Do we need to clear the field?
  if (await inputField.getValue()) await inputField.
setValue(newValue);

  // Send text to input field
  for (const letter of text) {
    await inputField.addValue(letter);
  }
  success = true;
} catch (error: any) {
  await log(`  ERROR: ${SELECTOR} was not populated with
${scrubbedValue}.\n        ${error.message}`
  );
  expect(`to be editable`).toEqual(SELECTOR);
  // Throw the error to stop the test, still masking password
  await inputField.setValue(scrubbedValue);
}
return success;
}
```

The following is an example of the masked credentials in our output:

```
[0-0] ---> Logging in with user role 'tomsmith'
[0-0] ---> Entering 'tomsmith' into #username
[0-0] ---> Entering 'Su***************d!' into #password
```

There are a lot of other features we could implement to customize the data input of our fields. We could use the same technique to inject SQL statements to always pull a valid order number for a search. Strings of random `Corporate Lorem Ipsum` filler words could be populated to check exact field length boundaries. Text with vulgar words could be tested to make sure they get flagged and notification emails are sent to test accounts. Take a few minutes to think about all the types of dynamic and special data that might be available to test against with an automated framework.

Summary

In this chapter, we added all sorts of custom-made gadgets to our `setValueAdv()` method. This method delivers a result indicating the success or failure of `true` or `false`. We conducted a background check to ensure that we had a valid element. Our approach involved wielding the power of time travel by replacing date-related tags with the present, future, or past date offset. We also kept security in mind and made sure to mask our output value when the field in question was a likely credential input.

Next, we will supercharge the `Select()` method with lists and comboboxes.

7

The Select Wrapper – Choosing Values in Lists and Comboboxes

In this chapter, we'll extend our suite of utility belt functions with a versatile method called `selectAdv()`. This function is designed to handle list elements effectively, similar to how our existing `clickAdv()` and `setValue()` functions operate. We'll incorporate a validation check to ensure the element passed to the function is a valid one. Moreover, we'll implement a retry mechanism that attempts to locate the element up to three times, scrolling it into view each time as necessary.

The true challenge, however, arises when dealing with comboboxes. These elements can be complex to interact with, especially when it comes to opening them to reveal a list of selectable items. Another point of concern is to clear any lingering text from the combobox before selecting a new value. We'll explore three distinct strategies to achieve this.

Once these hurdles are overcome, the next step is to identify the desired item from the list and select it. Here, another tool, `SelectorsHub`, comes into play as a life-saving sidekick, assisting us in pinpointing the correct item with precision.

We'll cover the following main topics in this chapter:

- Adding the base functionality of `Click` and `setValue`
- Selecting an item from a list
- Inspecting a list that closes when it loses focus with `SelectorsHub`

We will begin with the code that is common to the prior methods discussed.

Adding the base functionality of clickAdv() and setValueAdv() to selectAdv()

Just like our `clickAdv()` and `setValueAdv()` methods before, we will want to ensure that our elements are valid and scroll into view for our screen captures. If the test itself has already failed, we will not perform any further action, essentially stubbing out the function. The initial section of the method will be similar to the `clickAdv()` method:

```
exports.selectAdv = async (selector, text){
    element = await getValidElement(element, "list");
        let listName : String = getListName{element}
```

If the list element does not exist, we will make three attempts to find a similar node in the `getValidElement()` function. This first approach is to try to find a list using the `@id` property:

```
case 'list'
    newSelector = `//select[contains(@id,
      '${selector.toLowerCase()}']}`;
    length = await (this.countMatches(newSelector)));
    exists = length != 0
    element = await ${`${newSelector}`);
```

If there are no elements found with all-lowercase IDs, we will try again without the case:

```
if (length == 0){
  // Second chance List locator
  newSelector = `//select[contains(@id, '${selector}']}`;
  length = await (this.countMatches(newSelector)));
  exists = length != 0
  element = await ${`${newSelector}`);
}
```

Our final attempt will be to seek the child `select` node of any element that contains the text in the string. This is commonly a `Div` or `Span` node:

```
if (length == 0){
  // Second chance List locator
  newSelector = `//*[contains(text(),
    '${selector}')]/parent::*/select]`;
  length = await (this.countMatches(newSelector)));
  exists = length != 0
  element = await ${`${newSelector}`);
}
```

```
      break;

  }
```

Now that we have the list element, we have three ways to select the item from the list. Each way has its advantages and disadvantages.

Selecting an item from the list

WebdriverIO provides three ways to select an item from an element:

- `selectByVisibleText`: Matches the option based on its visible text
- `selectByIndex`: Matches the option based on its index location (0-based)
- `selectByAttribute`: Matches the option based on a specific attribute and its value

For example, if we wanted to select the third month from a list of months, each of these approaches could work:

```
await lstMonth.selectByVisibleText ("March");
await lstMonth.selectByAttribute ("value", "March");
await lstMonth.selectByIndex(2); // 0 based index
```

Often, the WebdriverIO `selectByVisibleText` method works fine as the default method in a wrapper, but there are times when a list element needs to interact with open of the alternative ways.

In each case, we should validate that the correct value has been selected:

```
await lstElement.selectByVisibleText (item);
let itemValue = await listElement.getText();
if (itemValue === item) return true
```

In addition, if an error is thrown, we should attempt to find a close match in the list.

One way is to send the down arrow in the list. Then, we check whether the selected value contains the expected value:

```
await listElement.click({ block: 'center' }) // Set focus
await browser.keys(["\uE015"]}; // Send down arrow key to open the
list
```

Then, we can loop through and note the match or print the list of non-matching values:

```
let item : String ="";
let arrItems: string[] = [];
let found : boolean = false
let lastItem : string = await listElement.getText()
arrItems.push(lastItem);
```

This is an infinite loop with two exit points. Either a close match was found or the last item of the list was reached and there was no match:

```
do {
  if (await listElement).getText().contains(item){
    found = true
    global.log ("Found a close match: " +
      listElement).getText()
    break;
  }
  await browser.keys(["\uE015"]}; // Send down arrow key
  item = listElement.getText()

  if (lastValue === item) {
    break;
 global.log (`'${item}' was not found in list: ${arrValues});
// Output the item and the list of values
}
    arrItems.push(item)

} while !(lastValue == listElement.getText()) // No match
```

If this loop never finds a match, we will output the item we sought and the list of available elements stored in `arrItems[]`:

```
if (found === false) {
  await this.log (`    Failed to select '${text}' from ${arrItems} in
${listName}
  return element;
}
```

This completes the most common list element. However, we can also support a path that interacts with a combobox, which can be a whole different type of beast.

Selecting from a combobox

Another reason to have a wrapper is to be able to identify and interact with an element that is not a true drop-down list. In this example, we have a combobox. This is both an input field and a selection from a list of potential matches. Take, for example, a list of countries.

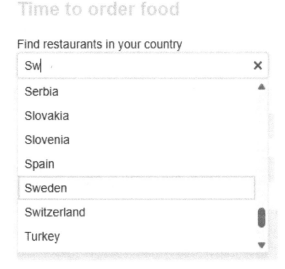

Figure 7.1 – A combobox with an item selected from partial text

In **WebdriverIO (WDIO)**, selecting an option from a combobox (or dropdown) can be done in multiple ways. A combobox in HTML is usually represented by a `<select>` element with multiple `<option>` child elements. Here are a few approaches.

Using selectByVisibleText

This method allows you to select an option by its visible text (the text displayed to the user):

```
const comboBoxSelector = 'select#yourComboBoxId';

$(comboBoxSelector).selectByVisibleText('Option Text');
```

Using selectByAttribute

This method allows you to select an option by its `value` attribute:

```
const comboBoxSelector = 'select#yourComboBoxId';
$(comboBoxSelector).selectByAttribute('value', 'option-value');
```

Using selectByIndex

This method allows you to select an option by its index (0-based):

```
const comboBoxSelector = 'select#yourComboBoxId';
$(comboBoxSelector).selectByIndex(1); // Index starts from 0
```

Then, we click the field and type the item text. If we find an element containing the text, we click it. However, writing that element locator in a self-closing list can be tricky. That's where `SelectorsHub` comes in handy.

Inspecting a list that closes when it loses focus with SelectorsHub

On occasion, it is difficult to get the locator of a list item because the list will only be open when the mouse cursor hovers over it. In this example, we can pause the execution of the web page in order to interact with the elements while the list is expanded. The pause feature in DevTools is located on the **Sources** tab:

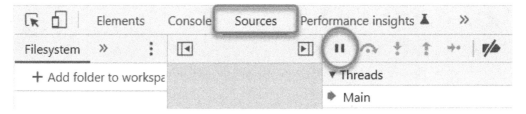

Figure 7.2 – The Sources tab selected to display the pause button

This is handy for catching elements that do not stay on the screen long, such as spinners and *loading...* mechanisms. Sometimes, we're just not fast enough to get to the pause button or the list simply closes once we move our mouse off of it. This is where a tool called `SelectorsHub` comes in handy. This tool is a Chrome browser add-on:

Figure 7.3 – SelectorsHub displayed in the browser tools' extentions menu

This tool can be installed by searching the Chrome browser extensions.

Once installed, the tool can be found on the **Elements** tab. Usually, it's the first tab listed, and sometimes, it's the last. One of the hidden features of this tool is **Debug** mode.

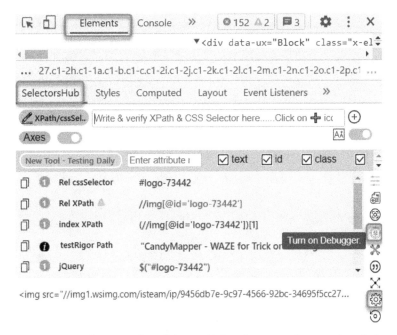

Figure 7.4 – Activating the pause from SelectorsHub to freeze a spinner and get its locator ID

By clicking the **Debugger** icon, SelectorsHub will automatically pause the web page after five seconds. This allows us to capture tricky elements in good time. Try pausing the *loading...* spinner page of the website at https://candymapperr2.com/launch-candymapper:

Figure 7.5 – An example of a spinner on a web page

The default setting of entering pause mode after five seconds is sufficient for most of these situations. To catch very brief elements, the **Settings** option allows us to change the delay to shorter or longer amounts as needed.

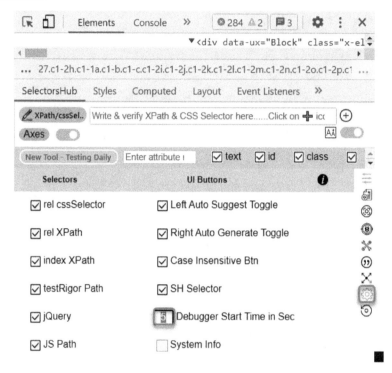

Figure 7.6 – Setting the time for the debugger to wait

This also works well with *loading...* **wait** mechanisms that are briefly displayed.

Writing a locator that is an element inside a list

Now, we have our list in a combobox and can clear any existing element text. There are a few ways this can be done. We can set the value, we can double-click to select all the existing text, and lastly, we can send *Ctrl + A* keystrokes to the field:

```
ListElement.setValue("");
```

However, that may not work for all input field elements. Perhaps a double-click to the field will work:

```
await listElement.doubleclick()
```

Well, it will work if there is a single word already in the field, such as Denmark, but not if it includes spaces, such as Trinidad and Tobago.

Surprisingly, a triple click on a field will select everything. However, at the time of writing, the authors know of no automation tool that supports triple clicks. Also, in case you were wondering, this is not a triple-click:

```
await listElement.click(); await listElement.click(); await
listElement.click()
```

Here is a way to clear a field. Set the focus on the field with a single click. Then, send a Home keystroke to place the cursor at the start of the field. Next, hit the *Shift* and *End* keys to highlight all the text in the field. Finally, send a *Delete* key to the field followed by the text, like this:

```
await listElement.click()
await browser.keys(['Home']);
await browser.keys(['Shift','End']);
await browser.keys(['Delete']);
await browser.keys(`${item}`)
```

In this situation, the combobox displays all the items that are available to choose. Inside a `try` and `Catch`, we can now get a collection of all the list items that match our expected value:

```
// Find the item in the list
try {
  listItems = await browser.$$(`//li/*`)
```

We search for a list item that is close to a perfect match.

If found, we break the loop and perform a click, using the custom `clickAdv()` method:

```
for (const listItem of listItems) {
  if ((await listItem.getText()).includes(item))
  // Found the element
  break;
}


  clickAdv(listItem)
} catch (error) {
```

If this fails, it means there was no item to click. The most important information we need to log now is what the available items displayed in the list were:

```
listItems = await browser.$$(`//li/*`)
for (const listItem of listItems) {
    textContent += await listItem.getText() + " | ";
    // Get the text content of the element



}


        await log(`   ERROR: "${item}" was not found in combobox: \n
${textContent}`)


}
```

Now, we have a robust custom method that will give actionable details to help us maintain our tests when they fail. From here, we can extend this method to report when there are multiple close matches.

Summary

In this chapter, we wrote a custom wrapper to select an item from a list element. We learned how to handle two separate types of objects with a single method, reducing test case code. The combobox path uses the `click()` method to open and navigate through a list, as well as clear the input field that filters matches in the list. We embedded reporting if no exact or close match exists, making debugging easier. This was done by sending a log error message, indicating what item was sought, the list element it was using, and the list of non-matching values. We also showed how to use `SelectorsHub` to provide a way to validate handwritten XPath selectors when the list closes, as soon as the object loses focus.

This completes three of the four most common methods used in test automation. In the next chapter, we will create an enhanced `Assertion` method that validates the state or text of an object, as well as validating generic text that appears on a page.

8

The Assert Wrapper – the Importance of Embedded Details

In this chapter, we will be writing our first assertion wrapper. Assertions allow us to pass or fail a test as well as add detail regarding the expected and actual results. WebdriverIO has at least three ways to implement assertions and each has its own style. First, there is the standard Jest **expect** assertion library, which is basic to evaluate numbers, strings, and even regular expression matchers. Then there is the **expect-webdriverio** assertion library, which is an extension of the Jest matchers. These take web objects and perform assertions on both values and states. Lastly, there is the **Chai** assertion library, which provides soft assertions and a variety of implementation styles. While the library choice is up to you, we will be using `expect-webdriverio` for all examples in this book. However, a little background on how these approaches differ should be noted.

We'll cover the following main topics in this chapter:

- expect, assert, and should
- Timeout
- Hard and soft expect assertions
- Allure reports

expect, assert, and should –how did we get here?

Let's take a look at a brief history of JavaScript assertion libraries to understand why we will be making some of the choices in our custom `assert()` wrapper.

What is Jasmine?

Jasmine was first released in 2010. It was designed to provide a simple and flexible way to add assertions. It provides a set of built-in assertion methods. Note that the interface is `expect` with chainable methods such as `.toBe`, `.toEqual`, and `.not`. Here is a sample assertion in Jasmine:

```
function addNumbers(arg0: number, arg1: number): number {
  return arg0 + arg1;
}
describe('My Math Library', () => {
  it('should add two numbers correctly', () => {
    const result = addNumbers(2, 3);
    expect(result).toEqual(5);

    expect(result).toEqual(6); //Intentional fail
  });
});
```

The preceding test calls a simple function that returns the sum of two arguments passed to the `AddNumbers()` function.

This is a basic arithmetic assertion. If we run it, we notice the pass result does not report anything. Only the failure is reported. It really does not provide much detail when passing or failing:

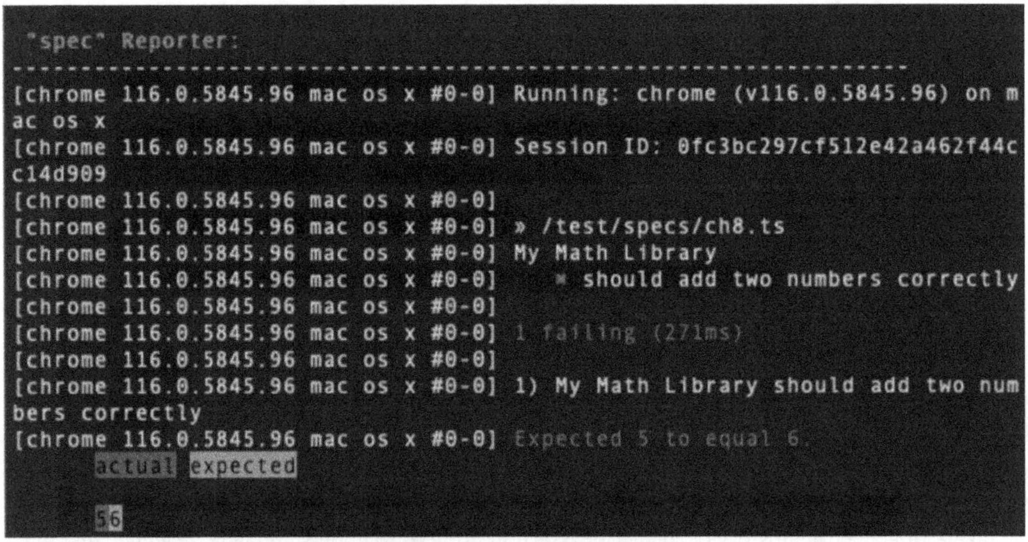

Figure 8.1: Results of a pass and intentional fail of the AddNumbers() function

In a test automation project, we would need to extract the object properties or values and validate that against the expected result. The detailed result may only report expected [true] actual [false]. To provide this output would require a lot of additional code to include if we had it performed at the test or feature file level.

What is Jest?

In 2013, Jest was released by Facebook and became widely adopted by the React community. It has a similar assertion syntax as Jasmine with additional features including snapshot testing and code coverage reporting. Note the interface is also expect. Here is the same assertion in Jest:

```
describe('My Math Library', () => {
  test('should add two numbers correctly', () => {
    let expected = 5
    let actual = 5
    expect(actual).toBe(expected);

    actual = 4
    expect(actual).toBe(expected);
  });
```

However, Jest on its own does not support any messages to report the details of the validation. The jest-expect-message package should be included to provide this functionality with npm or yarn:

```
npm install jest-expect-message
yarn add jest-expect-message
```

Now that we have added the expect message package for Jest, we can provide more descriptive results:

```
describe('My Math Library', () => {
  test('should add two numbers correctly', () => {
    Let expected = 5
    let actual = 5
    expect(actual,
`Expected: '${expected}' Actual: '${actual}'`).toBe(expected);

expected = 4
expect(actual, `Expected: '${expected}' Actual: '${actual}'`).
toBe(expected);

  });
});
```

Jest is included as part of the WebdriverIO package, but WDIO has an extended assertion library of its own. This allows us to pass elements directly for assertions rather than writing our own.

What is Chai?

Chai is a popular assertion library for JavaScript that provides three interfaces for making assertions:

- should (BDD)
- expect (BDD)
- assert (TDD)

Each of these interfaces has its own pros and cons, which we will look into in the subsections.

Should

The should interface extends all objects with a should property that can be used to make assertions. Here is a Chai should sample:

```
import 'chai/register-should'

describe('My App', () => {
  it('should have the correct title', () => {
    browser.url('https://example.com');
    browser.getTitle().should.be.equal('Example Domain');
  });
});
```

While this interface allows for readable and expressive code, it can lead to unexpected side effects in the way that it modifies object behaviors. For this reason, it will not be a part of our implementation.

Assert

The assert interface provides a more classical style of making assertions, using traditional methods such as assert.equal() and assert.notEqual(). This interface is useful for developers who are already familiar with other testing frameworks or who prefer a more traditional style of testing. However, it can be less readable and expressive than the should or expect interfaces, especially when dealing with more complex assertions:

```
const assert = require('assert');

describe('My App', () => {
  it('should have the correct title', () => {
    browser.url('https://example.com');
    const actualTitle = browser.getTitle();
    const expectedTitle = 'Example Domain';
    assert(actualTitle === expectedTitle);
```

```
  });
});
```

Expect

The Chai `expect` interface provides a more flexible and chainable way of making assertions. This interface is designed to be easy to read and write and provides a fluent syntax that can be used to make complex assertions in a clear and concise way. Here is a Chai `should` sample:

```
import assert from 'chai';

describe('My App', () => {
  it('expect to have the correct title with chai', () => {
    browser.url('https://example.com');
    expect(browser.getTitle()).to.equal('Example Domain');
  });
});
```

Using Chai's `expect` interface is the preferred way of making assertions. It provides a lot of flexibility without the side effects of `should` with a similar syntax to the Jest assertions. There is a problem, we don't get all the details. Consider this:

```
await LoginPage.open();
await expect(browser).toHaveUrlContaining('the-internet.herokuapp.com/
login')
[chrome 110.0.0.0 win32 #0-0]     ✓ Chapter 8: expectAdv Wrapper
should check if actual is equal to expected
0.0 win32 #0-0] 1 passing (844ms)
```

Sure, the tests passed, but what exactly did it do? There is no expected result, actual results, or any detail of what the assertion is doing. This is why we need wrappers to simplify our reporting of our results.

Let us look at a failing assertion:

```
await LoginPage.open();
await expect(browser).toHaveUrlContaining('the-internet.herokuapp.com/
bogus')
[chrome 110.0.0.0 win32 #0-0] Error: Expect window to have url
containing "the-internet.herokuapp.com/bogus"
Expected: "the-internet.herokuapp.com/bogus"
Received: "https://the-internet.herokuapp.com/login"
[chrome 110.0.0.0 win32 #0-0] error properties: Object({
matcherResult: Object({ pass: false, message: 'Expect window to have
url containing
[chrome 110.0.0.0 win32 #0-0]
[chrome 110.0.0.0 win32 #0-0] Expected: "the-internet.herokuapp.com/
bogus"
```

```
[chrome 110.0.0.0 win32 #0-0] Received: "https://the-internet.
herokuapp.com/login"' }) })
[chrome 110.0.0.0 win32 #0-0] Error: Expect window to have url
containing
[chrome 110.0.0.0 win32 #0-0] Expected: "the-internet.herokuapp.com/
bogus"
[chrome 110.0.0.0 win32 #0-0] Received: https://the-internet.
herokuapp.com/login
```

Now we are over-reporting as we had one validation. The error was reported three times to the output, and that is a problem.

There is one problem – all of these assertion packages are designed to perform a hard expect ending the test execution, not a soft expect that will allow the test to perform more validations:

```
Spec Files:       0 passed, 1 failed, 1 total (100% completed) in
00:00:06
```

Notice it takes 6 seconds for the validation to fail. Do we really need to wait that much time? We already have the pageSync() method consuming all the time needed.

Timeout – delay of game

The default timeout for a WebdriverIO expect matcher is 3 seconds and the interval is 100 ms. That is 30 checks over 3 seconds, which is far better than waiting 30 seconds as is the industry standard. Remember we are using the pageSync() method to burn the time that the page uses to build. It makes sense that our assertions should be available almost immediately. To adjust the timeout and interval of the expect-webdriverio assertion, we can make a change in the WebdriverIO hooks section of the wdio.config.ts file:

```
before: function (capabilities, specs){
require('expect-webdriverio').setOptions ({wait:5000, interval: 250});
}
```

This code will now change our expect assertions to be executed 20 times. The wait timeout will be 5 seconds. The check will be performed every 1/4 second:

```
Spec Files: 0 passed, 1 failed, 1 total (100% completed) in 00:00:05
```

The resulting time is now reduced to an optimal amount. It is just a second, but a little here and there saves minutes and hours.

What is expect-webdriverio?

For the purpose of this book, we will be using `expect-webdriverio`.

WebdriverIO uses the `expect-webdriverio` assertion library, which is an extension of the Jest expect interface. It adds browser and element assertions:

```
const expect = require('expect-webdriverio');
describe('My App', () => {
  it('should have the correct title', () => {
    browser.url('https://example.com');
    expect(browser).toHaveTitle('Example Domain');
  });
});
```

However, all these libraries are missing the ability to execute a soft assertion. For that, we turn to Chai and the `soft-assert` package.

What are hard and soft expect assertions?

By default, all of the assertion packages perform a **hard expect assertion**, which is more commonly known as a **hard assert**. This means that when an assertion fails, the test ends. What kind of superhero leaves the fight after the first punch? This is problematic as we might have four or five values on a single page that we want to assert. What is the point of failing on the first assertion and leaving the next four out of the results? We want the power to continue the fight even if we take one to the chin along the way.

That is why we strive to add the ability of a **soft expect** (more commonly known as **soft assert**) into the framework. This feature is built into Java's TestNG. It seems a shame that it is missing from all the popular JavaScript assertion libraries. If the buttons exist for navigation, the best testing frameworks will be able to get to the end point and have all validations executed, no matter whether they pass or fail. That is our ultimate dual goal: more results in our report and less repetitious piecemeal runs.

Putting it all together

Now, we need to protect our identities; to accomplish this feat, we use `expect-webdriverio`, which extends the Chai `expect` interface.

We can now perform a failing soft assertion on our **Bogus** button and still allow the next assertions to execute:

```
const btnBogus = $('button[name="Bogus"]');
softexpect(btnBogus.isEnabled()).to.be.true;
```

```
const btnAddToCart = $('button[name="Add To Cart"]');
softExpect(btnAddToCart.isEnabled()).to.be.true;
expect(addToCartButton.isClickable()).to.be.clickable;
```

We have our power rings. When we smash them together, we will take on multiple forms, as a helper expectAdv() wrapper will be used to increase the flexibility in the amount of detail being provided in a consistent format. This section will take us beyond generic fail messages and detail the pass results with the least amount of repeated code.

The expect-webdriverio library supports 23 different element matcher assertions. Eight are substring matchers of other full-string assertions. Others, such as .toBePresent, .toHaveChildren, and .toBeDisplayedInViewPort, are in the lesser part of the 80/20 relevancy.

What are soft assertions and why would we need them?

An efficient test will be able to perform multiple validations on a page, but if the first of three assertions fail, the test will immediately end. Maybe only the first assertion is failing, or maybe all three. We want the full count of assertions, not the least. Otherwise, it becomes a piecemeal process and slows us down.

Note that Expect.toBeExist, Expect.toBePresent, and Expect.toBeExisting only mean the element is in the DOM. They do not explicitly mean the element is visible to the user, so they are, for the most part, impractical.

WebdriverIO provides positive and negative checks of the status of elements:

```
Expect.toBeDisplayed
Expect.toBeFocused
Expect.toBeEnabled
Expect.toBeDisabled
Expect.toBeClickable
Expect.toBeChecked
Expect.toBeSelected
```

It also provides two ways to check whether an element contains text or a value:

```
Expect.toHaveText / Expect.toHaveTextContaining
Expect.toHaveValue / Expect.toHaveValueContaining
```

It also provides validations of IDs, elements, and attributes, which can be exact or string subsets:

```
Expect.toHaveElementProperty
Expect.toHaveAttribute
Expect.toHaveAttributeContaining
Expect.toHaveElementClass
Expect.toHaveElementClassContaining
```

```
Expect.toHaveId
Expect.toHaveLink / Expect.toHaveLinkContaining
```

Soft asserts – allowing a test to continue after an assertion fails

In our custom `expectAdv` wrapper, we will implement a few concepts that allow it to be read similarly to a plain English sentence. The first parameter, `actual`, is intentionally assigned the `any` type. This is because we want the flexibility to validate either an element or a string value:

```
function expectAdv(
actual: any,
assertionType: string,
expected?: any,
Description: string = 'A description of this assertion is
recommended.')
}
```

Here, `assertionType` is a string that indicates the assertion to perform. An element might *exist*; the element might *equal* an expected string.

The expected argument is optional as it would not be required if an element "is enabled".

> **Quick tip**
> The description is required. Every validation should have some detail about what is being performed. Thus, if it is missing, a helpful nudge to add transparency to our test case is provided.

In the case of a soft assertion, the method returns a Boolean `true` or `false` value. This means our test cases can be optimized with decision trees. This concept will be used in a later chapter when we discuss how to have steps that continue without failure even if the element does not exist.

Introduction to Allure reports

Allure is a powerful reporting framework that presents concise and well-organized reports. You can access this report template by installing the `@wdio/allure-reporter` and `allure-commandline` packages:

```
> yarn add @wdio/allure-reporter
```

Allure exports reports in a standardized format called Allure results format. To generate comprehensive reports, you can utilize the Allure framework through the command-line interface:

```
"node_modules/.bin/allure generate --clean ./reports/allure-results &&
allure open -p 5050"
```

The Allure Framework is a versatile and lightweight test reporting tool supporting multiple programming languages. It provides a succinct presentation of test results in HTML format, empowering all stakeholders in the development process to extract valuable insights from routine test executions:

```
// Code example using expect-webdriverio
export async function expectAdv(actual, assertionType, expected) {
  const softAssert = expect;

  const getAssertionType = {
    equals: () => (softAssert(actual).toEqual(expected)),
    contains: () => (softAssert(actual).toContain(expected)),
    exist: () => (softAssert(actual).toBeExisting()),
    isEnabled: () => (softAssert(actual).toBeEnabled()),
    isDisabled: () => (softAssert(actual).toBeDisabled()),
    doesNotExist: () => (softAssert(actual).not.toBeExisting()),
    doesNotContain: () => (softAssert(actual).not.
toContain(expected)),

    default: () => (console.info('Invalid assertion type:  ',
assertionType)),
  };
  (getAssertionType[assertionType] || getAssertionType['default'])();

  if (!getAssertionType[assertionType]){
    allureReporter.addAttachment('Assertion Failure: ', `Invalid
Assertion Type = ${assertionType}`, 'text/plain');
    allureReporter.addAttachment('Assertion Error: ', console.error,
'text/plain');
  } else {
    allureReporter.addAttachment('Assertion Passes: ', `Valid
Assertion Type = ${assertionType}`, 'text/plain');
  }
  allureReporter.endStep();
}
```

By adding these Allure statements into our framework, we can provide significantly more detail to stakeholders in a way that is visually informative.

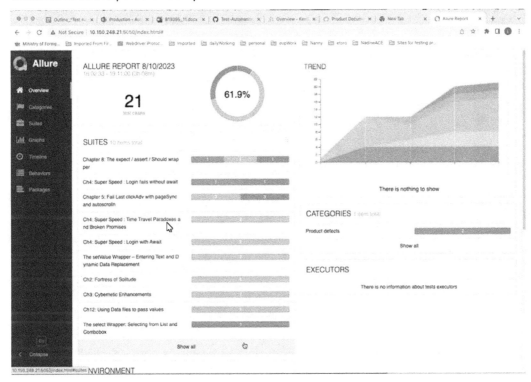

Figure 8.2: Samples of test results in Allure with historical trends

Allure reports can organize tests into subcategories. This makes it clear whether related tests are failing. It also shows how the runs have been performing over time. This can show both an increase in test case coverage as well trends where results are improving or recently worsening.

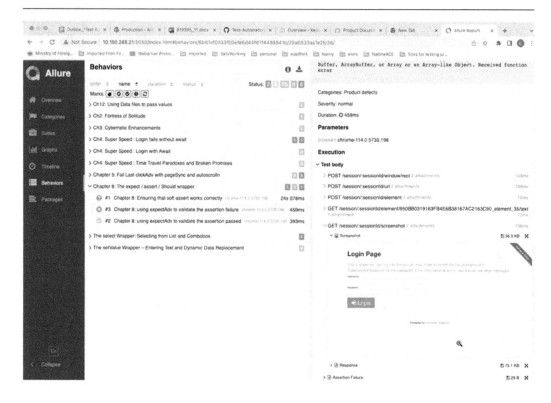

Figure 8.3: Sample of step-by-step execution with a screen capture of the Login page

These reports also provide the option to add screen captures such as X-ray vision. This can give vital clues as to what is occurring when the test fails, particularly if we are running in the cloud without a direct live view into the system as it runs.

Summary

In this section, we talked about the history of assert, expect, and should assertions. We introduced the concepts of hard and soft assertions, why they are important distinctions, and when they should be implemented. We also introduced Allure reports to provide details of all events being executed and the results of whether they pass or fail. Allure reports will further enhance our view in the future by providing a historical view of tests that pass and fail. In the next chapter, we'll build the page object model.

9
The Ancient Spell Book – Building the Page Object Model

All frameworks have three to four abstraction layers. This might best be visualized as a book of ancient spells. The easiest incantations are at the beginning. These are building blocks for more complex and powerful enchantments in the middle. And the darkest secrets are always at the end of the cryptic grimoire. Similarly, there is the Test layer, which calls upon the methods referencing objects in the middle Page Object Class layer, which in turn utilizes helper wrappers and other functionality at the bottom-most Core layer. In a Cucumber framework, there is an additional abstraction layer from the Test Feature File layer to the step definitions to the Glue code to the core code layer. In this chapter, we focus on creating page elements and the methods used to perform actions on the page.

Before that, here's a list of all the main topics we'll be covering in the chapter:

- Understanding what page object model is
- Creating a page class for the tests
- Adding object selectors
- The module.exports statement
- Reducing code with common objects and methods
- POM using Klassi-js

Technical requirements

All test examples can be found at this GitHub repository: `https://github.com/PacktPublishing/Enhanced-Test-Automation-with-WebdriverIO`

What is Page Object Model?

Page Object Model (POM) is a design pattern used in test automation to create a structured and maintainable framework for web application testing. It promotes the separation of test code from the implementation details of the web pages.

In POM, each web page is represented as a separate class, and the properties and behaviors of the page are encapsulated within that class. Test methods interact with the web pages using the methods provided by the page classes, rather than directly accessing the web elements or using low-level browser APIs.

POM can be implemented in Node.js using frameworks such as WebdriverIO or Klassi-js

What constitutes a good Page Object pattern?

A good Page Object pattern in test automation is one that promotes the maintainability, reusability, and readability of the code. Some characteristics of a well-implemented Page Object pattern are:

- **Adheres to the Single Responsibility Principle (SRP)**: Each page class should have a single responsibility and represent a specific page or component of the application. This ensures that the code is well-organized and easy to maintain.

- **Encapsulation**: The page class should encapsulate the details and behavior of the web page or component it represents. It should provide methods to interact with the page elements without exposing the underlying implementation details. This abstraction simplifies test code and makes it more readable.

- **Modular and reusable**: Page classes should be modular and reusable across different tests and test suites. They should provide a consistent interface to interact with the page elements, allowing for easy reuse and reducing code duplication.

- **Adheres to separation of concerns (SoC)**: The Page Object pattern separates the test logic from the implementation details of the web pages. Test methods should utilize the methods provided by the page classes rather than directly interacting with the web elements or using low-level browser APIs. This separation improves code maintainability and makes it easier to update the tests when the application changes.

- **Independent of test framework**: Page classes should be independent of the specific test framework being used. They should not have any dependency on the testing framework, such as assertions or test execution logic. This ensures that the page classes can be easily reused with different testing frameworks or tools. Take a look at the following example:

```
class LoginPage {
  get usernameField() { return $('#username'); }
  get passwordField() { return $('#password'); }
  get loginButton() { return $('#login'); }
```

```
      enterUsername(username) {
        this.usernameField.setValue(username);
      }
```

- **Clear naming conventions**: Page classes, methods, and variables should have meaningful and descriptive names that accurately represent their purpose and functionality. This helps improve code readability and understanding:

```
      loadPage: Async (url, seconds) => {
      Await browser.url(url, seconds)
      }
```

- **Undergoes regular maintenance**: Page classes should be regularly maintained and updated as the application evolves. They should be kept in sync with the changes in the application's UI and functionality. Regularly reviewing and updating page classes helps ensure their accuracy and reliability.

Creating a page class for the tests

We have created a `LoginPage` class that represents a specific page of the web application. The web element selectors are defined as getters using the $ function from WebdriverIO, which allows us to locate elements on the page using CSS selectors.

The class also includes page methods such as `enterUsername`, `enterPassword`, and `clickLoginButton`. These methods encapsulate actions that can be performed on the page, such as entering text into input fields and clicking buttons.

The `mkdir` command in Linux/Unix allows users to create or make new directories. `mkdir` stands for "make directory":

Go to your **command prompt** | **Terminal** and pass the desired name to the `mkdir` command:

```
mkdir loginPage.ts
homePage.ts
testClass.ts
```

Adding object selectors

The `TestClass` test class utilizes the exported instances of the page classes. In the test case, we interact with the web pages using the methods defined in the page objects.

// LoginPage.ts

`LoginPage`: This class encapsulates the properties and behaviors of it respective web pages:

```
class LoginPage {
  get usernameField() { return $('#username'); }
  get passwordField() { return $('#password'); }
  get loginButton() { return $('#login'); }

  enterUsername(username) {
    this.usernameField.setValue(username);
  }

  enterPassword(password) {
    this.passwordField.setValue(password);
  }

  clickLoginButton() {
    this.loginButton.click();
  }
}

module.exports = new LoginPage();
```

// HomePage.ts

`HomePage`: This class encapsulates the properties and behaviors of their respective web pages:

```
class HomePage {
  get welcomeMessage() { return $('#welcome'); }
  get logoutButton() { return $('#logout'); }

  getWelcomeMessage() {
    return this.welcomeMessage.getText();
  }

  clickLogoutButton() {
    this.logoutButton.click();
  }
}
```

module.exports = new HomePage();Calling methods to be used in the test

The `module.exports` statement is used to export an instance of each page class as a module:

```
module.exports = new HomePage();
module.exports = new loginPage();
```

// TestName.ts

The `TestName` test file utilizes the exported instances of the page classes. In this example test case, we interact with the LoginPage and the HomePage web pages using the methods and objects defined in the respective page classes:

```
import LoginPage from('../PageObjects/LoginPage');
import HomePage from('../PageObjects/HomePage');
import assert from('assert');
describe('Test Name', () => {
  before(() => {
    // Set up WebDriverIO configuration

  });

  it('should perform login and logout', () => {
    LoginPage.enterUsername('username');
    LoginPage.enterPassword('password');
    LoginPage.clickLoginButton();

    const welcomeMessage = HomePage.getWelcomeMessage();
    assert.strictEqual(welcomeMessage, 'Welcome, User!');

    HomePage.clickLogoutButton();
  });

  after(() => {
    // Quit WebDriverIO instance
  });
});
```

Reducing code with common objects and methods

Reducing code duplication and improving maintainability can be achieved by leveraging common objects and methods in your Page Object pattern. Some strategies to achieve code reduction are set out here:

- **Base page class**: Create a base page class that contains common objects and methods shared across multiple pages. This base class can encapsulate elements and behaviors that are common to multiple pages, such as a **Home** button, **Halloween Party** button, and then a **Find My Candy!** button, to reduce duplication:

Figure 9.1 – Header of CandyMapper party page website with links common to all pages

These elements appear in the header of every page of the website. So, it makes sense to declare them in the top-level page class and extend it to all other pages.

Figure 9.2 – Header page of the Candymapper landing page with three common links

If the selectors were in every page class, there would be an increasing level of maintenance over time. So, we will create selectors in the common page class like this:

```
get homeButton() {return $(`//a[text()='Home']`); }
```

Figure 9.3 – Highlight of HOME link from the link selector

Let's take a moment to look at these three examples as some changes could be made. These selectors match buttons in the header and the footer of the page. We could lock into just the first element match like this:

```
get homeButton() {return $(`(//a[text()='Home'])[1]`); }
get halloweenPartyButton() {return $(` (//a[contains(text(),
'Party')])[1]`); }
```

Figure 9.4 – Locator identified for first Halloween Party link

Since these elements are common to all our pages, it would make sense to create a common base `Page` class and store all of them there:

```
export default class Page {
  get homeButton() {return $(`//a[text()='Home']`); }
  get halloweenPartyButton() {return $(` (//a[contains(text(),
'Party')])[1]`); }
}
```

Other page classes can now inherit from this base `Page` class all its common objects and functionality. We can use the `extends` keyword to add these object to any `Page` class:

```
import * as helpers from "../../helpers/helpers";
import Page from "./page";

class CandymapperPage extends Page{
  await helpers.clickAdv(await
    super.halloweenPartyButton);
}
```

Last, we use the `super` keyword to reference objects and methods in the common parent class to reduce repeated code.

If we find only the case of the text of common elements is different from page to page or is frequently changing release to release , we can use this next approach to reduce maintenance. Consider the 'FIND MY CANDY' link element below:

```
 get findMyCandyButton() {return $(`
(//a[contains(translate(normalize-space(),
'ABCDEFGHIJKLMNOPQRSTUVWXYZ', 'abcdefghijklmnopqrstuvwxyz'),
'my candy') and not(contains(@style, 'display: none')) and
not(contains(@style, 'visibility: hidden'))])[1]`); }
```

Figure 9.5 – Case insensitive match Locator for Find my candy! link

This is done via the display or visibility property of the element style. There is a single trick to find only elements that are visible. Ultimately, a collection of elements could be returned and each check for immediate visibility.

Other page classes can be inherited from this base class and inherit its common functionality.

- **Page components**: Identify common components or sections within your application's pages that are repeated across multiple pages. Create separate page component classes to represent these reusable components. Then, include these components within your page classes to reuse the common functionality and reduce code duplication.

- **Helper methods**: Identify common operations or actions performed across multiple pages, such as logging in, navigating between pages, or handling popups. Extract these operations into helper methods that can be called from different page classes. This centralizes the implementation and avoids duplicating the code for these common actions.

- **Parameterization**: If you have similar elements or actions that vary based on input parameters, you can create parameterized methods in your page classes. These methods can accept parameters and perform the desired actions based on the provided input, reducing the need for separate methods for similar functionality.

- **External configuration**: Move configurable values such as URLs, timeouts, or test data into external configuration files. This allows you to centralize and reuse the configuration across multiple tests and pages, reducing the need for hardcoding values in individual page classes.

- **Maintainable selectors:** Use a reliable and maintainable way to locate elements on the page, such as CSS selectors or XPath expressions. Avoid using hardcoded selectors in your test methods. Instead, define selectors as properties within your page classes, making it easier to update them if the UI changes.

POM using Klassi-js

Klassi-js is a robust and versatile **behavior-driven development** (**BDD**) JavaScript test automation framework that empowers developers and QA professionals to create and execute comprehensive tests for web and mobile applications. At its core, Klassi-js leverages the power of WebdriverIO, which is a cutting-edge automation framework for Node.js. This foundation allows Klassi-js to seamlessly interact with web browsers and mobile devices, making it an excellent choice for cross-browser and cross-platform testing.

One of Klassi-js's standout features is its seamless integration with cucumber.js, a popular BDD testing tool. This integration allows for the creation of human-readable, expressive test scenarios that foster better collaboration between developers, testers, and other stakeholders. It promotes a common language for discussing application behavior and helps in building more reliable tests.

Klassi-js goes a step further by offering integrated visual, accessibility, and API testing capabilities, ensuring that your application not only works but is also user-friendly, compliant with accessibility standards, and delivers the expected API responses. Moreover, Klassi-js provides the flexibility to run tests locally or harness the power of cloud-based testing platforms such as LambdaTest, BrowserStack, or Sauce Labs, allowing for scalable and efficient testing across various environments.

POM is a design pattern for organizing your UI automation code to make it more maintainable and readable. When using Klassi-js with Cucumber, you can implement the POM design pattern as follows.

Project structure

First, organize your project structure to separate different concerns. A common structure might look like this:

```
project-root
-- features
    -- login.feature
-- step-definitions
    -- login.steps.ts
-- pages
    -- login.page.ts
-- index.ts
-- runtime
-- world.ts
-- package.json
```

Let's break this down:

- `features`: Stores your Cucumber feature files

- `step-definitions`: Stores your Cucumber step definitions

- `pages`: Stores your page objects

Cucumber feature files

Create Cucumber feature files in the features directory of your project. These feature files describe the behavior of your application in plain text. For example, you can create a `login.feature` file:

```
Feature: Login functionality
  Scenario: Successful login
```

```
Given I am on the login page
When I enter my username and password
And I click the login button
Then I should be logged in
```

Page objects

Create a page object for each web page or component you want to interact with. Here's an example, login.page.ts:

```
class LoginPage {
    get usernameInput() { return $('#username'); }
    get passwordInput() { return $('#password'); }
    get loginButton() { return $('#login-button'); }
    get welcomeMessage() { return $('#welcome-message'); }
    open() {
        browser.url('/login'); // Adjust the URL as needed
    }

    login(username, password) {
        this.usernameInput.setValue(username);
        this.passwordInput.setValue(password);
        this.loginButton.click();
    }
}

module.exports = new LoginPage();
```

Cucumber step definitions

In your step definitions, use page objects to interact with web elements. Here's an example, login.steps.ts:

```
const { Given, When, Then } = require('cucumber');
const LoginPage = require('../pageobjects/login.page');

Given('I am on the login page', () => { LoginPage.open(); });

When('I enter my username and password', () => {
    LoginPage.username.setValue('your_username');
    LoginPage.password.setValue('your_password');
});

When('I click the login button', () => { LoginPage.loginButton.
```

```
click(); });
Then('I should be logged in', () => {
    expect(LoginPage.welcomeMessage).toHaveText('Welcome, User');
});
```

Running tests

You can run your Cucumber tests as usual with Klassi-js. Use a command such as this:

```
> node index.ts --tags @login
```

Klassi-js will automatically discover your Cucumber feature files and execute the corresponding step definitions.

With this structure, your UI automation code becomes more modular and easier to maintain. Each page object encapsulates the functionality and interactions with a specific page or component, making it easier to update and manage your tests.

Summary

Following the aforementioned principles, you can create a Page Object pattern akin to the meticulous planning of a superhero, ensuring your code becomes more maintainable, reusable, and readable. Just as a superhero fine-tunes their abilities to be more effective, by adhering to these strategies, you can reduce code duplication and enhance maintainability in your Page Object pattern. Reusing common objects, methods, and components across pages is like harnessing the compartments of a superhero's utility belt, streamlining your code and ensuring that modifications are easy to implement and maintain.

In the next chapter, we will continue to amplify our framework's prowess by leveraging system variables and dynamic configurations, much like a superhero adapts to different environments, to seamlessly switch between dev and stage landing pages.

10

Increased Flexibility – Writing Robust Selectors and Reducing Maintenance

Maintenance is the ever-growing villain of a test automation project. Each release has more tests and more elements that can go stale, causing a test to fail. If you are new to the test automation field, you may not realize just how much maintenance will increasingly impact your project release after release. I (Paul) would like to share with you this story that inspired several unique solutions.

Several years ago, my client's development team decided to change the entire underlying architecture supporting the application under test. My automation team only became aware of this change when we found nearly all 100 of our test cases suite failed to reach a passing state. In fact, the only test case that passed was the LogIn test we wrote on the first day of the project. We realized that hundreds of element objects had changed their tag name to different types and used different properties. We were faced with the daunting task of rewriting hundreds of element selectors one by one. We estimated the rework of the page objects might take 2 days to be returned to a working state.

Add to this that the client had been used to receiving a detailed summary of the regression test suite results in under 2 hours, along with our smoke tests detecting issues within 15 minutes. We were faced with the task of explaining that release results would not be available for another 2 days or more. The manual team of six resources would likely complete their testing in that amount of time.

My coworker set about the task of updating selectors in the page object tags. I had a different idea. From my analysis, I realized that just one element tag had changed. Many of the <a> link anchors were now <button> tags. Luckily, none of the strings used to locate elements had changed, they were just in different object properties. I proposed adding a thin layer to our framework that would search for alternate tag elements to the one that was no longer found.

The code change was completed in under an hour. The number of test cases that were executed increased to 95% completion. Two test cases failed the release, and another three needed to be maintained by hand to get to a working state. This was in line with the maintenance work on the previous release iterations. Our client understood the challenge the architectural change presented, and she was overjoyed we could provide actionable results within 4 hours.

On similar lines, we will cover the following main topics in this chapter:

- Reducing page object maintenance with generic selectors
- Anatomy of an XPath selector
- Leveraging `data-qa` and **Accessible Rich Internet Applications (ARIA)** attributes
- Writing an XPath element that contains a textual substring
- Second chances – getting valid objects from stale selector

Technical requirements

All test examples can be found at this GitHub repository: `https://github.com/PacktPublishing/Enhanced-Test-Automation-with-WebdriverIO`

Reducing page object maintenance with generic selectors

Before we get into the advanced concepts of making our object flexible like plastic, let's begin with several ways we can write better selectors. A robust selector is extremely important to reduce the maintenance of your test automation framework. We will move beyond exact matches to use substring matches to be sure that we can find an element even if it changes slightly.

We begin with a simple question. Which is better—XPath or CSS? There is a common idea that CSS is the preferred method for writing a selector because it executes faster. While this may be true, the speed difference today is minimal. I would rather spend a few more milliseconds finding an element over the minutes spent repeatedly updating object selectors. In addition, CSS selectors are harder to write syntactically. Furthermore, CSS selectors are not as flexible when we need to find one element relative to another—for example, locating one of many generic **Span** or **Input radio** button objects relative to a unique `label` object:

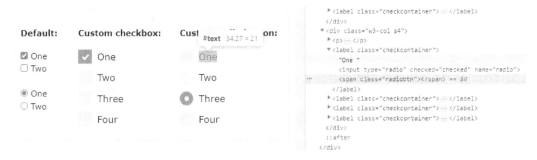

Figure 10.1 – A generic radio button relative to a Label element named "One" on the DOM

In the preceding example, there is no way to uniquely identify any of the radio buttons by their text. This is because the uniquely identifiable text is contained in a Label element relative to the **Span radio** button.

We must leverage the XPath axis of a parent and child element to uniquely locate these elements by relative location. We write a selector to the parent object that has the text One:

```
//label[text()='One']
```

We then follow it with the generic child radio button:

```
span[@class='radiobtn']
```

We then combine them:

```
//label[text()='One']/span[@class='radiobtn']
```

That was an easy riddle to solve. But what if we have text that has extra spaces, forced carriage returns, or even a mix of quotes and single quotes, as in the following example? To solve issues such as this, we will take a deeper dive into more ways that we can locate and identify elements:

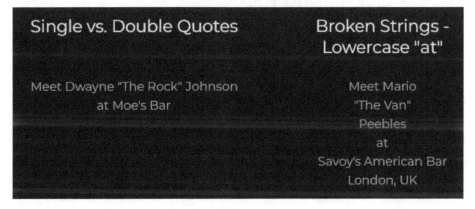

Figure 10.2 – Extra spaces, mixed single and double quotes, and embedded carriage returns

Thus far, we have seen examples of XPath and CSS selectors. Let us take a moment to further explore the components to retrieve collections of elements in WebdriverIO.

Anatomy of an XPath selector

Selectors are comprised of one or more node tag types followed by an optional [predicate] in square brackets. The predicates have operators and functions to filter certain node matches. Lastly, they include path separators with generic *axes* with double colons to further refine the path of the element. This makes it more likely to find an element regardless of its location in the DOM.

XPath selectors are written as *absolute* or *relative*. This is an example of an absolute-style selector to the **Find My Candy** button on the *Candymapper* website:

```
public get myElement() {
  const selector: string = "/html[1]/body[1]/div[1]/div[1]/div[1]/
div[13]/div[1]/div[1]/div[1]/div[2]/div[2]/a[1]";
  return $(selector);
}
```

Now that you have seen an absolute selector, use it only as a red flag. The point of this exercise is the fluid nature of the numeric indexes inside the square brackets. The exact location will be dynamic from release to release, causing endless maintenance. If you see a lot of selectors with this format in your code base, it is all but certain your selector is not robust. Furthermore, it is a devilish riddle for another developer to figure out the intended element since the text "Find My Candy" does not appear in the selector string. Let's look for better ways to write selectors.

> **Rule of thumb**
>
> Always take extra time to replace an absolute selector with a relative selector and use a descriptive element name. The myElement name in the preceding example is of no help and should be renamed findMyCandy or, better still, btnFindMyCandy.

Relative selectors

Most relative selectors begin with a double slash (//) followed by a single slash indicating the next element in the path. Let's look at this in a bit more detail:

- // (**double slash**): Denotes any descendant relationship between elements. When you use a double slash between elements in an XPath expression, it selects all descendants of the preceding element, regardless of their depth in the hierarchy.

  Example: //div selects all <div> elements anywhere in the document.

- / **(single slash)**: Denotes the direct child relationship between elements. When you use a single slash between elements in an XPath expression, it selects the child elements of the preceding element.

  Example: `/html/body/div` selects all `<div>` elements that are direct children of the `<body>` element inside the `<html>` root.

- * **(star)**: Denotes a wildcard match.

To start, we will get a collection of all the elements on the page using the * wildcard matcher for all node types:

```
const allElementsByXPath: ElementArrayType = await browser.$$('//*');
```

Node test functions – text() versus normalize-space()

Several of the element selector tags shown here, including anchors, buttons, and lists, can be matched with exact text using the `text()` Node test function:

```
//a[text()=`FIND MY CANDY!`]
```

This is an easy sample, but what if there were some strange formatting embedded in the text?

Broken strings

There can be times when extraneous spaces or carriage returns make a selector match challenging. In such cases, it is recommended to use `normalize-space()` instead of `text()`:

```
//a[normalize-space()=`FIND MY CANDY!`]
```

We can check if this selector is valid with the `SelectorsHub` Chrome extension:

Figure 10.3 – SelectorsHub indicates more than one element will match the selector

The XPath selector is valid, but it matches four additional elements on the screen. Another way is to get the button element relative to the container page:

```
//*[contains(@class,"popup")]//following::a
```

This element can be located with the parent class and converted to a CSS selector with a period (.) as a shortcut for a class name:

```
.widget-popup a
```

Similarly, we can perform a close match with a popup on the class name to find an anchor link child using the CSS containing a *= shortcut in this way:

```
[class*="popup"] a
```

We can also narrow down the parent element to a specific tag type:

```
div[class*="popup"] a
```

There are five common web page elements we will seek: links, buttons, lists, fields, and text elements.

Here are common ways to find these elements with an exact string as well as a substring match in XPath:

- Links:

  ```
  //a[normalize-space()='Link Text']
  //a[contains(normalize-space(),'Link')]
  //a[@href='https://example.com']
  ```

- Buttons:

  ```
  //button[normalize-space()='Click Me']
  //button[contains(normalize-space(),'Click')]
  //button[@id='submit-button']
  ```

- Lists (unordered and ordered):

  ```
  //ul/li[normalize-space()='Item']
  //ul/li[contains(normalize-space(),'Item')]
  //ol/li[position()=2]   // Not recommended
  ```

- Fields and multiline text areas:

  ```
  //input[@type='text']
  //input[contains(@id,'input')]
  //textarea[@placeholder='Enter text']
  ```

- Text:

  ```
  //span[normalize-space() ='Some Text']
  //span[contains(normalize-space(),'Text')]
  //*[starts-with(normalize-space(),'Hello')]
  ```

Leveraging data-qa and ARIA attributes

There have been two new developments in website design where developers can help SDETs maintain robust low-maintenance selectors. Consider this web page element snippet:

```
<div data-qa="product-card" role="article" aria-label="Product
Details">
        <a href="#" data-qa="add-to-cart">Add to Cart </a> </div>
```

This can be accomplished by adding the data-qa attribute, which is unique and static. Alternately, if the developer team follows the ARIA standard, many text elements can be identified by the aria-label attribute:

```
//div[contains(@aria-label, 'Product Details')]
//a[contains(@data-qa, 'Add to Cart')]
```

Here is an example leveraging data-qa and ARIA attributes to ensure that your web application's elements are accessible and interactable:

```
describe("Accessibility Testing", function () {
  // Simulate loading a web page or application
  beforeAll(function () {
    // Load your web page or application
  });

  it("should have proper ARIA attributes", function () {
    // Find an element by its data-qa attribute
    const buttonWithQA = element(by.css('[data-qa="login-button"]'));

    // Verify that the ARIA role is set to "button"
    expect(buttonWithQA.getAttribute('role')).toEqual('button');

    // You can also check other ARIA attributes like "aria-label",
"aria-describedby", etc.
    // Example: expect(buttonWithQA.getAttribute('aria-label')).
toBe('Login Button');
  });

  it("should be keyboard accessible", function () {
    // Find an element by its ARIA label
    const buttonWithARIA = element(by.css('[aria-label="Login
Button"]'));

    // Trigger a click event using Protractor
    buttonWithARIA.click();
```

```
    // Verify that the element is focused after the click
    expect(browser.driver.switchTo().activeElement().
getAttribute('aria-label')).toEqual('Login Button');
    });
});
```

In the example, we have two test cases. The first one verifies that an element with a `data-qa` attribute has the correct ARIA role. The second test case checks the keyboard accessibility of an element with a specific ARIA label. This is just a basic example, and you can adapt it to your specific application's needs to ensure that your elements are properly accessible and have the right attributes.

> **Rule of thumb – alternatives to CSS selectors**
>
> Unfortunately, CSS selectors do not provide a direct way to filter elements based on their text content, like the `text()` and `normalize-space()` functions in XPath.

So, while CSS selectors are hailed as being faster, they can be limited in functionality in test automation. The next example utilizes CSS to quickly gather all elements on the page:

```
const allElementsByCss: ElementArrayType = await browser.$$('*');
```

For fetching particular types of elements, a combination of XPath and CSS can be employed. Here are some supplementary element selector types:

- Text:

  ```
  //span[text()='Vital Signs']
  ```

- Links:

  ```
  a[href='https://example.com']
  //a[@href='https://example.com']
  ```

- Buttons:

  ```
  button#submit-button
  //button[text()='Login']
  ```

- Lists:

  ```
  ol li:nth-child(2)
  ```

- Fields:

  ```
  input[type='text']
  input[id*='input']
  textarea[placeholder='Enter text']
  ```

Finding an element only by text

Elements can be found with an XPath selector with an exact matching string. For example, a **Next** button with an exact match would be formatted as such:

```
//a[text()='Next >']
```

However, while the text is likely to remain constant, the angle bracket and spacing could change. We can reduce our chance of future maintenance with a selector that has a substring.

Writing an XPath element that contains a textual substring

By adding `contains()` to the selector, the object can be found with just a small part of the text:

```
//a[contains(text(),'Next']
```

This works for many elements, but checkboxes and radio buttons are tricky.

Finding an element relative to another element

In this next example, we want to click the checkbox next to the name *John Smith*. We have several checkboxes but none has a unique identifier by name:

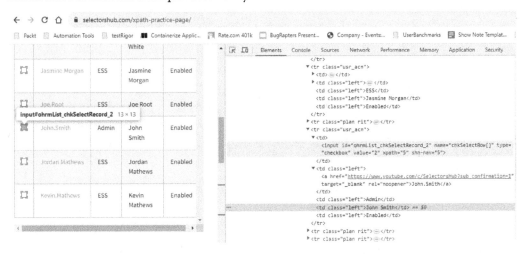

Figure 10.4 – The name John Smith and its associated checkbox are two separate elements

This selector will identify all the checkboxes:

```
//input[contains(@name,'chkSelect')]
```

To locate this checkbox element, we need to use the link and find the input checkbox preceding it. Here's how we can do that:

```
//a[normalize-space()='John.Smith']//preceding::input[@id='ohrmList_
chkSelectRecord_2']
```

Case-insensitive partial matches

What if we learn a developer sometimes changes the case of the text? A solution to that is to add a `translate` option and convert the text to match either upper- or lowercase:

```
//a[translate(normalize-space(), 'ABCDEFGHIJKLMNOPQRSTUVWXYZ',
'abcdefghijklmnopqrstuvwxyz')='john.smith']//preceding::input[@
id='ohrmList_chkSelectRecord_2']
```

The problem now is that the element the selector returns is not always visible. Here is how we handle that.

Finding only visible elements

One of the biggest challenges in test automation is to return a collection of visible elements. This reminds us of a very famous quote delivered by Michael Keaton: "*Want to get nuts? Let's get nuts!*"

This extensive selector is provided as one example. It will eliminate most objects that are not visible in multiple ways. We addressed the opacity being 0, the overflow or visibility being hidden, the display being none, and the width or height being set to 0:

```
(//a | //input | //select | //textarea)[
not (
contains(@style,'opacity: 0;') or contains(@style,'visibility:
hidden;') or contains(@style,'display: none;') or contains(@
style,'overflow: hidden;') or contains(@style,'width: 0') or
contains(@style,'height: 0')) and
not(ancestor::*[contains(@style,'opacity: 0;') or
contains(@style,'visibility: hidden;') or
contains(@style,'display: none;') or
contains(@style,'overflow: hidden;') or
contains(@style,'width: 0') or
contains(@style,'height: 0')])]
```

This selector also eliminates any elements that have an ancestor that is hidden. Here is another place where the 80/20 rule applies. Even if this selector only eliminates about 80% of non-visible elements, we will still need to parse through a collection of elements to find the first one that is visible. So, why not let XPath or CSS handle more than half of the work getting our visible elements?

The reason we want to do this is to give our methods a second chance at trying to find an element if it has been changed from its class. It's never too late for a second or third chance to find an element.

Second chances – getting valid objects from stale selectors

Now that we have our four primary method wrappers, let us make them more robust with self-healing code. The biggest drawback in automation is the maintenance to fix elements in the **Page Object Model (POM)** when selectors become stale. In this section, we look at self-healing techniques to find elements that have changed their node type.

Self healing techniques

Let's go over some self-healing techniques in this sub-section.

Reducing code for case-insensitive matches

All these functions will require a conversion to case-insensitive matches. We start by creating two constants to reduce the repeated use of the upper- and lowercase alphabet:

```
const A_Z = 'ABCDEFGHIJKLMNOPQRSTUVWXYZ';
const a_z = 'abcdefghijklmnopqrstuvwxyz';
```

Next, we will need a function that will extract unique text from a stale locator.

Extracting selector text

This function will try to return the first match of any unique text encased in double or single quotes. This will be injected into a close match locator:

```
function extractSelectorText(selector: string): string {
const singleQuoteCount = (selector.match(/'/g) || []).length;
  let newSelector = selector;
```

First, we check for a single quote, such as a possessive apostrophe, embedded in the selector string. For example, "Moe's Bar" would result in an odd number of single quotes:

```
if (singleQuoteCount === 1 || singleQuoteCount === 3){
  const parts = selector.split("'");
  if (singleQuoteCount === 1) {
```

Handle cases where there is one single quote by surrounding it with a concat function:

```
      newSelector = `concat('${parts[0]}', "'", '${parts[1]}')`;
```

This converts "Moe's bar" to "concat("Moe","'","'s bar")" to support a single-quote match.

```
    } else if (singleQuoteCount === 3) {
```

In any other language, it would be impossible to have a locator with both a single quote and a quoted string in a single locator. But because JavaScript allows literal strings with backticks, there could be a string like this:

```
`//*[text()=Meet Dwayne "The Rock" Johnson at Moe's Bar]`
```

So, we handle the case where there are three single quotes and only the second single quote should be escaped like this:

```
        newSelector = `concat('${parts[0]}${parts[1]}', "'",
'${parts[2]}')`;
    }
  }
```

This extracts as the following:

```
`concat(Meet Dwayne "The Rock" Johnson at Moe","'"'s Bar"`
```

Extract text between two double or single quotes as follows:

```
    let match = newSelector.match(/"([^"]+)"$/) || newSelector.
match(/'([^']+)'$/);
```

If no match is found, or the matched group is not valid, return the original selector. In fact, the locator string passed is likely not robust enough to be given a second chance. We return a string clearly identifying the issue, as returning a Null value would throw an error, and an empty string likely would match all elements:

```
    if (!match || match.length < 2) {
      return "NO TEXT FOUND IN LOCATOR";
    }
```

Otherwise, we return the captured group between single or double quotes modified if a single quote is detected:

```
    return match[1];
    }
```

Now that we have extracted the text of a locator, we can inject it into a similar one for each class of elements.

From links to buttons

On the main page of the *Candymapper* sandbox website, there is exactly one <Button> element. It is the **Send** button. But not too long ago, it was an <A> anchor link like the other ones on the page. and it was in all caps. I've since fixed that, but do I need to spend time fixing the locator in my code?

Figure 10.5 –The Send button element on the Candymapper website

This was the original locator that used to work:

```
//a[text()='SEND']
```

What if we could pull the text and inject it into a button class like this?

```
//button[normalize-space()='SEND']
```

If it still did not work, we made a third attempt to make a case-insensitive match:

```
//button[translate (normalize-space(), 'ABCDEFGHIJKLMNOPQRSTUVWXYZ',
'abcdefghijklmnopqrstuvwxyz') = 'send']
```

Now, we have a solution that allows us to find our elements regardless of case sensitivity. We can now move on to optimizing this with a mutant merge power.

Finding an element by text alone

This can be wrapped together as a function in use by `getValidElement()` to give our buttons a second chance to be identified without refactoring the code:

```
function transformLink(selector: string): string {
let extractedText = extractSelectorText(selector)

// Create the new selector string
const newSelector = `//button[contains(translate (normalize-
space(),'${A_Z}','${a_z}'), '${extractedText.toLowerCase()}')]`;
return newSelector;
}
```

Now, the **Send** button can be reached even if it changes case and class:

```
public get sendLink () {
    return $(`//a[text()='Send']`);
}
await helpers.clickAdv(await this.sendLink)
```

Fields and lists

Fields could change from `<input>` to `<textarea>` objects. To find them, this change can be done with the `@placeholder` property:

```
function transformField(selector: string): string {

let extractedText = extractSelectorText(selector)

// Create the new selector string
const newSelector = `//textarea [contains (@placeholder,
'${A_Z}','${a_z}'), '${extractedText.toLowerCase()}')]`;
return newSelector;
}
```

And of course, `<select>` objects might change to a `<input>` combobox:

```
function transformList(selector: string): string {

let extractedText = extractSelectorText(selector)

// Create the new selector string
const newSelector = `//input [contains (@placeholder,
'${A_Z}','${a_z}'), '${extractedText.toLowerCase()}')]`;
return newSelector;
}
```

Short substrings

One last trick before we leave this rabbit hole. Sometimes, small text changes can still be located accurately. `"Select all active files"` becomes `"Select all activated files"`. Divide the text into thirds. If the remaining length is greater than five characters, there is a good chance of matching on the middle string, `"all activ"`, as long as it is a unique match:

```
function getMiddle(s: string): string {
  const len = s.length;

  // Return the string as it is if its length is less than or equal to
5
```

```
  if (len <= 5) {
    return s;
  }

  // Divide the string into three parts
  const oneThird = Math.floor(len / 3);
  const twoThirds = 2 * oneThird;

  // Extract the middle part
  return s.substring(oneThird, twoThirds);
}

console.log(getMiddle("Select all active files")); // Output: "all
active fi"
console.log(getMiddle("small")); // Output: "small"
```

Statistically, this will return a unique element about 40% of the time.

On thin ice

Scrolling elements pose a particularly difficult challenge. Occasionally, they will end up partially outside of the view area of the browser. Let's take a look at this example:

Figure 10.6 – Text area object of upper-left corner 0,0 located above the browser view
area; center of a second text area object located off the bottom of the browser

And what if your site supports side-scrolling element animation? If your framework activates a sliding menu and immediately tries to click an element inside, there are bound to be some strange results:

Figure 10.7 – Example of clicking the center of a sliding menu item

What makes it more frustrating is that should this issue occur, the screen capture at the end of the test will likely occur once the slider animation has been completed. The only clue you might get is a message indicating the element was not clickable at point 2050, 250 which is just beyond the right edge of a display with a 1920 x 1080 pixel resolution.

The intrinsic WebdriverIO .click() method should never have an issue interacting with an offscreen element. The major reason the clickAdv() wrapper function scrolls the element into the browser view area is to have a better chance of having the element appear in a screen capture if an error occurs.

Attempting to use a fancy JavaScript click can throw errors if the element is not in the viewport. It depends if the click is being executed at the top-left corner of the object or at its calculated center. Here is an example of a JavaScript click call using the browser.execute method to execute the arguments[0].click(); code string:

```
async function jsClick(element: WebdriverIO.Element): Promise<void> {
await browser.execute("arguments[0].click();", element); }

// Usage example
  await jsClick('#some-button-id');
```

There is another good reason this approach can cause issues. In GUI automation, we always want to emulate the user as much as possible. What happens if we have a modal popup displayed over the desired element, as seen here?

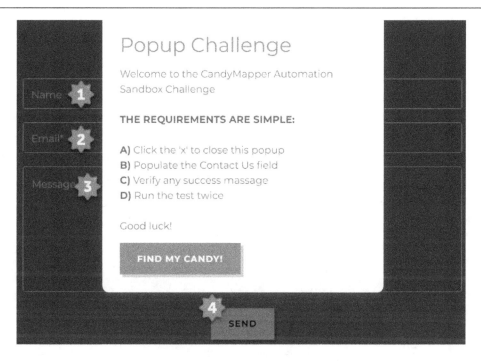

Figure 10.8 – Calling jsclick() to force interaction with an element
below a modal popup will be problematic

If the element we are seeking is sliding in on a control from off-screen, you often might get an error that the element click is out of bounds. It can occur if the element is an item in an expanding list that is still animating. Occasionally, an error can occur when the object has scrolled a few pixels out of the viewport. To counter this, we need to know if the element is moving when the error is thrown and when the movement has stopped. Here's how we can do that:

```
async function scrollOneClickUp(): Promise<void> {
await browser.execute(() => { const event = new
WheelEvent("wheel", { deltaY: -50 });
document.dispatchEvent(event); });
}
```

Scroll down one mouse wheel and click, like so:

```
async function scrollOneClickDown(): Promise<void> {
await browser.execute(() => { const event = new
WheelEvent("wheel", { deltaY: 50 });
document.dispatchEvent(event); });
}
```

Writing the isMoving() method

The days of clicking on an element by an *x* or *y* coordinate are long past us. It does not mean the coordinates of an element are of no value. Surprisingly, in some instances, a click is sometimes performed relative to an element's screen location. With coordinates, we can determine if an element is in motion to ensure there is a higher degree of accuracy in our framework. Consider this line of code:

```
const currentLocation: WebdriverIO.LocationReturn = await element.
getLocation();
```

This will return an object with the current *x* and *y* screen coordinate location of the element. By looping through with a brief pause of a few milliseconds, we can implement a dynamic wait that ensures our object scroll animation has been completed:

```
export async function waitForElementToStopMoving(element: WebdriverIO.
Element, timeout: number): Promise<void>
  const initialLocation = await element.getLocation();
  return new Promise((resolve, reject) => {
    let intervalId: NodeJS.Timeout;
    const checkMovement = () => {
      element.getLocation().then((currentLocation) => {
        if (
            currentLocation.x === initialLocation.x &&
            currentLocation.y === initialLocation.y
          ) {
            clearInterval(intervalId);
            resolve();
          }
      });
    };
    intervalId = setInterval(checkMovement, 100);
    setTimeout(() => {
      clearInterval(intervalId);
      reject(new Error(`Timeout: Element did not stop moving within
${timeout}ms`));
    }, timeout);
  });
}
```

The best practice is to implement this just after any `browser.execute` scroll and before any similar click-based method.

Summary

In this thrilling installment of our superhero coding saga, we've journeyed through the enigmatic world of element targeting, mastering the art of locating elusive HTML entities in the wilds of the web. Our quest led us to conquer the shifting shapes of `<a>` anchors, transforming them into mighty `<button>` sentinels, and evolving simple `<input>` fields into vast expanses of `<textarea>` elements. We've navigated the morphing mazes of dropdowns metamorphosing into comboboxes, deploying our powers to match text with a disregard for case, and even to seek out the hidden meanings within the midst of strings.

Our toolkit expanded, and we've embraced the arcane arts of self-healing locators, weaving spells to mend themselves when the digital winds change. We stood firm as elements danced and darted across the screen, phasing in with animations that would baffle a lesser Tech Mage.

As we stand at the precipice of discovery, we pose a question that defies the very reality of our craft: What if the need for a page object locator were but a mere illusion? What if, in the shadowy recesses of the UI, we could summon a **Send** button with nothing but a whisper to the framework? The answer beckons us—dare we leap into the unknown? The next chapter awaits, promising wonders beyond the limits of our imagination.

11

Echo Location – Skipping the Page Object Model

So far, we have used the **Page Object Model (POM)** to encapsulate the UI elements and interactions with a page within an object. We can usually see our target objective *clearly* with the XPath or CSS locator, but consider the superheroes who get the job done blindly in the dark. While the POM has many merits, there are scenarios where finding objects by text alone, in the dark, based on some clues, can offer advantages:

- **Quick prototyping and simplified test creation**: For quick and dirty testing or prototyping, it might be overkill to establish a full-fledged POM of thousands of objects. In such cases, directly locating elements can speed up the initial test development process.

- **Handling elements with dynamic content**: In modern web applications, the content can be highly dynamic. Elements may not have fixed IDs, classes, or other attributes. Text content is often more stable in later releases behind the scenes in the DOM.

- **Code readability**: Tests written with direct text queries can sometimes be more readable and self-explanatory. Anyone reading the test can understand the user interactions being mimicked, without needing to dive into the page objects to understand what each method does.

In this chapter, we'll cover the following main topics:

- A reduced code base

- Automation in plain English

- Getting a visible button, field, and list by name

- Getting a visible element from a collection

A reduced code base

Skipping the POM reduces the amount of code you have to maintain. This can be particularly beneficial in smaller projects or proof-of-concept implementations, where quick development is more important than long-term maintainability.

While a "text-based" approach has its merits, it's crucial to note that this is not a one-size-fits-all solution. It is intended to remain highly reliable, reducing the amount of maintenance required.

In this chapter, we will enhance our element location by passing just text. Which method is used will provide a clue as to the node types to return for consideration. What does it mean if we can just click **Add To Cart**, enter `setValueAdv("First name", "Paul")` into the **First Name** field, or even select **2** from the **Number of Guests** list?

We will enhance our three custom functions, allowing them to identify elements only based on a string. In addition to passing an object, a simple text string will be passed to the `clickAdv()`, `setValueAdv()`, and `selectAdv()` methods. This way, we can eliminate some of the page objects entirely.

This chapter covers the following main topics:

- Automation in plain English
- Clicking a named button or link
- Entering text into a named field
- Selecting an item from a named list
- Chasing a rabbit hole more than three layers deep

Automation in plain English

We will continue to further modify our custom methods by allowing two different types of classes to be passed. Our methods still support a `WebdriverIO WebElement`, but now, we will enhance them with a string. For example, let's say we want to click the **HALLOWEEN PARTY** button at the top of the CandyMapper site. Consider this code:

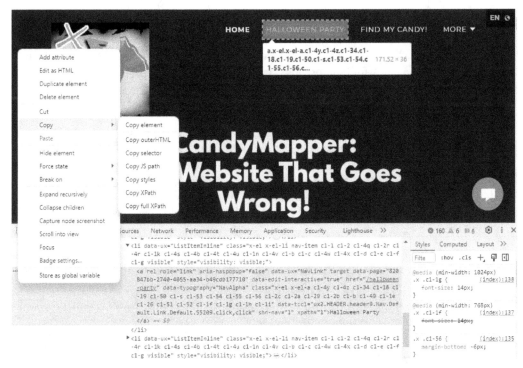

Figure 11.1 – A DevTools view of the HALLOWEEN PARTY link

Here is the POM approach to find the link:

```
public get btnHalloweenParty () {
    return $(`#nav-55206 > li:nth-child(2) > a`);
}
Helpers.clickAdv (btnHalloweenParty);
```

By using the echo location superpower, this line of code could be smart enough to find the proper link with just this:

```
Helpers.clickAdv ("Halloween Party");
```

Alternatively, you could enter an email into a field:

```
Helpers.setValueAdv ("Email", "me@mydomain.com");
```

You could also add a total of two guests to accompany you to the party:

```
Helpers.selectAdv ("Guests","2");
```

Now, we can enhance the method to split along a path that is either an object or a string; in this case, we can use our `getValidObject()` to return a collection of visible elements that contain the string. In addition, we can deduce the type of elements to seek, based on the verb of the action being called. `ClickAdv()` will look for buttons, links, and similar elements. `SetValue()` will look for input fields or `textarea` nodes. `SelectAdv()` will interact with lists.

> **Quick tip**
>
> While we could extend this to our `assertAdv()` function, it is not recommended. The problem is that the `assertAdv()` function with a string would need a lot more context. It would be nearly impossible to determine whether we are validating a button state, a field value, a list item, or some displayed text. It is better to keep this simple and just confirm that the text we seek is visible on the page and highlight all potential matches. For anything else, just pass the `WebElement` class.

Our first step is to extend a code path that will interact with both `WebElement` and a string in the `clickAdv()` method. This same process will apply to the `getValidElement()` function, which we'll do in the following section. Lastly, the `SetValueAdv()` and `Selectadv()` functions will be modified with their relative sections in `getValidElement()`.

Getting a named button

In each of the three custom functions, we will extend the element types that are passed to include strings like this:

```
export async function clickAdv(
element: WebdriverIO.Element | string,
text: string ) {
```

If a string is passed, we will use it to identify a valid element of the type passed:

```
// If button element is a string, find the elements using the string
if (typeof element === 'string') {
element = await getValidElement(element, "button");
}
```

In this example, we provide a clue that this element will be a button. The same will be done next for returning a field to set a value.

Getting a named input field

The same will be modified for `setValueAdv` in a similar fashion. However, we will instruct `getValidElement` to seek out an input or `textarea` field class:

```
export async function setValueAdv(
inputField: WebdriverIO.Element | string,
text: string ) {
// If inputField is a string, find the elements using the string
if (typeof inputField === 'string') {
inputField = await getValidElement(element, "field");
}
```

As with the last two functions, we will extend `selectAdv()` with a final clue string.

Getting a named list

Finally, `selectAdv()` will be modified as well. The types of elements that might match will be listed:

```
export async function selectAdv(
inputField: WebdriverIO.Element | string,
text: string ) {
// If inputField is a string, find the elements using the string
if (typeof inputField === 'string') {
inputField = await getValidElement(inputField, "list") as Element;

}
```

Now that these three methods are updated, we need to enhance the `getValidElement()` method to return an element that fits each verb type.

Getting a visible button by name

The first enhancement in the `getValidElement()` method is to allow a string to be passed, as with the three preceding methods:

```
export async function getValidElement(
   element: WebdriverIO.Element | String,
   elementType: string
): Promise<WebdriverIO.Element> {
```

The first check that we can perform is to see whether there are *any* elements that might match what we seek. In this case, we can leverage both an XPath and a CSS locator for a second time. This XPath locator will seek any node that contains the text passed to the method:

```
if (typeof element == "string") {
    // Try finding "Halloween Party" element by xPath text
    elements = await browser.$$(`//*[contains(normalize-
space(),'${eleText}')]`)
```

If there are no elements returned, a second attempt will be done with a CSS selector using the `href` property. This property often contains the text string in a lowercase set, oriented by dashes:

```
    // No such elements by element
    if (elements.length == 0) {
      //Try finding CSS href contains "halloween-party"
      const elements = await browser.$$(`[href*='${eleText}.
toLowerCase().replaceAll(" ", "-")}']`)
    }
```

Now, we have three types of elements to sort through. Let us deal with each one separately, starting with a button for a click:

```
If (elements.length > 0 and elementType === "button"{
let buttonElements = await browser.$$(`(//a|//button)
[contains(normalize-space(),'${element}')]`)
    }
```

If this returns no matching element, we can try this case-insensitive approach:

```
  if (elements.length === 0) {
let buttonElements = await browser.$$(` (//a|//
button)[contains(translate(normalize-space(text()),
'ABCDEFGHIJKLMNOPQRSTUVWXYZ', 'abcdefghijklmnopqrstuvwxyz'),
'${element}')]
`)
}
```

Now, we have a good shot at finding a button based solely on a string passed into the function. Let us do the same for input fields and text areas.

Getting a visible field by name

Next, we have to gather a collection of fields:

```
If (elements.length > 0 and elementType === "field"{
elements = await browser.$$(`//label[
normalize-space()='${element}']//preceding::input `)
    }
```

If there are no matches, we will take a second shot at finding text areas relative to a label:

```
If (fieldElements.length === 0 and elementType === "field"{
elements = await browser.$$(`//label[normalize-space()='${element}']//
preceding::textarea`)
}
```

Finally, we will do the same for a collection of lists.

Getting a visible list by name

Next, we will try to find a list element based on the text:

```
If (lelements.length > 0 and elementType === "list"{
elements = await browser.$$(`//select[@id='${element}'] `)
    }


If no Select element matches that we take a second chance by searching
for by the name attribute.

If (elements.length === 0 and elementType === "list"{
elements = await browser.$$(`//select[@name='${element}'] `)
    }
///
```

If no `Select` element matches either of these, then we take a final shot by searching for a combo box relative to a label:

```
If (elements.length === 0 and elementType === "list"{
listElements = await browser.$$(`//label[contains(@for,'#{element}')]/
following::select`)
    }
```

We are not done quite yet. The collection of elements returned must be filtered for visibility.

Getting a visible element from a collection

Now that we have a collection of potential elements, we will parse through them to find the first one that is visible:

```
for (let element of elements) {
const tagName = await element.getTagName();
// const tagName = await element.getAttribute('class'); // Alternate
class match
await element.waitForDisplayed({ timeout: 0 });
const isVisible = await element.isDisplayed();
// const isVisible = await highlight(element);
// Alternate visible validation.
If (isVisible)
//Found a matching button or an element with anchor class. Exiting
loop
break;
}
```

At this point, we have made an educated guess as to which element is being referenced. All we need to do is return the element to be interacted with from the calling method:

```
return element;
}
```

At this point, you might see ways to further identify collections, We encourage you to modify the two or three sample locators to work with your particular framework, but...

Beware the endless rabbit hole!

As we come to the end of this section, you may have noticed that we have given no more than three examples to dynamically locate multiple nodes by text. And for good reason. You might spend hours trying to find a fifth or sixth template that will return the perfect collection of elements. We recommend limiting the search to just three attempts. It is just not worth the time to go deeper down this rabbit hole, reducing accuracy and slowing the result search time.

Summary

In this chapter, we demonstrated how to dynamically locate elements using just a string, much like how a superhero uses their keen senses to pinpoint villains just by their silhouette. We employed a clue from each action, narrowing down the pool of potential elements to those pertinent to the requested action, akin to a superhero zeroing in on their target. Lastly, we established a boundary on the number of attempts to identify a valid element, similar to how a superhero might limit their efforts in a search before changing tactics.

In the next chapter, we will explore expanding our testing to multiple environments, paralleling how a superhero adapts to different challenges in various suburbs of Metropolis.

12

Superhero Landing – Setting Up Flexible Navigation Options

The city our superhero framework lands in is always changing and they often don't know what they are up against when on patrol. Our next step is to make the landing page URL more flexible. We will need to be able to switch from testing in the QA environment to staging. At the same time, they should be robust enough to be able to handle small differences. In this chapter, we'll look at handling elements that exist in one release or environment but not in another. In addition, we will enhance the log wrapper to include colors.

We'll cover the following main topics:

- Using system variables
- Adding data configuration files
- Configuration allure reporting

> **Quick tip**
>
> Avoid testing in the development environment because there will constantly be changes . Stay focused on the QA and staging environments. Promising to keep tests in a running state in dev will generate more maintenance time. More maintenance means less time creating new tests and analyzing existing results, which means more bugs slip into production, increasing the chance we have money leaving the bottom line. If the powers that be insist, make it clear a small subset of 4-10 tests can be provided just to give the developers a "warm fuzzy" about the state of their environment. We do want to shift left, but spreading our team too thin will be counterproductive.

Technical requirements

All test examples can be found in this GitHub repository: `https://github.com/PacktPublishing/Enhanced-Test-Automation-with-WebdriverIO`.

Using system variables

When running our tests from the command line, we can set up user variables easily to indicate which test environment to use or run. This can be done with an environment {`process.env.ENV`} variable:

```
> Env=dev
```

This variable can then be read inside our framework and redirect our login method to the proper environment, like this:

```
prod=www.candymapper.com
dev=www.candymapperr2.com
```

> **Quick tip**
>
> Be extra vigilant when testing in production. Discuss with leadership the potential impact it can have. Slowing down the production database with inefficient SQL calls that return a million results will overshadow any bugs that are found. Set up your job runs with a marker that indicates your production environment's safe test cases.

Adding data configuration files

Legend has it that data files were created by a brilliant and enigmatic scientist whose name is whispered only in hushed tones by those who know of its existence. They are said to contain ancient knowledge, sacred algorithms, and hidden codes that can unravel the mysteries of the application under test.

Where data is stored for test use

Adding data files to your test code with TypeScript is exactly like how you do it for JavaScript, but with TypeScript, you have the added benefit of leveraging TypeScript's static typing and modules that will help you catch type-related errors early, making your tests more robust and maintainable.

Organizing test data

First, create a directory to store your test data files. You can name it something such as `test-data` or `shared-data`. Place your data files (e.g., JSON, CSV, etc.) in this directory.

Setting up TypeScript configuration

Ensure that your TypeScript configuration (`tsconfig.json`) includes the appropriate settings for test files and modules. Take the following example:

```
// Json file
{
  "compilerOptions": {
    "target": "es6",
    "outDir": "./dist",
    "esModuleInterop": true
  },
  "include": ["src", "shared-data", "tests"]
}
```

Include the `test-data` directory and the `tests` directory in the `include` section of the `tsconfig` file.

Reading data from files

Here, we use the `fs` module to read data from the files:

```
import * as fs from 'fs';

const jsonData: string = fs.readFileSync('./shared-data/data.json',
'utf-8');
const parsedData: MyDataInterface = JSON.parse(jsonData);
```

Once we have a file system object, we can begin to build data-driven tests

Using test data in tests

In your test files, you can import the necessary data and use it in your test cases, like so:

```
import { expect } from 'expect-webdriverio';
import { someFunction } from '../src/someModule';
import testData from '../shared-data/data.json';

describe('someFunction', () => {
  it('should return the correct value', () => {
    const result = someFunction(testData.input);
    expect(result).toEqual(testData.expectedOutput);
  });
});
```

In the preceding example, we are pulling some data from the `data.json` file in the shared-data directory. The input data is then compared to the actual result and asserting the values are matching.

Beyond masking – making confidential data invisible

As mentioned earlier, superheroes often go to great lengths to protect their identity, such as by wearing masks or donning a pair of glasses. But if they truly want to be stealthy, nothing beats a vault of secrets.

The use of data files to keep confidential information such as usernames and access keys is very commonplace today. For security reasons, these should *never* be uploaded into your code repository. A good DevSecOps team will parse GitHub and GitLab repos for terms such as "password" and flag your team for being out of compliance with **System and Organization Controls 2 (SOC II)** if they find any matches.

Create a `.env` file at the base of your project to store all your confidential data, then add `dotenv` to your dependencies once done. This will give `process.env` access to all the data in the `.env` file:

```
// content of .env
# LambdaTest Credentials
LT_USERNAME=LT_USERNAME
LT_ACCESS_KEY=LT_ACCESS_KEY
LT_HOST_URL=LT_HOST_URL
```

For this, we need another node package called `dotenv`. This package allows developers to store configuration data in a plain text file named `.env`. Each line in the `.env` file typically represents an environment variable in the form of KEY=VALUE, such as API_KEY=your_api_key_here. Installing it is simple enough:

```
> yarn add dotenv
```

Next, we place this at the top of `wdio.config` file just below the `import` statements:

```
require('dotenv').config()
// usage in wdio config
module.exports = {
    // ….
    user: process.env.LT_USERNAME,
    key: process.env.LT_ACCESS_KEY,
    // ….
};
```

In this case, we are creating a system variable to hold LT_USERNAME and LT_ACCESS_KEY. This is how we pass sensitive data without storing our credentials in our repo.

Spec and Allure – cub reporter versus star journalist

In many comic books, there are several reporters documenting the big events and crimes in the city. The cub reporter gives inside knowledge for our superhero to save the day and the star journalist provides flashy front-page headlines. Spec and Allure reporters are similar reporting mechanisms in WebdriverIO. They serve different functions and provide different levels of detail. The Spec reporter is best for SDETs to use to debug failing test runs on the fly. It tells you if the test passed or failed, shows the name of the test, and reports the time it took to run. If a test fails, the Spec reporter provides the error message and stack trace in the console. This provides you with an immediate understanding of what has happened, but it's up to you to help provide in-depth contextual data about the test run.

Allure provides flashy historical graphs that are better suited for showing results to project managers and senior executives. It goes beyond the basics to give you a more complete picture. It produces a stylish and informative report with a lot of additional information, such as the following:

- Test and suite descriptions
- Attach screenshots on failure
- Attach text/plain context to the test report
- Mark your tests with BDD labels and severity
- Test case categorization for tests of a common application area
- Trend history and failure analysis
- Environment information

So, the Allure reporter provides a much richer, more detailed report than the Spec reporter. It allows for a better understanding of what is happening during testing and offers a more holistic view of your test suite. You can think of it as the difference between a simple headline (Spec reporter) and a full news article complete with photos, analysis, and context (Allure reporter).

The first step is to add Allure to our project:

```
> yarn add @wdio/allure-reporter
> yarn add allure-commandline
```

Then, inside the wdio.conf.ts file, we will add the configuration:

```
reporters: ["spec", ["allure",
{
   outputDir: "./reports/allure-results",
   disableWebdriverStepsReporting: false,
   disableWebdriverScreenshotsReporting: false,
}]],
```

This section directs where the reporting detail will be stored and includes two options that can be enabled or disabled. Both options are enabled by default (`false`), allowing Allure to provide detailed step-by-step reporting and include relevant screenshots to enhance the visibility and understandability of your test results. The only reason to disable these options would be to save disk space, which is not recommended. Excluding Webdriver steps reporting and screenshots reporting from the generated report only makes our analysis job harder.

Configuring Allure reporting

If you did not set `Allure` as a reporter previously, it can be done manually. This is a two-step process: **installation** and **configuration**. If you did set `Allure`, skip to *step 2*:

1. To install Allure, type the following:

    ```
    > yarn add @wdio/allure-reporter
    ```

    This will install Allure as a `devDependancies`. We can verify the package is added to the `package.json` file.

```
1   {
2       "name": "my-new-project",
3       "type": "module",
4       "devDependencies": {
5         "@types/jasmine": "^5.1.1",
6         "@wdio/allure-reporter": "^8.20.0",
7         "@wdio/cli": "8.20.5",
8         "@wdio/jasmine-framework": "^8.20.5",
9         "@wdio/local-runner": "^8.20.5",
10        "@wdio/spec-reporter": "^8.20.0",
11        "ts-node": "^10.9.1",
12        "typescript": "^5.2.2"
13      },
14      "scripts": {
15 ▷      "wdio": "wdio run ./wdio.conf.ts"
16      }
17    }
18
```

Figure 12.1 – Allure reporter dependency is added to package.json

2. The Allure package is added to the dev dependencies. Next, the output directories for the HTML report and screen captures must be configured in `wdio.config.ts`:

```
134    reporters: ["spec"][
135      [
136        "allure",
137        {
138          outputDir: "allure-results",
139          disableWebdriverStepsReporting: true,
140          disableWebdriverScreenshotsReporting: true,
141        },
142      ]
143    ],
```

Figure 12.2 – Adding Allure configuration to the wdio.config.ts file

In the `wdio.config.ts` file, `outputDir` directs where the HTML files and screen captures are to be stored. Let's use `allure-results`. Now run the test again:

```
> yarn wdio
```

This will launch the `example.e2e.ts` test. It also generates results in the `allure-results` folder for Allure to build a dashboard.

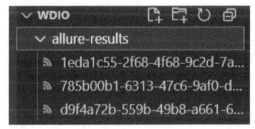

Figure 12.3 – New support files created by Allure to create the HTML report page

3. To display the results, type the following:

```
> allure generate --clean && allure open
```

4. The Bash terminal can also execute combined statements like this:

```
> allure generate -clean; allure open
```

We have installed and configured both WebdriverIO and the Allure dashboard service to display pretty result graphs for our stakeholders. But there is one constant in test automation, and that is change. We need to keep the versions of all our support packages up to date. If there are conflicts, there is bound to be trouble. Fortunately, there is an easy solution for that.

This information does not need to be stored in the repository, so we will add it to our `.gitignore` file:

```
allure-report
allure-results
Screenshots
```

At the top of each test, we should be consistent with an Allure reporting tag to help organize and categorize our test cases in the report. This includes tags for test owners (authors), features, stories, and descriptions. Advanced reporting can include links back to Jira tickets using TMS links. Let us begin with the `Owner` tag:

```
AllureReporter.addOwner("Paul Grossman");
```

The first question any caped crusader wants answered is, "Who did it?" In earlier chapters, we noted that code can be quickly traced back to its owner in VS Code with GitLens. Since the original author of the test knows the tests they wrote best, your team members should be in the habit of adding their names to each test they write. Next, we need to organize our tests by feature:

```
allureReporter.addFeature("Automation Hello World");
```

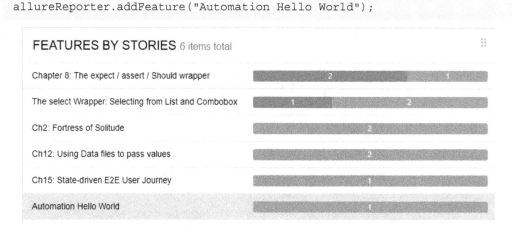

Figure 12.4 – Allure report displaying one passing test under the "Automation Hello World" feature

A `Feature` tag describes what area of the application is being tested by this and other tests. Test cases can be grouped for more efficient execution. This could be a small subset of tests that relate to only one area. This would eliminate separating tests by smoke and regression suites. Tests also need some detail regarding the functionality of the test itself.

This is the command for adding a descriptive tag name to the test in the report:

```
AllureReporter.addDescription("Verify the user can login");
```

This description can be seen in the following screenshot, highlighted in blue.

Figure 12.5 – Description indicating the test will assert the login functionality

The `Description` tag is the summary of the validation performed by the test itself. This is generally copied word for word from the title of a ticket in an issue-tracking tool referencing an existing manual test. It could also be the title of a ticket in a separate automation project that links across to the manual test in a separate project. Those ticket numbers should be matched with a `Story` traceability tag.

This is how we add a story description to a test report:

```
allureReporter.addStory("TA-001");
```

This information is then attached as the name of the test.

Figure 12.6 – The "TA-001" story added with a Jira ticker reference

Tests need traceability to individual story detail information. There is little point in duplicating the text in the actual story ticket, so just providing the ticket number can be sufficient. It can be appended to a saved URL in a browser for a quick lookup.

Adding custom comments to the Allure report

In *Chapter 8*, we discussed creating a wrapper for Expect. We can add custom reporting with the addattachment() function:

```
allureReporter.addAttachment('Assertion Failure: ', `Invalid Assertion
Type = ${assertionType}`, 'text/plain');
```

In this example, we intentionally fail with an invalid assertion verb, equa. expectAdv reports a detailed error to the Allure report describing the cause.

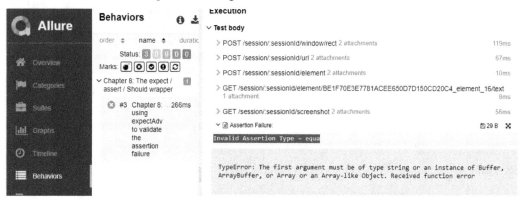

Figure 12.7 – The problem string "equa" is reported as an error

The best advice is to be as efficient as possible. Traceability could be combined with a single description:

```
AllureReporter.addDescription("TA-001 : Verify the user can login");
```

Within the Log wrapper, we can provide details to both reporters. But not everything. That would cause a high signal-to-noise ratio. So, let us just log errors and warnings:

```
let SEND_TO_ALURE = false
```

In addition, the Spec reporter can be made a little more flashy with some color. Let's say we want any text that indicates a result passed to be displayed in the console in green, while a test that failed is displayed in red. The Log wrapper can be amended to watch for the PASS: and FAIL: text. These strings can be surrounded by lines with ANSI color markers.

First, let's add Allure to our project:

```
const { addFeature, addDescription } = require('@wdio/allure-
reporter').default;
describe('My feature', () => {
    it('should do some things', () => {
        browser.url('https://webdriver.io');
```

```
        // Add a step to the report
        addFeature('Navigate to WebdriverIO website');
        browser.url('https://webdriver.io');

        // Add a description to the report
        addDescription('This is a description of what the test should
        do');
    });
});
```

Next, let's identify the basic colors at the top of our helper file starting with green:

```
const ANSI_GREEN = `\x1b[38;2;140;225;50m` // PASS
```

The color escape sequence is broken down here:

- \x1b is the escape character, which starts the sequence.
- [is the **Control Sequence Introducer** (**CSI**), which tells the terminal to interpret the following characters as a command.
- 38 is the **Select Graphic Rendition** (**SGR**) code for setting the foreground text to a custom ANSI color. 48 sets the background color. Use 30–37 to set the color to one of the eight default foreground colors and 40–47 for the eight default background colors.
- 2 specifies that the color will be faint set using RGB values. Other options include 3 for italics, 5 and 6 for blinking text, 7 for inverse text, and 9 for crossed-out text.
- 140;225;50 are the red, green, and blue values, respectively, for the color to be set. In this case, they define a shade of green.
- m is the final character, which marks the end of the escape sequence.

As you can see, we can get quite creative with the color and formatting of the text. Next, we add red for failing messages and yellow for warning messages:

```
const ANSI_RED= `\x1b[38;2;145;250;45m`    // FAIL
const ANSI_YELLOW = `\x1b[38;2;145;226;45m`  // WARNING
```

When we output locators, they should have their own color as well:

```
const ANSI_PURPLE= `\x1b[38;2;250;235;80m`  // Locator
```

Any text encased in single quotes could be auto-formatted to its own color as well:

```
const ANSI_WHITE= `\x1b[97m`  // TEXT entered into a field
```

Finally, we want to reset any color settings back to the default so we can distinguish between messaging from our framework from that of WebdriverIO:

```
const ANSI_RESET= `\x1b[0m` //Reset
```

These colors may not be perfect for everyone. You can find a palette of ANSI RGB color combinations to customize to your liking here: `https://github.com/hinell/palette-print.bash`.

Now let's enhance the log wrapper to get some color:

```
if (message.includes("Warning: ")) {
    message = ANSI_YELLOW + message + ANSI_RESET
    SEND_TO_ALLURE = true
else if (message.includes("Error: ") || message.includes(Promise") {
    message = ANSI_RED + message + ANSI_RESET
    SEND_TO_ALLURE = true
} else {
    message = ANSI_GREEN + message + ANSI_RESET

}
```

When we output out strings using accent marks, we can uniquely identify them and colorize them:

```
message  = message .replace(/`([^`]+)`/g, `${ANSI_WHITE}$1${ANSI_RESET}`);
```

We could embed color for our xPath locators from the log method too:

```
message = message.replace(/\/{1,2}[\w\-\.\:]*\[[^\]]*\]/g, `${ANSI_PURPLE}$1${ANSI_RESET}`);
```

The same goes for CSS locators:

```
message = message.replace(/[#.|]?[a-zA-Z]+\s?)+[{] /g, `${ANSI_PURPLE}$1${ANSI_RESET}`);
```

Now, when passing a result, it could be displayed at runtime in color based on the content:

```
global.log(`FAIL: Invalid Assertion Type = ${assertionType}`);
```

But it would be more reliable to do this from the `Click`, `Select`, `Enter`, and `Expect` method wrappers instead.

Finally, we can redirect any error logging to an Allure report like this:

```
if (SEND_TO_ALURE){
addStep(str);
}
```

Webhooks and screen captures

Our final step is to add a screen capture at the end of our test cases. It is your decision whether you want to take a screen capture only on failing test cases. However, based on our experience, we think taking a screen capture regardless will give you the opportunity to see what the difference between a passing versus a failing test is when you're looking at a historical run saved in Jenkins:

```
    /**
     * Function to be executed after a test (in Mocha/Jasmine only)
     * @param {object}   test              test object
     * @param {object}   context           scope object the test was
executed with
     * @param {Error}    result.error      error object in case the test
fails, otherwise `undefined`
     * @param {*}        result.result     return object of test
function
     * @param {number}   result.duration   duration of test
     * @param {boolean}  result.passed     true if test has passed,
otherwise false
     * @param {object}   result.retries    information about spec
related retries, e.g. `{ attempts: 0, limit: 0 }`
     */
    afterTest: async function (
        test,
        context,
        {error, result, duration, passed, retries}
    ) {
      if (!passed) {
        await browser.takeScreenshot();
      }
    },
```

This is accomplished by adding the preceding lines of code to the afterTest hook of the WDIO. config file.

> **Note**
>
> The `onPrepare`, `onWorkerStart`, `onWorkerEnd`, and `onComplete` hooks are executed in a different process and therefore cannot share any global data with the other hooks that live in the worker process.

Summary

In this chapter, we embarked on a heroic journey akin to traversing the dynamic realms of a superhero multiverse. We mastered the art of directing our test scenarios to various domains of operation—be it QA, stage, or, when the situation demands it, dev and even production. Alongside this, we infused our console log with a spectrum of hues, akin to a caped crusader's vibrant costume. Our Allure reports, much like a meticulously organized utility belt, now display information with precision and clarity. We also unlocked the power of data files, safeguarding the keys to our digital city—sensitive credentials—from the prying eyes of nefarious adversaries.

Navigating through these diverse environments mirrors the complex task of a guardian navigating through parallel universes—each familiar in contour but unique in content. As we prepare to soar into the next chapter, we will fortify our tests with the resilience of a superhero's shield, ensuring they withstand the trials of missing elements that may have vanished into the ether. Furthermore, we will broaden our horizons into the vast expanse of cross-browser testing, ensuring our digital endeavors are as versatile as a shape-shifting hero's array of abilities.

13

The Multiverses – Cross-Browser Testing and Cross-Environment Testing

In this chapter, we will begin adding the mutant power of horizontal scaling to browser operating systems and other platforms. This is in contrast to vertical scaling, which involves adding more tests to our suites, such as adding more floors to a superhero base that's hiding in plain sight. Horizontal scaling is like expanding to more buildings up and down the city block. Our tests can run in multiple browsers, versions, operating systems, and other platforms. What this means is that if we are using a Mac as opposed to a Windows PC, then we will be confident that our applications and tests run well on our chosen browser. Chrome is typically the target browser because of the large number of users on both Windows and Mac. But many Mac users prefer Safari and Windows users prefer Edge. So, how do we ensure these combinations get tested?

That's where the standalone Selenium WebDriver service becomes useful. This service is used to automate the testing process across various browsers and platforms, which helps in identifying issues that might occur in specific environments. Utilizing this service can be a creative solution to streamline the test automation framework as it allows for more comprehensive testing coverage with less manual effort. However, it can also become quickly overwhelming.

Think of this as a crossover between the multiple superhero universes. We will be extending testing beyond Chrome to Edge on a Windows machine as well as extending Chrome to Safari on a Mac. Then, we will use cloud-based solutions for various combinations.

The main topics in this chapter are:

- Horizontal scaling
- Using built-in functionality via the wdio config file
- Using LambdaTest online to automate browser testing grid

- Using Selenium Standalone server to locally build the testing grid
- Avoiding the rabbit hole of horizontal scaling
- Handling environment-specific logic

Horizontal scaling – cross-browser testing

There are three ways in which you can do cross-browser testing for your projects:

- Using the built-in functionality via the wdio config file
- Using LambdaTest online to automate the browser testing grid
- Using Selenium Standalone server to locally build the testing grid

Although we will discuss all three ways, in this book, our examples will be completed using the built-in functionality provided by the wdio config file.

Using built-in functionality via the wdio config file

Cross-browser testing involves setting up the testing environment, writing tests using Jasmine syntax in TypeScript, and running the tests on different browsers. This is accomplished in the config file of WebdriverIO in the capabilities section. We will extend from Chrome to Edge in the capabilities section. This also controls how many concurrent browsers will be launched in parallel with the **maxInstances** parameter.

Extending the wdio config file so that it supports multiple browsers

Set up wdio.conf.ts so that it defines your test settings and browser capabilities:

```
// wdio.conf.ts
exports.config = {
  specs: ['./tests/**/*.spec.ts'],

maxInstances: 2,

capabilities: [
    {
      browserName: 'chrome',
    },
    {
      browserName: 'safari',
    },
```

```
      {
        browserName: 'edge',
      },

    ],
    framework: 'jasmine',
    jasmineOpts: {
      defaultTimeoutInterval: 60000,
    },
    Services:[
  "chromedriver",
  "safaridriver",
  "edgedriver"


    ]
  };
```

In the `Services` section, we must provide the drivers to interact with the browsers. `chromedriver` runs the Chrome browser, which we have been using all along. To drive Safari, `safaridriver` will be used. Keep in mind that the number of concurrent browsers that can be used is limited to the resources available to the local machine.

The following is an example of the type of test that can be run:

```
// test/example.spec.ts
import { browser } from '@wdio/globals';

describe('Example Test', () => {
  it('should open a website', async () => {
    await browser.url('https://example.com');
    const title = await browser.getTitle();
    expect(title).toContain('Example Domain');
  });
});
Yarn
```

Finally, we must execute the test in multiple browsers by running this command:

```
yarn wdio wdio.conf.ts --spec ./test/example.spec.ts
```

This will execute the preceding example test on all browsers configured in the `wdio.conf` file's capabilities section, namely Chrome, Safari, and Edge.

Handling browser-specific issues

If your application has browser-specific code or issues, you can use conditional checks or feature detection to handle them gracefully.

Test responsiveness

Besides functional testing, ensure that your application is responsive and works well on different screen sizes and devices. This will require some next-level platform support. Companies such as LambdaTest, Browser Stack, and Sauce Labs provide custom environment configurations to ensure our application runs correctly under different architectures. These include iOS and Android mobile devices, tablets, and laptops of differing screen sizes. It is here that trying to maintain all these physical devices with the latest updates can become unfeasible.

Using LambdaTest online to automate the browser testing grid

Cross-browser testing with LambdaTest allows you to test your web applications or websites across a wide range of browsers and operating systems. LambdaTest is a cloud-based platform that provides real browsers that run on virtual machines, enabling you to perform comprehensive testing without the need to set up physical devices or virtual machines locally.

To perform cross-browser testing with LambdaTest, follow these steps:

1. First, you need to sign up for a LambdaTest account. Once you've registered, you can access the LambdaTest dashboard:

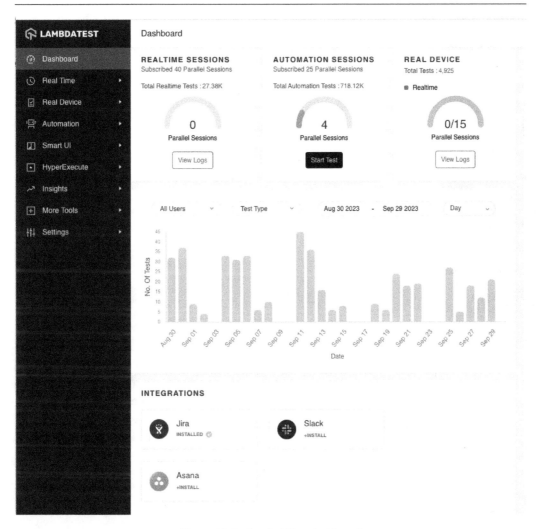

Figure 13. 1 – LambdaTest dashboard

2. On the LambdaTest dashboard, you can select the browsers and operating systems you want to test your website on. A large variety of browsers and versions are available, including Chrome, Safari, and Edge on different operating systems such as Windows and macOS, as well as iOS and Android mobile devices:

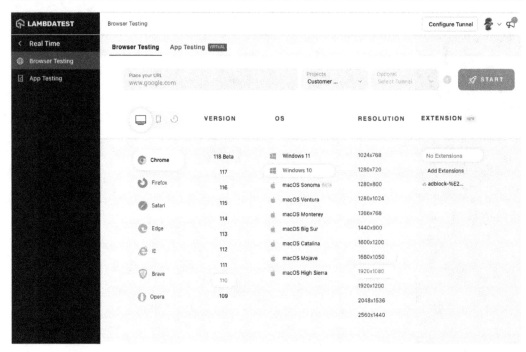

Figure 13.2 – LambdaTest browser, operating system, and screen resolution selections

3. You can choose to run tests on either the *live interactive testing* environment or the *automated screenshot testing* environment.

Live interactive testing

In this mode, you can interact with browsers in real time, just like using a physical device:

Figure 13.3 – LambdaTest live interactive testing for manual testers

You can navigate your website, perform actions, and manually check for multiple issues. Interactive live testing is a pivotal feature in modern test automation frameworks that aligns well with a focus on inspecting tests mid-execution.

The live interactive testing feature provided by LambdaTest allows testers to interact with a website or web application in a real-time environment. This mirrors the experience a user would have on a physical device.

Automated screenshot testing

In this mode, LambdaTest takes screenshots of your website on different browsers and operating systems automatically. This is useful for quick checks and to see how your website looks on various configurations:

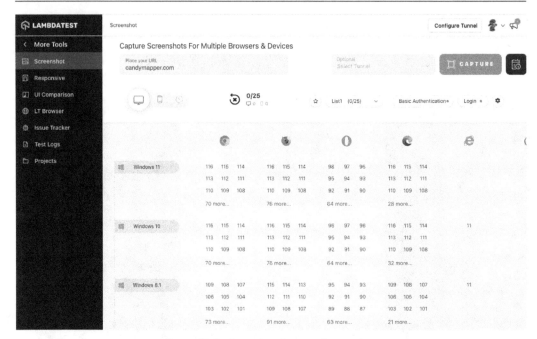

Figure 13.4 – Automated screenshot testing

Once you've selected the browsers and testing mode, you can enter your website's URL in LambdaTest and start the testing process. The platform will open virtual machines with the chosen browsers and load your website for testing.

During the testing process, you can inspect elements, use developer tools, and debug any issues you encounter. You can also take screenshots and save them for further analysis and reporting.

LambdaTest provides detailed test reports, including screenshots and logs, which can help you identify any discrepancies across browsers and operating system configurations. You can share these with your team to discuss and address any issues that are found during cross-browser testing.

They also offer integrations with various testing and collaboration tools, making it easier to incorporate cross-browser testing seamlessly into your existing development workflow. By using LambdaTest for cross-browser testing, you can ensure that your web application performs consistently and optimally across different browsers and operating systems.

Using Selenium Standalone server to locally build the testing grid

Cross-browser testing with Selenium Standalone server allows you to test web applications or websites across multiple browsers and operating systems using the Selenium WebDriver API. The standalone server acts as a hub that connects to different browsers and executes test scripts on them.

To perform cross-browser testing with the Selenium Standalone server, follow these steps:

1. Download the Selenium Standalone server JAR file from the official Selenium website and run it on your machine or a dedicated server. This server acts as a central hub that manages browser sessions and receives test commands from your test scripts.

2. Install the browsers you want to test on the machine where the Selenium Standalone server is running. Ensure that you have the necessary browser drivers installed for each browser (for example, ChromeDriver for Chrome, GeckoDriver for Edge) and that they have been added to your system's PATH.

3. Develop your test scripts using your preferred programming language and Selenium WebDriver bindings (for example, JavaScript, Python, C#, and so on). In your test scripts, set the desired capabilities to specify the browser and operating system configurations you want to test. The desired capabilities define which browser, browser version, and operating system Selenium Standalone server should use for the test. Use the Selenium WebDriver API to request a new browser session from the Selenium Standalone server, specifying the desired capabilities. The server will then launch the specified browser on the configured machine.

Once the browser session has been established, your test scripts can interact with the web elements by using WebDriver commands. You can navigate pages, click buttons, fill out forms, and perform other actions to test the functionality and user interface of your web application. During the test's execution, the server will collect test results, logs, and any errors that were encountered during cross-browser testing.

Cross-environment testing with a shared configuration file

Cross-environment testing involves configuring WebdriverIO to run tests on different environments, such as test and staging. Occasionally, this might include development as well as production environments. This approach allows you to ensure compatibility and functionality across different environments, helping you catch potential issues early in the development process:

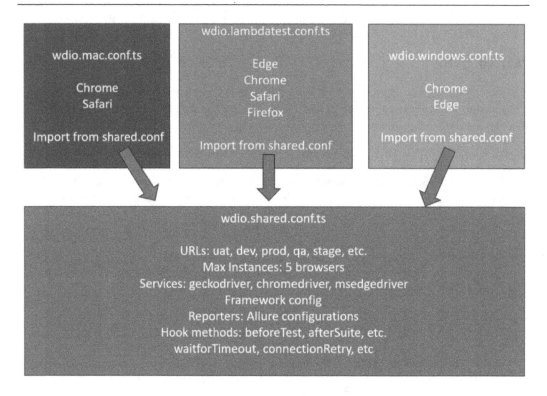

Figure 13.5 – Three wdio conf files sharing a common config file

But we don't want to repeat all the settings in multiple files. Fortunately, WebdriverIO allows us to share values across all environments. We created a `shared.conf` file that holds all the settings that are shared across all environments. If any settings need to be changed, we can make the necessary changes in a single location.

The way this is accomplished is by creating individual files for each operating system and environment, such as `windows.conf` and `mac.conf`. We will do this in a cloud environment with `lambdatest.conf` shortly.

In the `wdio.shared.conf.ts` configuration file, define multiple environments (for example, development, test, and production) with the appropriate settings for each environment. Here's an example:

```
// wdio.shared.conf.ts
/**
 *  The baseUrl will only be used if you don't specify a url in your
script
 *  loadPage('/')
 *  if you specify on then its ignored
 *  loadPage('https://candymapper.com/')
 */
```

```
let baseUrl: string
let env = process.env.Env
let urls = {
    uat: 'https://the-internet.herokuapp.com',
    dev: 'https://candymapperr2.com/',
    prod: 'https://candymapper.com/'
}
baseUrl = urls[env]
    exports.config = {
      // ... other configurations ...
      baseUrl: baseUrl,
      // ... other configurations ...
    };
```

Regardless of the operating system, every browser will navigate to the same URLs without having the information copied multiple times.

This can be quite complex for a project on local machines with potentially different resources and configurations. So, the next step is to leverage cloud resources to ensure all testing configurations are consistent, such as on LambdaTest. This is how the shared.conf file is used in windows.conf, mac.conf, and a cloud-based service such as lambdatest.conf.

The following is an example of a windows.conf.ts or mac.conf.ts file using the shared.conf.ts file:

```
import { config as sharedConfig } from './wdio.shared.conf'

export const config: WebdriverIO.Config = {
    ...sharedConfig,
    ...{
        capabilities: [
            {
                browserName: 'chrome',
                'goog:chromeOptions': {
                    args: ['--disable-gpu']
},
      acceptInsecureCerts: true,
      },
      {
       browserName: 'safari'
      }
     ]
    }
}
```

However, `LambdaTest.conf.ts` or other cloud-based services (SauceLabs, BrowserStack, and so on) will require different sets of configurations.

The following is an example of a cloud-based service using the `shared.conf` file:

```
import { config as sharedConfig } from './wdio.shared.conf';

export const config = {
    ...sharedConfig,
    ...{
        services: [
            ["lambdatest",
                {
                    tunnel: false,
                    lambdatestOpts: {
                        logFile: "tunnel.log"
                    }
                }
            ]
        ],
        user: process.env.LT_USERNAME,
        key: process.env.LT_ACCESS_KEY,

        capabilities: [
            {
                "LT:Options": {
                    browserName: "Edge",
                    version: "latest",
                    name: "Test WebdriverIO Single",
                    build: "WebDriver Selenium Sample"
                }
            },
        ],
        logLevel: "info",
        coloredLogs: true,
        screenshotPath: "./errorShots/",
        waitforTimeout: 100000,
        connectionRetryTimeout: 90000,
        connectionRetryCount: 1,
        path: "/wd/hub",
        hostname: process.env.LT_HOST_URL,
        port: 80
    }
}
```

In this example, we use the `baseUrl` variable to select the appropriate environment based on the "`Env=uat`" environment variable that's set when running the tests.

Use `baseUrl` from the configuration to navigate to different URLs for each environment:

```
// tests/ch13.spec.ts
describe('Cross-Environment Test', () => {
  it('should open the website', () => {
    browser.url('/');
    const title = browser.getTitle();
    expect(title).toContain('Example Domain');
  });

});
```

From the command line, we can change the environments the tests run against. In this example, we are running against uat, which is `the-internet`, and dev, which is `candymapperr2.com` on Windows on Chrome and Edge browsers. Lastly, the `prod` example runs against `candymapper.com` on Mac on Chrome and Safari:

```
Env=uat wdio wdio.conf.ts --spec ./test/specs/ch13.ts
Env=dev wdio wdio.dev.conf.ts
Env=prod wdio wdio.prod.conf.ts
Env=uat wdio wdio.lambdatest.conf.ts --spec ./test/specs/ch13.ts
```

From this, we can see how we might start getting to a point where we're trying to support large combinations of operating systems, browsers, and even older versions. This level of architecture support alone will not be sustainable, so the next logical step is to move testing to the cloud. This brings us some unique advantages. The console output of the tests is still available when it's run in a cloud environment:

```
"spec" Reporter:
-------------------------------------------------------------------
[chrome 117.0 win10 #1-0] Running: chrome (v117.0) on win10
[chrome 117.0 win10 #1-0] Session ID: DWXEV-KGQP1-716MW-FUYE8
[chrome 117.0 win10 #1-0]
[chrome 117.0 win10 #1-0] » /test/specs/ch13.ts
[chrome 117.0 win10 #1-0] Ch13: Cross Browser and Cross Environment Testing
[chrome 117.0 win10 #1-0]    ✓ should login with valid credentials
[chrome 117.0 win10 #1-0]    ✓ should open a website on Chrome
[chrome 117.0 win10 #1-0]    ✓ should open a website on Firefox
[chrome 117.0 win10 #1-0]
[chrome 117.0 win10 #1-0] 3 passing (18s)
-------------------------------------------------------------------
[safari 15.0 macos 12.0 #2-0] Running: safari (v15.0) on macos 12.0
[safari 15.0 macos 12.0 #2-0] Session ID: EHX2M-NT5VY-QS3YZ-PWNK1
[safari 15.0 macos 12.0 #2-0]
[safari 15.0 macos 12.0 #2-0] » /test/specs/ch13.ts
[safari 15.0 macos 12.0 #2-0] Ch13: Cross Browser and Cross Environment Testing
[safari 15.0 macos 12.0 #2-0]    ✓ should login with valid credentials
[safari 15.0 macos 12.0 #2-0]    ✓ should open a website on Chrome
[safari 15.0 macos 12.0 #2-0]    ✓ should open a website on Firefox
[safari 15.0 macos 12.0 #2-0]
[safari 15.0 macos 12.0 #2-0] 3 passing (18s)
-------------------------------------------------------------------
[MicrosoftEdge 116.0 win10 #0-0] Running: MicrosoftEdge (v116.0) on win10
[MicrosoftEdge 116.0 win10 #0-0] Session ID: 5AN6E-ZDZ36-SRNO4-Z6JU1
[MicrosoftEdge 116.0 win10 #0-0]
[MicrosoftEdge 116.0 win10 #0-0] » /test/specs/ch13.ts
[MicrosoftEdge 116.0 win10 #0-0] Ch13: Cross Browser and Cross Environment Testing
[MicrosoftEdge 116.0 win10 #0-0]    ✓ should login with valid credentials
[MicrosoftEdge 116.0 win10 #0-0]    ✓ should open a website on Chrome
[MicrosoftEdge 116.0 win10 #0-0]    ✓ should open a website on Firefox
[MicrosoftEdge 116.0 win10 #0-0]
[MicrosoftEdge 116.0 win10 #0-0] 3 passing (23.3s)
-------------------------------------------------------------------
[firefox 117.0 win10 #3-0] Running: firefox (v117.0) on win10
[firefox 117.0 win10 #3-0] Session ID: LO6YR-IODJW-WVJK7-LE67Y
[firefox 117.0 win10 #3-0]
[firefox 117.0 win10 #3-0] » /test/specs/ch13.ts
[firefox 117.0 win10 #3-0] Ch13: Cross Browser and Cross Environment Testing
[firefox 117.0 win10 #3-0]    ✓ should login with valid credentials
[firefox 117.0 win10 #3-0]    ✓ should open a website on Chrome
[firefox 117.0 win10 #3-0]    ✓ should open a website on Firefox
[firefox 117.0 win10 #3-0]
[firefox 117.0 win10 #3-0] 3 passing (23.7s)


Spec Files:      4 passed, 4 total (100% completed) in 00:00:34
```

Figure 13.6 – Results from the terminal window in LambdaTest

In the cloud, the test cases can be assigned to run in multiple browsers, versions, and operating systems, but without the need to configure and support the underlying architecture:

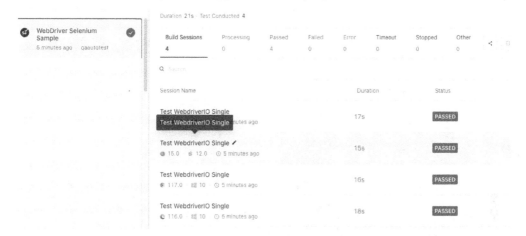

Figure 13.7 – Results of the test cases in multiple operating systems and browsers in the cloud

The following example shows the multiple browsers and operating systems that we can run against. Now, if we were to click on a single item, we could dive deeper into the details of a particular system and run results:

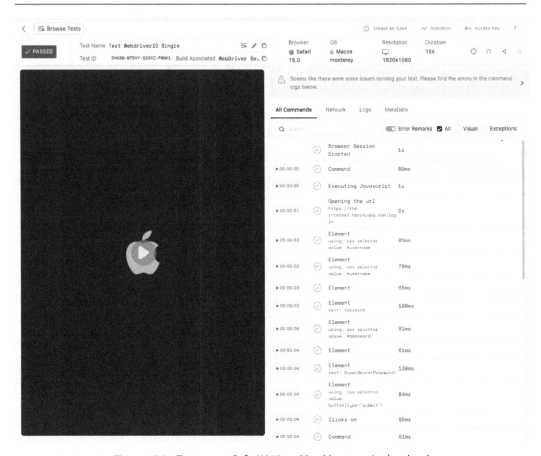

Figure 13.8 – Test run on Safari V.15 on Mac Monteray in the cloud

And while screen captures are nice, it's even better to watch an entire video that's been recorded. This provides a clear look into the interactions of a test run:

Figure 13.9 – A video still of the test case running in LambdaTest

Again, video storage space and cleanup are less time-consuming. The costs can be compared to having one or two team members dedicated to developing, enhancing, and maintaining such large files generated on-site becoming prohibitive when they could be spending more time writing more test cases, analyzing results, and writing defects.

Avoiding the rabbit hole of horizontal scaling

It is important to the 80/20 rule and the rule of threes in mind. We do not want to try to support 80% of the popular browser and operating system combinations when our customers are using only 20%. It may sound pro-active to try to support Safari on Mac when our customers only use Chrome on Windows. Attempting to do a regression test in a new browser on every environment becomes logarithmically impossible. You may not have the time to execute all test cases on all browsers and all environments. We only want to test on the browsers that are used by more of our users, so that might be a maximum combination of three: one browser in two operating systems or two browsers in one operating system. In addition, time can be taken away from creating new tests if we are trying to determine the root cause of why one test runs in one browser or operating system and fails in another.

Handling environment-specific logic

If your application has environment-specific code or issues, use conditional checks or feature detection to handle them gracefully:

```
If (process.platform === 'mac'){
  // do something specific thats mac only
} else {
 // contine as usual
}
```

> **Rule of thumb**
>
> Try not to get bogged down in getting All-Pass on every browser and operating system. Expand to one additional browser, then one additional operating system. It is best to only perform smoke testing on peripheral configurations. It can easily consume your time supporting logarithmically.

What if we have a new field that has been added to our testing environment but does not exist in production? Can we build a test that will support both? At this point, we can introduce a new set of `IfExist()` custom commands. Each base method, including `click()`, `setValue()`, and `select()`, will have a corresponding function: `clickIfExist()`, `setValueIfExist()`, and `selectIfExist()`, respectively. We can also add a `verifyIfExist()` method. The goal is that rather than have separate versions of every test for each environment, we have one set of tests that is highly likely to reach the endpoint of the journey, even if there are minor differences along the way.

The multiverse – one test, two environments

The advantage is that these `IfExist()` methods will not stop the test if the object doesn't exist. Our tests can now be executed in a test environment where new functionality exists, as well as a production environment where the functionality is yet to be pushed. For example, a page may ask for a month to be selected from a list on a long survey navigation path. In the staging environment, this requires the **Next** button to be explicitly clicked to move to the page. However, in QA, the **Next** button is removed and the page implicitly moves on once the user selects an item from the list:

```
Helpers.clickIfExists(await this.btnNext);
```

There are two approaches to this implementation. First, we could enhance the `clickadv()` method with an optional property:

```
export async function clickAdv(element: WebdriverIO.Element, ifExists:
boolean = false) {
// isExist code branch here ...
}
```

However, this leads to code that is less clear about the intention, with the potential of a magic Boolean argument being used:

```
await Helpers.clickAdv(this.btnNext, true); // may not exist
```

Instead, let's create an alternative function with `ifExists` appended. This function uses the automation switchboard to tell the initial wrapper to act differently if the element does not exist:

```
const IF_EXISTS = "IF_EXISTS";
export async function clickAdvIfExists(element: WebdriverIO.Element) {
ABS(IF_EXISTS) = true;
```

```
let result = await this.clickAdv(element);
ASB(IF_EXISTS) = false;
return result;
}
```

Second, we store the state of the element when we check that it is valid. We will also save the locator of the element if it has not already been saved in the beforeCommand hook:

```
export async function getValidElement(
  element: WebdriverIO.Element,
  elementType: string
): Promise<WebdriverIO.Element> {
...
  if (!found) {
    ABS.set ("ELEMENT_SELECTOR") = element.selector)
    await log(`  ERROR: Unable to find ${selector}`);
  }
  ASB.set ("ELEMENT_EXISTS") = found;
  return newElement;
}
```

Lastly, we return immediately from the clickAdv() method:

```
if (ASB.get("ELEMENT_EXISTS") == false){
await log(`  IfExist: Skipping clicking
${ASB.get("ELEMENT_SELETOR")}`);
return true;
}
```

Now, we can add the feature just by adding IfExists:

```
await Helpers.clickAdvIfExists(this.btnNext); // may not exist
```

We can do the same to enhance the setValueAdv() method:

```
export async function setValueAdvIfExists(
element: WebdriverIO.Element),
text: string
)
ABS(IF_EXISTS) = true;
let result = await this.setValueAdv(element, text);
c;
return result;
```

```
}

export async function setValueAdv(
  inputField: WebdriverIO.Element,
  text: string
) {
If (ABS(IF_EXISTS) == true)
return true;
}
```

We must do the same to create `selectValueAdvIfExists`:

```
export async function selectAdvIfExists(
element: WebdriverIO.Element),
text: string
)
ABS(IF_EXISTS) = true;
let result = await this.clickAdv(element);
ASB(IF_EXISTS) = false; // Reset for next element
return result;
}
```

Now, we can have tests that are robust enough to run in slightly different test environments and still get to the conclusion of an end-to-end test.

For example, in the following figure, we have two websites:

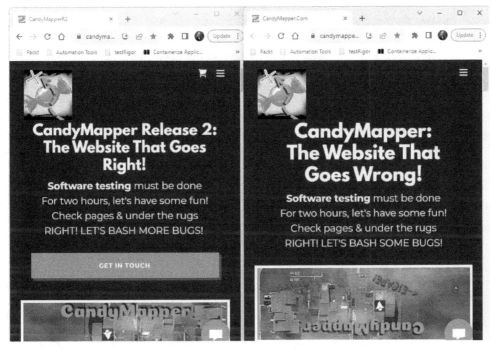

Figure 13.10 – Production versus pre-production environments
where a button element has been removed

The production site on the left has a **GET IN TOUCH** button that scrolls down the page to a customer detail input support page.

On the right is the new release of the site. Note that this site doesn't include the **GET IN TOUCH** button.

With the option to click the button only if it exists without failing the test, we can begin to have tests that are more flexible in slightly differing environments. If the button only exists in one environment, the test can continue to execute without failing in both. This changes our focus from maintaining test cases to having an increased chance of reaching the end path. Finally, even if the method fails because the locator is different, the next few steps will execute on the wrong page and still bring the test to a halt for maintenance.

Summary

In our epic journey, we've unlocked a new superpower for our scripts by integrating the automation switchboard. This newfound capability ensures that our scripts remain as adaptable as the ever-evolving world of superheroes. They can now seamlessly operate across various browsers and operating systems, making them as versatile as a superhero's toolkit.

As we turn the page to the next thrilling chapter, get ready to witness our web hero, WebdriverIO, taking flight into the clouds of cloud-based test automation and scheduling. Just like a superhero soaring through the skies, we'll delve into the extraordinary realm of executing tests in the cloud. This chapter promises to be a riveting adventure, showcasing the incredible potential of our superheroic scripts as they conquer new heights and challenges in the world of testing.

14

The Time-Traveler's Dilemma – State-Driven End to End User Journeys

This chapter addresses a different but common type of test automation – navigating through a survey, page by page, to reach a common endpoint. The challenge here is that decisions made by a user along the way can change the order of the pages displayed downstream – that's if they appear at all. In this case, we need a fluid user journey that can take many branches to get to a common endpoint, as well as report if a path ended with an error page. It is inefficient to try to create an expanding path of pages for end-to-end automation. The amount of `if/then` branches or `select/case` options would be infinite and complex. To solve this, we will explore ways to identify each page by its URL and look at ways to decouple page paths, allowing tests to handle sequential pages in any order with minimal maintenance. Imagine this approach as a ball bouncing randomly through multiple pegs of a giant Pachinko game.

This chapter covers the following main topics:

- Dividing by sections
- The happy path
- Extracting page name from the current URL with `getPageName()`
- A page processing loop
- Common exit points

Technical requirements

All test examples can be found at this GitHub repository: `https://github.com/PacktPublishing/Enhanced-Test-Automation-with-WebdriverIO`.

Divide and conquer!

In this approach, we will be considering a non-deterministic way to navigate from our start point to our endpoint. We will not be working on the traditional assumption that one page follows another. Instead, our script will pass through every potential page repeatedly and interact only if the current page matches one of the page classes. Then, based on high-level flow requirements, we can make different choices and even enter varied and unique data. We might even find a bug along the way!

In this small example, we will automate the Halloween Party feature of the Candymapper website. This provides customers with a limited set of options to plan a themed party. Party guests use the same site to attend, or avoid, these spooktacular events. The following paths are included for customers and guests:

- Customers can choose to host a zombie theme party

- Customers can choose to host a ghost theme party

- Guests can choose to attend a Zombieton party

- Attend a Ghostville party

- Scared guests can exit back to the **Host or Attend** choice page

At least one of these paths will go awry on the www.Candymapper.com production website. This journey is fixed on the new release of the website at www.CandymapperR2.com, as well as the order of the pages and new options for attending guests to bring friends.

In the first four of these paths, we will end at the common **Party Countdown** timer page. In the last path, we will end up back at the **Halloween Party** Host or Attend page. The pages we will encounter include these actions:

- **Main page**: clear the popup, and click **Halloween Party** in the page header.

- **Halloween Party page**: a choice to host or attend a party

- **Host party page**: a location address and "a **Find Out More**" button (Guest Path Only)

- **Party location**: a page with a choice of Zombieton or Ghostville

- **Attend Party page**: with two location choices and a **Scared** return button

- **Party Location choice page**: Zombieton or Ghostville:

  - A guest list (dev only)

  - An email field with "a **Remind Me**" button (dev only)

- **Party Time Countdown page**: the final destination

The core of this test is the `PartyPath()` driver, which takes a single string that can be parsed to make decision point changes at multiple milestones. This function is a giant loop that passes through every known page repeatedly. For each page, we will create an object model and a `build()` method. This method executes only if the current page matches the class page type. It returns `true` if all actions are successful. If the current page is not this page, it is a `null` function and returns `false`. This method will reference a test data model that is preconfigured with happy path data, which can be overridden from the `Switchboard` object. This will allow choices to be modified in the page flow from beginning to end.

Simplifying the complexities of a dynamic journey

In a real-world application, we might be navigating through multiple pages of job applications with different data requirements on each one. Some decision points might include adding a current address, military status, prior employers' contact information, and personal references. The application process flow might include additional pages for someone who is under 21 or a driver who requires proof of a specialized license to drive a truck. The multiple paths might ask increasingly more information from someone who is single, married, divorced, or widowed with dependents.

The challenge is that no one can predict the next page in the user journey that eventually leads to the final successful page destination. However, each of those milestones can be described with high-level terms that indicate what to do at each decision point.

What if we had a dictionary of terms that could be passed to the tests in almost any order, describing the type of applicant applying for the real-world job?

- `Happy Path`: Single, civilian, over 21, no dependents, and no job history or references

- `married dependents cdl`: This path includes the spouse, children, and CDL license information

- `military underage cu dd`: Uses company-known acronyms for **Credit Union** and **Direct Deposit**

For the Halloween Party example, these are the paths that we will follow:

- `Happy Path`: Host a zombie-themed party, with a countdown timer as the final destination
- `Attend/ ""Attend zombie""`: Attends a party with a decision point for a zombie theme over the default ghost theme
- `Scared`: Begins the path to attend a party but returns to the main choice Host or Attend choice page

The secret to this approach is a path generator, `partyPath()`. This is a loop that repeatedly executes every page `build()` method in the Page Object model until the final page is reached. Each page determines whether the current page is the one to process. Then, the test data is used to interact with the values on that page. Every field and list population method will be executed on their respective object. If there is no data provided for a particular input field, the interaction is executed.

There will be four reasons to exit the infinite loop:

- The final Party Countdown page is reached (`Happy Path`)
- An unknown page is encountered
- The same page persists after two loop attempts
- The scared journey encounters the Host or Attend page

Ultimately, the `build()` method will always attempt to explicitly move to the next page. In most cases, this would be a **Next** button, which is likely to be common to all pages and declared in the `Page` class, from which all other pages extend. In other cases, moving to the next page will be implicit by simply entering the final required field where no **Next** button exists. In this case, the `clickIfExists()` feature mentioned in earlier chapters will come into play. The goal is always to try to reach the end of the process, not find bugs.

It is expected in some cases that a page will not move on, expecting more data from the user after a selection has been made. While this might be handled within the same path, it could be a path detected on a second pass of the same page. So, if the navigation does not move forward after two loop attempts, the test exits with the user path incomplete, with a detailed error of the problem in the Allure report.

The first component we need to add is to determine which page we are currently on. While this is different from project to project, we often find that a unique identifier can be found in its URL. Let us begin by extracting a unique identifier from the last segment of the page URLs:

- `https://candymapperr2.com/halloween-party`
- `https://candymapperr2.com/party-location-1`
- `https://candymapperr2.com/party-time`

To capture the URL that the framework has navigated, the `getPageName()` function will give us a description at the end of the URL. The following function would return `halloween-party`, `party-location-1`, and `party-time` from the aforementioned URLs, respectively.

```
/**
 * Gets last segment of current URL after splitting by "/".
 * @returns {Promise<string>} The last URL segment.
 */
export async function getPageName(): Promise<string> {
  const currentURL = await browser.getUrl();
  const urlSegments = currentURL.split('/');
  return urlSegments[urlSegments.length - 1];
}
```

This will be executed in the main `partyPath()` loop and stored in the automation Switchboard object's page key. Note that we use only the ending portion of the URL, as this allows us to have similar functionality in different environments:

- `https://candymapper.com/party-time`
- `https://candymapperr2.com/party-time`

Each page class includes the `pages` object model that might be on the page:

```
import Page from './page.tjs';
import * as helpers from "../../helpers/helpers.tjs";
/**
 * sub page with selectors for a specific page
 */
class HalloweenPartyPage extends Page {
    /**
     * define selectors using getter methods
     */
    public get hostParty () {
        return $(`//a[contains(normalize-space(),'ost')]`);
    }

    public get attendParty () {
        return $(`//a[contains(normalize-space(),'ttend')]`);
    }
```

Note that the generic locators use `normalize-space` and also skip the first letter in case capitalization changes. This makes them more robust and less likely to become stale, even if the text changes from release to release.

Next, we have the `build()` method that is common for all pages. This will check first whether the identifier in the URL string matches the page and immediately returns `false` if it is not a match:

```
public async build () {

    // Is this the page to process?

    if (await ASB.get("page") !== "attend-a-party") {

        return false // Not the right page
    }
    if (ASB.get("hostorattend") === `attend`){
      return await helpers.clickAdv(
          await this.attendParty);
    }
    return helpers.clickAdv(await this.hostParty);
}
export default new HalloweenPartyPage();
```

This path example by default will host a party. The `HostOrAttend` milestone in the switchboard can be switched to make it a user journey that attends a party instead. After the click, the next page that appears will be different, depending on which button we click, as well as which environment we run this test in. So, it is vitally important where we disassociate the expected page in the user journey, as it may not always be the same. However, we need to start somewhere and that is the happy path.

The last feature we would introduce is a `beforeEach()` function which will help us reduce our code significantly when writing the tests. Since we have multiple test cases and we are writing the `loginPage.open(``)` each time. This can be simplified by placing the function in a `beforeEach()` function. This refactoring is performing the exact same process, but with less lines of code:

```
describe("Ch14: State-drive Automation - Host a Party (Default in
Ghostville)",  () => {
  it("should loop around until the final page is found", async () => {
    await LoginPage.open(``);
    await stateDrivenUtils.partyPath("Host");
  });
});

describe("Ch14: State-drive Automation - Host a Party (Default in
Ghostville)",  () => {
  it("should loop around until the final page is found", async () => {
    await LoginPage.open(``);
   await stateDrivenUtils.partyPath("Host");
  });
```

```
});
```

In this refactored version we move the await LoginPage.open(``) into the beforeEach(async () function. This code will now execute before every test case.

```
beforeEach(async () => {
  await LoginPage.open(``);
});

describe("Ch14: State-drive Automation - Host a Party (Default in
Ghostville)", () => {
  it("should loop around until the final page is found", async () => {
    await stateDrivenUtils.partyPath("Host");
  });
});

describe("Ch14: State-drive Automation - Host a Party (Default in
Ghostville)", () => {
  it("should loop around until the final page is found", async () => {
    await stateDrivenUtils.partyPath("Host");
  });
});
```

Keep in mind this works because we are not building a test that moves from one page to another specific page. We are simply populating whatever page is currently active, attempting to move to the next in a loop. Let's take a look at our state-driven flow driver, pathyPath(testData) – which will navigate through the milestone decision points of our website.

The happy path

If the testData argument is empty, the default Happy Path will be performed. This is configured in a userData.json file in the shared-data folder. The two milestones include HostOrAttend and location:

```
  }
  "journeyData": {
    "_hostOrAttend_comment": "'host' (default Happy Path), 'attend' or
'scared' ",
    "hostOrAttend: "host",
    "_location_comment": "'zombieton' (default Happy Path) or
'ghostville' ",
    "location": "zombieton",
  }
}
```

> **Rule of thumb – documenting JSON files**
>
> No developer worth their salt would ever design a data file without some documentation close at hand. However, JSON files do not allow for comments, as we can do in JavaScript files with double forward slashes (//). The workaround is to add a matching key, beginning with an underscore and ending with the word "comment". Each key can now be documented to ensure others on the team can understand the intent behind the design.

This file is first extracted into the Switchboard object. Then, any overriding values are parsed out of the `testData` argument or from a `JOURNEY` system variable:

```
public parseTestData(testData: string = '') {

    if (process.env.JOURNEY !== undefined) {
      testData = process.env.JOURNEY;
    }
```

At this point, we must plan for the future. In our final chapter, we will drive these test cases from Jenkins using the `JOURNEY` system variable. If this variable is populated, it will supersede the `testData` argument.

When we build this driver, we should have a list of known company terms that can be used to adjust the milestone decision points.

In our example, we have `host` and `attend` for the path verbs, and `zombie` and `ghost` and `scared` for decision points:

```
    if (testData != "") {
        testData = " " + testData.toLowerCase(); // Add space to make
    sure we match whole words and convert to lowercase once

    // Overriding default values
        if (testData.includes(" host")) {
          ASB.set("hostOrAttend", "host");
        }
        if (testData.includes(" attend")) {
          ASB.set("hostOrAttend", "attend");
        }
        if (testData.includes(" zombie")) {
          ASB.set("location", "zombieton");
        }
        if (testData.includes(" ghost")) {
          ASB.set("location", "ghostville");
        }
        if (testData.includes(" scared")) {
```

```
      ASB.set("location", "scared");
   }
```

Next, the default data values are parsed into the ASB Switchboard:

```
   parseToASB("path/to/userdata.json")
```

Then, any overriding key:value data in the testData string is parsed into the ASB object:

```
   parseToASB(testData)
```

Inside the test data string, we will allow the test to assign specific values to keys in our switchboard. For example, we might want to set a zip code to 12345. In this case, we will need a regular expression to parse values that are connected with an equal sign. Strings with and without spaces can be address=""123 main"" as well as zip=12345:

```
export function parseToASB(testData: string) {
  const regex = /(\w+)=("([^"]*)"|\b\w+\b)/g;
  let match;

  while ((match = regex.exec(testData)) !== null) {
    let key = match[1];
    let value = match[2];

    // Remove quotes if present
    if (value.startsWith('"') && value.endsWith('"')) {
      value = value.slice(1, -1);
    }

    let keyLower = key.toLowerCase();
    let oldValue = ASB.get(keyLower);

    // Always save value as a string
    ASB.set(keyLower, value);

    if (oldValue !== undefined) {
      console.log(`ASB(«${keyLower}") updated from "${oldValue}" to
"${ASB.get(keyLower)}"`);
    } else {
      console.log(`ASB(«${keyLower}") set to "${ASB.get(keyLower)}"`);
    }
  }
}


import fs from 'fs';
```

```
import xml2js from 'xml2js';

export async function parseXMLFileToASB(filePath: string) {

  const data = fs.readFileSync(filePath);
  const result = await xml2js.parseStringPromise(data);
  for (let key in result) {
    let newValue = result[key];
    let oldValue = ASB.get(key.toLowerCase());

    // Always save value as a string
    ASB.set(key.toLowerCase(), newValue);

    if (oldValue !== newValue) {
       console.log(`ASB(«${key.toLowerCase()}") updated from
"${oldValue}" to "${newValue}"`);
    }
  }
}
```

While the testData string argument tells us what will change at each milestone point, this is first transferred into the ASB switchboard object that all pages will reference when they execute. A data file will contain the default values that are populated into the switchboard, and then testData is parsed to customize these values. In preparation for our final chapter, this function also gets data from the JOURNEY system variable that will be sent from Jenkins:

```
import { ASB } from "../../helpers/globalObjects";
import candymapperPage from "../pageObjects/candymapper.page";
import halloweenAttendPartyPage from "../pageObjects/
halloweenAttendParty.page";
import halloweenPartyPage from "../pageObjects/halloweenParty.page";
import halloweenPartyLocationPage from "../pageObjects/
halloweenPartyLocation.page";
import halloweenPartyThemePage from "../pageObjects/
halloweenPartyTheme.page";
import halloweenPartyTimerPage from "../pageObjects/
halloweenPartyTimer.page";
import * as helpers from "../../helpers/helpers";
import AllureReporter from "@wdio/allure-reporter";
import Page from "../pageObjects/page";

class StateDrivenUtils extends Page {
```

The big driver loop

The partyPath() method is actually a utility, rather than a test, so we will store it in a Utilities folder in the project root folder:

```
export async function partyPath (testData) {
    let complete: Boolean = false;
    let lastPage: string = ""
    let retry = 2

    this.parseTestData(testData);    // Parse the known milestone verbs
                                     // to the switchboard
    helpers.parseToASB(testData);    // Parse the key=value data to set
                                     // the switchboard
```

The next step is to navigate the start of the Halloween Party path. This will require an is a loop that processes every page repeatedly, seeking one of four exit points:

```
    while (complete === false) { // Loop until final page
      //Get Page Name
        let pageName = await browser.getUrl();
        pageName = extractPathFromUrl(pageName)
        ASB.set("page", pageName);
```

This puts the name of the current page into the Switchboard. This object will be read in every page's build() method. Next, we will call every known page, using logical OR, to determine whether any were successfully identified:

```
    // Pass through every known page
  knownPage =
        await halloweenLocationPage.build() ||
        await halloweenAttendPartyPage.build() ||

    await halloweenHostPartyPage.build() ||

    await halloweenPartyPage.build() ||
  // Add new pages along the journey here.
```

Note that these pages do not need to be in any particular order. In fact, our designs have placed the first processing page list last and others in roughly reverse order. This tends to ensure only one page gets parsed per loop. Having multiple pages executing per loop is just as acceptable.

> **Rule of thumb – refactoring**
>
> In this small example, we are using only six pages. Real-world projects may have 50 to 100 web pages to navigate. It is always recommended to reduce code to smaller, more manageable units. In this case, the longer the lists of pages, the more they should be refactored into their own function.

We now add the first of the four exit points. Note that in the preceding list of pages, one is missing – the final countdown page. This is the success page where our journey ends. Nothing else matters at this point:

```
// Exit Point #1: Success reached the timer page
    if (await halloweenPartyTimerPage.build()) {
        knownPage = true; // Skip Exit point 2
        console.log("Success: Reached the timer page")
        complete = true; // Exit the loop

break;
    } // End of all paths except unknown page
```

If this page is processed, we report the successful end of the journey. It also sets out the `knownPage` flag as `true` for any additional reporting or cleanup at the end of the function. Then, we break out.

Our job here is done, unless there is something unknown lurking out there?

```
// Exit Point #2: Unknown page encountered
    if (knownPage === false) {
      //None of the build methods returned true
      AllureReporter.addAttachment(`Unknown Page detected:
${pageName}`, "", "text/plain");
        console.log(`Unknown Page detected: ${pageName} - Exiting
Journey`);
        expect(pageName).toBe("a known page");
        break;
    }
}
```

In this case, no page returned `true`. We output the name of the unknown page. We also use a clever `expect` to set the test to a failed status, while further documenting the issue at hand, the URL of the new page. In our example, the production website `Candymapper.com` will generate an `Error 404` page when a guest is too scared to go to a party and expects to return. This page is never expected, but if we can screen-capture it.

Next, we need to handle a situation where a page just did not move forward from the last one:

```
// Exit Point #3: Page did not change
if (lastPage === pageName) {
  retry--; // Give two additional attempts
  if (retry === 0) {
    console.log(`Page did not change: ${lastPage} - Exiting Journey`);
    expect("Page did not move on from").toBe(lastPage);
  } else {
    // Page moved on, reset retry for next page
    retry = 2;
  }
}
```

As superheroes, we are always open to second chances. In this case, a page could have two or three states itself. A point of sale page might add one product if the cart is empty and a different item if the cart has one item, before moving on. Calling such a method twice could be required and offer flexibility.

Lastly, there could be a journey that expects an alternative page as its final destination. This is rare but presented as an option. This path is one where we return to a prior step in the process. This works because the page was identified and processed as the first step in the loop, moving to the next page before reaching this point:

```
// Exit Point #4: We were scared and went back - Halloween Party Home
page reached - only works in dev, prod has an intentional Error 404
issue.
if (ASB.get("page") === "halloween-party") {
    console.log("Halloween Party Home page reached")
    complete = true;
}
```

Is that all the exit points? We are certain there are other ways journeys must end prematurely. We can think of one more example – an infinite loop journey. This would require tracking an array of all the URLs visited. It would be triggered when a page has been visited for the third time. We have given you all the tips and tricks to pull this off. Now, it is time to work this one out on your own.

Our final step before cycling back again is to set the current page name to the last page name:

```
      lastPage = ASB.get("page"); // Save the last page name
    }
```

This ensures that exit point #3 works correctly when determining whether we are stuck on the same page.

Next, the test data file object is used to determine what fields are populated. If the test data object does not contain the data for a particular field, a warning is added to our results, but the test continues.

Finally, the method to move on to the next page is performed. Note that we will use the `ClickIfExits()` method to ensure our engine remains robust, even if the element does not exist in future test environments.

In the loop, we check to see whether the page has moved on with an increment counter, starting at 2. If the page did not move on in the first loop, we decrement the loop counter. If the loop counter reaches 0, we have failed to successfully move on, and we exit. If successive loops do result in a new page URL, the counter is reset to perform two additional loops.

Some pages may have code that can resolve issues generated by incomplete data. This may not have been detected in the first execution of the `build` method for the page; thus, the build method must be executed at least twice before the test user journey is abandoned.

Once we have completed this process for each page, we can begin to add milestones, based on the values passed from the JOURNEY user variable. In this example, we will have a path that plans a zombie party by default but will switch to a user attending a party, by passing `attend` in the JOURNEY string. This, in turn, will be injected into the test data object and read by the proper page.

If we encounter a page that is new, the test will stop. We will report the URL of the page to Allure and provide a screen capture of the results. Our reporting automatically tells us the path that led us to that new endpoint.

It's all in the details

Similarly, we could detect the string `error` in the URL on our page report with a screen capture, or we could capture all the text on the screen this way – `const allText = await $('body').getText();`.

Another way to capture the scree text would be to send *Ctrl-A / Ctrl-V* to the browser and send the clipboard to the Allure report:

```
import { clipboard } from 'electron';

const operatingSystem = process.platform;

let selectAllKeys: string[];
let copyKeys: string[];

if (operatingSystem === 'darwin') {
  selectAllKeys = ['Command', 'a'];
  copyKeys = ['Command', 'c'];
} else {
  selectAllKeys = ['Control', 'a'];
  copyKeys = ['Control', 'c'];
}
```

```
await browser.keys(selectAllKeys);
await browser.keys(copyKeys);

const allText = clipboard.readText();
```

This makes it more likely we will capture only the visible text of the browser.

This loop also provides the opportunity to interact with any known page, regardless of the order it appears in the path. Consider this path in the candymapperR2 website hosting a party:

1. Host a Party

2. Party Venue Address Confirmed

3. Party Theme

4. Party Countdown

And consider the path to attend a party:

1. Attend a Party

2. Choose a Party Venue or Return

3. Party Venue Location Address

4. Party Countdown

Note that these two paths encounter the same **Party Venue Location Address** page but from different pages. In addition, the paths of these two journeys are different from the production Candymapper website. Thus, we can have the same test case run in two environments with dissimilar paths and still complete its goal.

Our final path would be to set our final expected page. In this example, the path returns us to the `Plan` or `Attend` page indicating the user journey; although it did not end at the common endpoint, it was still a success.

Changing decision points

The way we pass the string that customizes a path is through a single environmental variable, like so:

```
Set JOURNEY=""; yarn ch15
```

This way, we can create test several paths. In this example, the user does not attend the party and instead clicks the **I'm scared** button:

```
Set JOURNEY="attend scared"; yarn ch15
```

With this example, the user takes the path to host the party with a zombie theme:

```
Set JOURNEY="Host ZOMBIE"; yarn ch15
```

A single environmental value can modify multiple decision points from the Happy Path baseline. While an empty string by default will create a Happy Path, the best practice is to assign the string so that the path is shown in the results, with the parsing being case-insensitive.

```
let journey: string = " " + (process.env.JOURNEY || "Host").
toLowerCase();

if (journey===" ")) {
    journey = " host"; //Default Happy Path
}
```

Note that there is a space prepended to the journey variable. The reason for this is to make it less likely to match a similar string in the path. We have a host command and a ghost party. Writing this line of code could potentially take the host command from the ghost string:

```
Set JOURNEY="Attend Ghost"; yarn ch15
if (journey.includes(" host").toLowerCase()) {
// Host path being taken in error.
}
```

This is resolved, as every command that is acted upon always has a prepended space. Now, there is less chance of an incorrect path match. For our example, we will go one step further, making Host the default Happy Path and Attend the deviation from the path:

```
if (journey.includes(" attend").toLowerCase()) {
// Attend a party path, case insensitively
Helpers.click(attend)
} else {
    // The JOURNEY variable contains "host" Happy Path
Helpers.click(host)
}
```

This completes the first method to choose a decision point on the first page. The function exits and loops around. The next page could be next, but it does not have to be in sequential order. It could be further down the list inside the loop. All the following pages will not match the URL, and the build() method will simply return immediately as a null function. The next page could be earlier in the loop. It would have executed as a null function before this page and now executes as the loop starts from the top again.

Wash, rinse, repeat

The same principle applies to modifying the type of data in the page classes. As an example, the custom `date` tokens could be passed like this:

```
Set JOURNEY="host <today+7>"; yarn ch15


const match = journey.match(/(<.+>)/);
const dateToken = match ? match[0] : "";
Helpers.setValueIfExists(dateField, dateToken);
```

Now, we have a date token extracted from the journey value. The token is passed to `dateField`, if it exists, and set to next week's date. If there is no token, the date is set to an empty string, which the method will return immediately as there is nothing to do.

At this point, we have covered all the processes of a non-deterministic engine. New pages will be reported in the results and must be added to extend the path coverage. If a page is never encountered in a particular path, it does not stop the test. If an error is encountered, it is reported. If the path gets stuck, it is also reported. The data and the paths can be customized. These build methods can be called from other test cases.

Why not generate these Artifacts with API calls?

Using API calls for a task does mean quicker and more stable testing, as it directly communicates with an application. It can be implemented earlier in the development process. This could lead to early detection of issues, making the development process more flexible and agile.

Conversely, using an automated GUI could provide a richer understanding of the user experience, as it can simulate the exact paths a user might take, including interactions with visual elements that API tests might overlook. This approach might be more intuitive and can encompass a broader analysis, including the appearance and layout, which are crucial for user satisfaction.

In fact, there is no reason to support once approach over another. The GUI approach confirms the system works correctly for the user. The API approaches generate the artifacts with greater speed. We can implement the differences in the approaches by adding another keyword value to the journey parsing code:

```
Set JOURNEY="military references api"; yarn job-app-engine


if (journey.toLowerCase().includes(" api")) {
// API path
} else {
// GUI path
}
```

In this example, the default GUI approach is overridden with an API path in the same `build()` methods.

Summary

In this chapter, we delved into a sophisticated approach to test automation, reminiscent of a superhero strategizing for dynamic and complex missions with multiple potential outcomes based on choices made. Our method involved a loop that continuously navigates through each page, engaging only upon recognizing a known resource. The journey is non-deterministic shaped by high-level objectives and occasionally encountering unexpected obstacles like dead ends or logic loops.

This approach is flexible, allowing for the adjustment of user paths based on various variables and can be adapted to different environments, highlighting its robustness and versatility. It also aids in data generation for manual testers, significantly reducing the time and effort needed to create data records for testing when paired with tools like Jenkins, enhancing the efficiency of the testing process overall.

In the final chapter, this approach will have additional advantages, making manual testers more efficient. The worst idea is to assume automation replaces "costly" manual testers. We should aways strive to augment their efforts. Manual testers could reduce a lot of setup time creating complex test artifacts when they only need to validate the results. But do we want to have them install a coding tool and teach them how to run a script like this? This is where we employ our final magical item and let a CI/CD tool provide an effortless way to do the heavy lifting. Something like a mystic sentient cloak of levitation perhaps?

15

The Sentient Cape – Running Tests in a CI/CD Pipeline with Jenkins and LambdaTest

Have you ever wondered how some superheroes manage to be courtroom lawyers by day and crime fighters by night? When do they catch a wink of sleep?

In this final chapter, we will get our WebdriverIO scripts to execute by scheduling test executions. This can be accomplished by using an execution pipeline in a continuous execution environment to run our jobs that run in a virtualized cloud-based environment rather than our local **operating system (OS)**. Think of this as an accessory that seems to have a mind of its own – an ever-vigilant silent assistant whose sole purpose is to help out by taking time-consuming tasks off your plate, often while you sleep. This is where we'll cover Jenkins and LambdaTest **continuous integration (CI)** with cross-OS usage.

Before we start, let's recall what was noted back in *Chapter 1* – automation requires more than average computing resources. Virtualization requires even more. We used two machines to write code in this book: a Windows 11 system – that is, a **Micro-Star International (MSI)** Raider GE76 12UE gaming machine purpose-built with 2 TB of SSD drive space and 64 GB of RAM. It has a 12th-generation Intel i9-12900H Core CPU with a 2.90 GHz base speed. The CPU is equipped with 14 cores and supports 20 threads. We also used two Apple MacBook Pros with M1 chips with a 1TB hard drive using Parallels to virtualize a Windows OS.

> **Quick tip – how to profile your PC**
>
> You can't be a good detective without a tool that gives insight into your system in one convenient location. The profiler we have used for over 15 years in Windows is Belarc Advisor Personal Edition.

We did this just to be sure there was little chance our resources would run low, causing random transient issues that might cause false positives. If your RAM goes below 15% availability, you will most likely experience issues. If your Windows machine has a red dot indicating an upgrade is required, give it the priority it deserves.

The following main topics will be covered in this chapter:

- What are Jenkins and Slack
- Installing Jenkins
- Creating a WebdriverIO project with Jenkins
- Reporting Slack from Jenkins
- On-demand and scheduled suite runs
- Types of debugging runs with Jenkins
- CI/CD pipeline

Technical requirements

To complete this chapter, you must meet the following technical requirements:

- Install and configure Jenkins
- Configure Slack to receive messages
- Modify the `wdio.config.ts` file
- Create a Jenkins job run an individual test and report to Slack
- Organize tests into categories
- Create a Jenkins job to run each category
- Organize tests into Sanity, Smoke, and Regression suites
- Create a Jenkins job to run each suite
- Set up and configure the jobs to run nightly
- Manual testers can run a parameterized job on demand

All the test examples can be found in this book's GitHub repository at `https://github.com/PacktPublishing/Enhanced-Test-Automation-with-WebdriverIO`.

What are Jenkins and Slack?

In the realm of test automation, particularly when working with frameworks such as WebdriverIO, Jenkins and Slack hold a significant place due to their functionalities, which streamline and enhance the test deployment process. They can be configured to send update messages to a Slack channel when the test run has finished. Jenkins can schedule test suite runs or they can be launched on demand by any team member.

We will begin this final chapter by preparing for a Jenkins installation.

Installing OpenJDK for Jenkins

Before installing Jenkins, we need to ensure we have the correct version of the Java Development Kit. OpenJDK version 17 should be used and the latest version is recommended. The Java 17 SDK can be downloaded from `https://www.oracle.com/java/technologies/downloads/#java17`.

The easiest way to install Java 17 on Windows is to download and execute the MSI file and save it to the default path under the `Program Files` folder. Copy the path and add it to the `JAVA_HOME` environmental system variable's path:

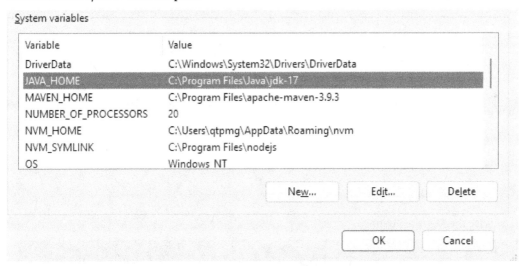

Figure 15.1 – Adding the path to the system variables in Windows

Then, add %JAVA_HOME%/bin to the Path variable:

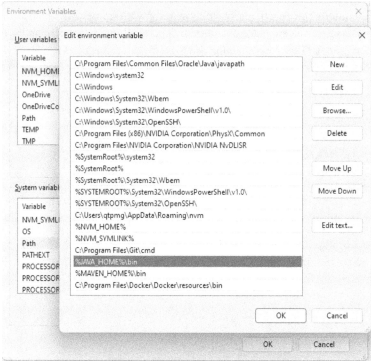

Figure 15.2 – Adding the JAVA_HOME\bin to the Windows Path variable

Next, we must confirm Java is installed.

From the command prompt, type the following:

```
> java -version
```

You will see the following output:

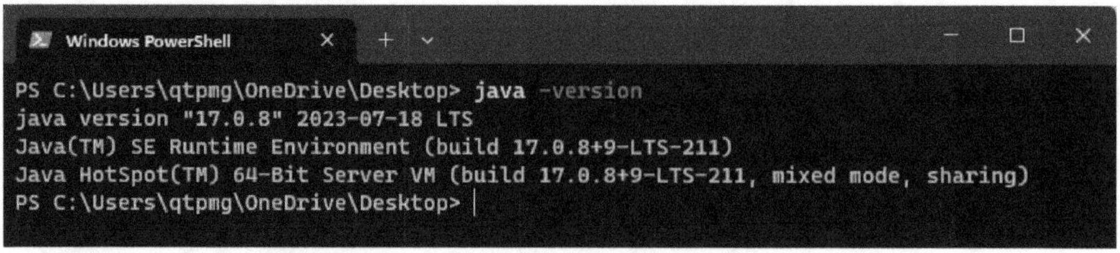

```
PS C:\Users\qtpmg\OneDrive\Desktop> java -version
java version "17.0.8" 2023-07-18 LTS
Java(TM) SE Runtime Environment (build 17.0.8+9-LTS-211)
Java HotSpot(TM) 64-Bit Server VM (build 17.0.8+9-LTS-211, mixed mode, sharing)
PS C:\Users\qtpmg\OneDrive\Desktop>
```

Figure 15.3 – Verifying that version 17 of Java has been installed

Now, we can proceed to install Jenkins.

Installing Jenkins as a standalone application

IMPORTANT: Jenkins will provide a temporary password for an admin account. Save this information as we will need it after the installation has been finalized.

Installing Jenkins

Installing Jenkins is fairly straightforward. Download the latest version of Jenkins for your Mac, Windows, or Linux OS from `https://www.jenkins.io/download/` and use the default path for the installation.

Once it's been downloaded, drag the `jenkins.war` file to the desktop. From the command prompt, navigate to the desktop and type the following:

```
> java -jar jenkins.war
```

You will see the following output:

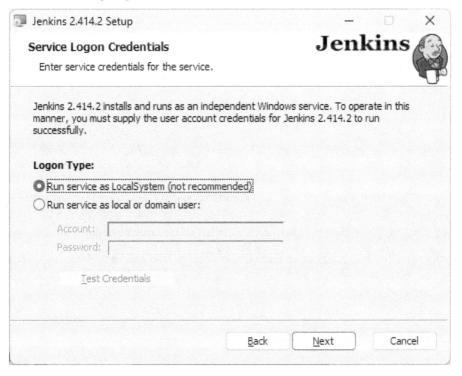

Figure 15.4 – Select LocalSystem for this example. In the real world, the IT
DevOps team would install an admin domain user account for security

While the service is installed as LocalSystem, it is recommended to change to local or domain user credentials. Next, we must set the port. Use the default port of 8080 and test that we get a green checkmark for the assigned port number:

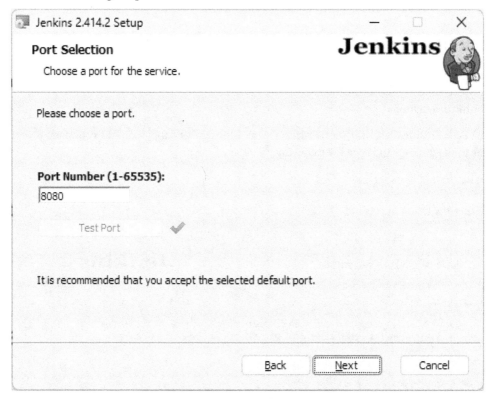

Figure 15.5 – Using the default port of 8080 and testing that we get a green checkmark

If the port is blocked, it will need to be opened; otherwise, an alternate open port must be assigned.

The next page specifies the custom setup features. Leave them as-is and click **Next**. The path where Java is installed should be picked up by the JAVA_HOME environmental variable we set in Windows earlier. Otherwise, set the path to where JRE was installed:

Figure 15.6 – Click Install and Jenkins will be ready

Our Jenkins server will be now accessible at `https://localhost:8080/` and will require the temporary admin password we were provided earlier to be entered and then changed for security purposes. The path to the log file where the generated credential can be found is listed on the web page.

Jenkins will then ask you if you wish to install the suggested plugins:

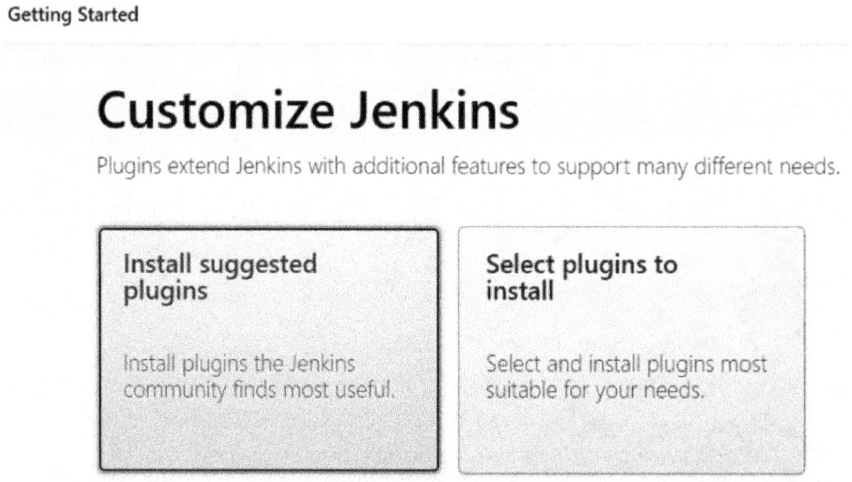

Getting Started

Customize Jenkins

Plugins extend Jenkins with additional features to support many different needs.

Install suggested plugins	Select plugins to install
Install plugins the Jenkins community finds most useful.	Select and install plugins most suitable for your needs.

Figure 15.7 – Installing the suggested plugins

Continue with the suggested plugins:

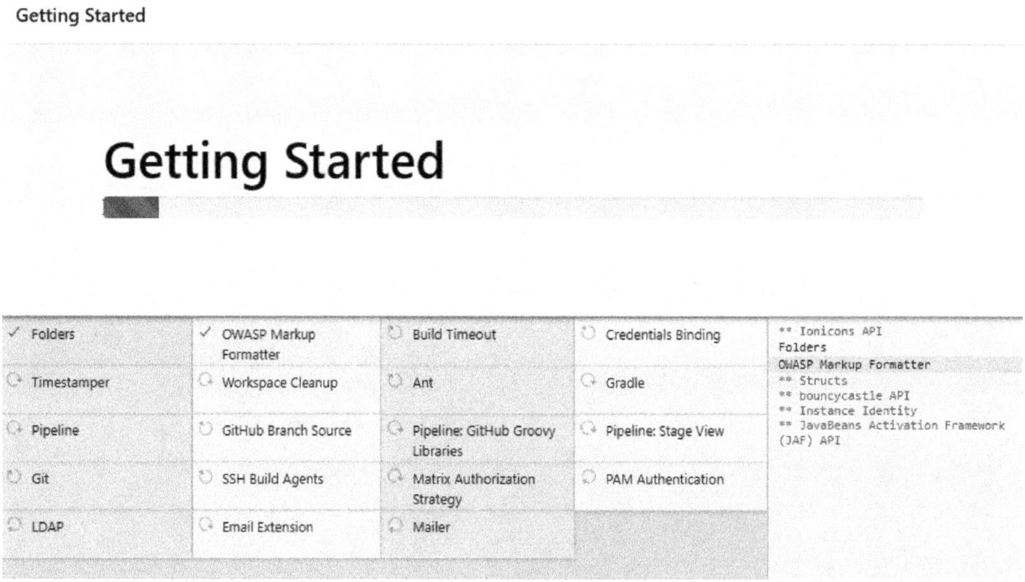

Getting Started

Getting Started

✓ Folders	✓ OWASP Markup Formatter	⟳ Build Timeout	⟳ Credentials Binding	** Ionicons API
				Folders
				OWASP Markup Formatter
⟳ Timestamper	⟳ Workspace Cleanup	⟳ Ant	⟳ Gradle	** Structs
				** bouncycastle API
				** Instance Identity
⟳ Pipeline	⟳ GitHub Branch Source	⟳ Pipeline: GitHub Groovy Libraries	⟳ Pipeline: Stage View	** JavaBeans Activation Framework (JAF) API
⟳ Git	⟳ SSH Build Agents	⟳ Matrix Authorization Strategy	⟳ PAM Authentication	
⟳ LDAP	⟳ Email Extension	⟳ Mailer		

Figure 15.8 – Suggested plugins

Finally, we must create the first admin user's account credentials:

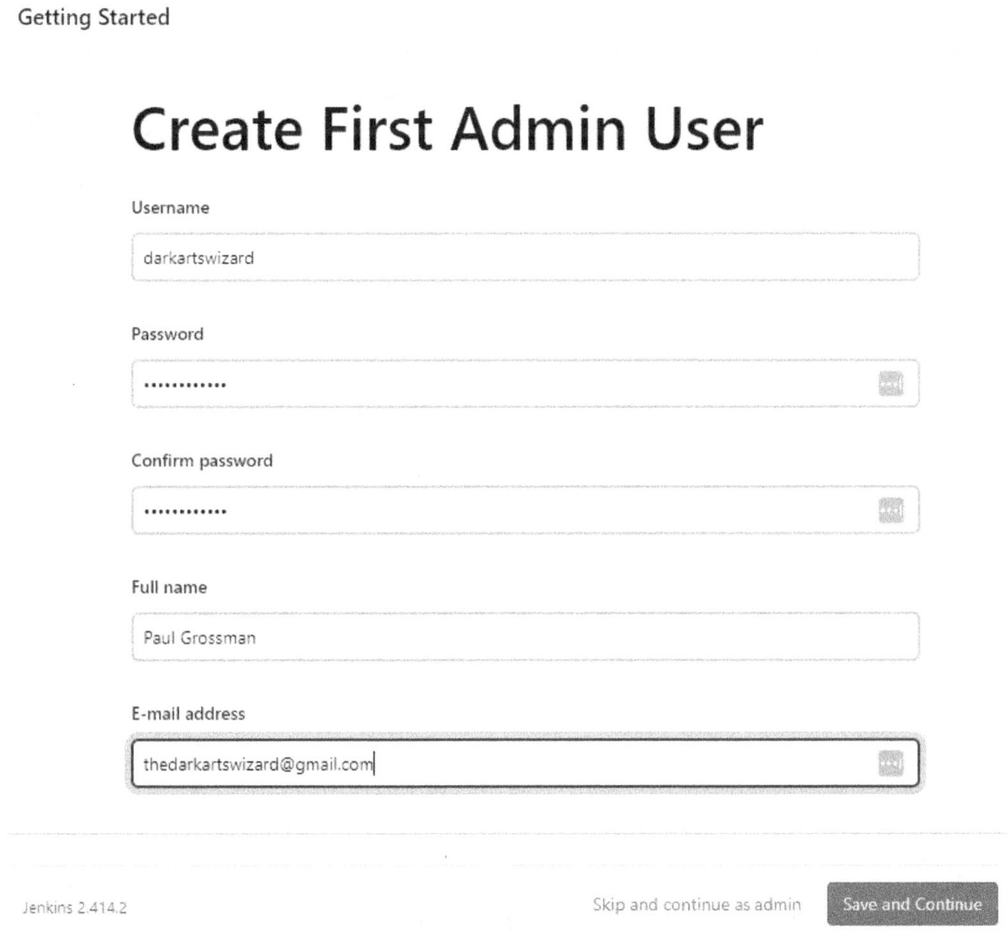

Getting Started

Create First Admin User

Username

darkartswizard

Password

••••••••••••

Confirm password

••••••••••••

Full name

Paul Grossman

E-mail address

thedarkartswizard@gmail.com

Jenkins 2.414.2   Skip and continue as admin   Save and Continue

Figure 15.9 – Create First Admin User

Click **Save and Continue**. Jenkins will provide its URL again. Click **Save and Continue** one last time. Click **Start Using Jenkins** to be redirected to the main page. We recommend that you save this link to your browser's bookmarks bar. Our faithful Sentient Cape is now ready to do our bidding:

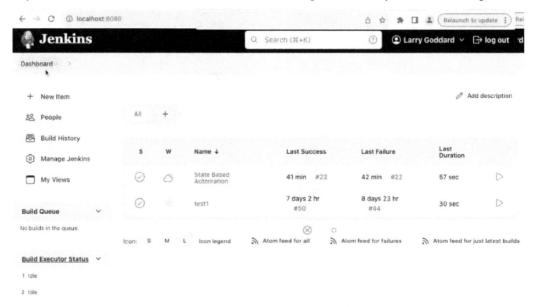

Figure 15.10 – The Jenkins main page

Here, we can create new projects and jobs and run them on demand or a scheduled cadence. With that, it is time to run our first test job.

Creating a WebdriverIO project with Jenkins

From the main dashboard view, click the **+ New Item** button. Jenkins provides us with several project options and organizational tools. **Freestyle project** is a streamlined approach to building a job, while **Pipeline** allows more granular customization with the Groovy programming language:

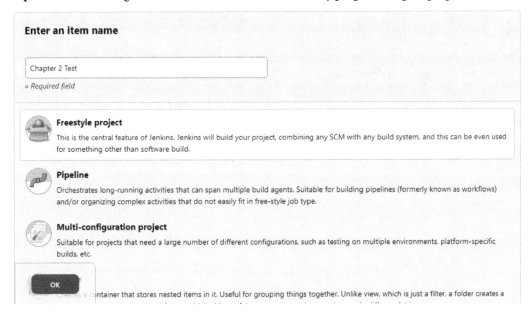

Figure 15.11 – Creating a Freestyle project

For our purposes, **Freestyle project** will suffice. Several options will be displayed. We will only need a few to get our first test from *Chapter 2* to be checked out of our GitHub **source control manager (SCM)** and run:

Build Steps

Figure 15.12 – Adding build steps

Under the **Build Steps** section, select **Add a Build step** to execute terminal commands. For Mac, select **Execute shell** and for Windows, choose the **Execute Windows batch command** option. Using the command prompt, we will navigate to the workspace path.

Next, add a `run a npm command` build step. This is required when we run our tests in LambdaTest. In this section, we will execute the commands listed in the `package.json` file. In this example, we'll run the tests from *Chapter 2* with `npm ch2`.

But before that, we need to add one last add-on to support job notifications.

Installing the Jenkins plugin for LambdaTest

To install the Jenkins plugin for LambdaTest, follow these steps:

1. Click **Manage Jenkins**, then **Manage Plugins**.

2. Click the **Available** tab.

3. In the **Filter** box, type LambdaTest.

4. You will see a list of plugins; select **LambdaTest**.

5. To install the **LambdaTest** Jenkins plugin, you must select the checkbox in front of **LambdaTest**. Once the plugin has been installed, and Jenkins has been restarted, you will be able to find the LambdaTest Jenkins plugin under **Installed plugins**:

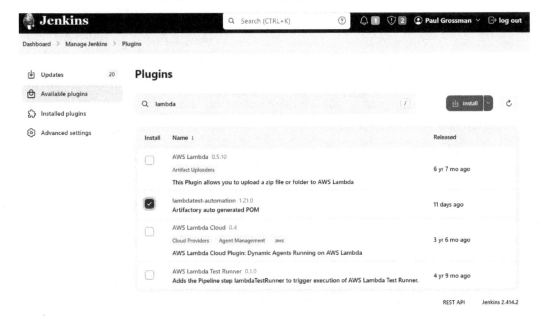

Figure 15.13 – Searching for the LambdaTest Jenkins plugin

Configuring LambdaTest using Jenkins

Follow these steps to configure LambdaTest with Jenkins:

1. On the Jenkins home page, click **Credentials**.

2. Under **Credentials**, click **System**.

3. On the **System** page, click **Global credentials (Unrestricted) domain**. The **Global credentials** page will open.

4.   Click **Add Credentials**. The **Add Credentials** page will open.

5.   Enter the relevant data in the fields and click **Verify Credentials**. After verification, click the **OK** button. Jenkins will generate an ID, which is visible on the **Credentials** page.

6.   Save your changes:

Figure 15.14 – Adding the necessary credentials to the LambdaTest plugin

Once you've added your credentials, Jenkins will generate an ID. To retrieve this ID for LambdaTest Credentials, you must go to the Jenkins home page and click on **Credentials** from the left navigation menu.

From the Jenkins home page, click **Credentials** from the left menu. You can copy the ID for LambdaTest Credentials.

Creating a freestyle project and job

From the Jenkins dashboard, click + **New Item**. This provides us with several options, including **Freestyle project** and **Pipeline**. The **Freestyle project** option is for beginners, while the **Pipeline** option is for advanced users who wish to create a custom pipeline script in Groovy. Let's begin by entering Enhanced Test Automation with WebdriverIO as the name and selecting **Freestyle project**.

This will display several tabs, including **General**, **Source Code Management**, **Build Triggers**, **Build Environment**, **Build**, and **Post-build Actions**. We will choose to run using code from our local machine. Advanced users can use a cloud-based corporate Jenkins to check out code from a private repository:

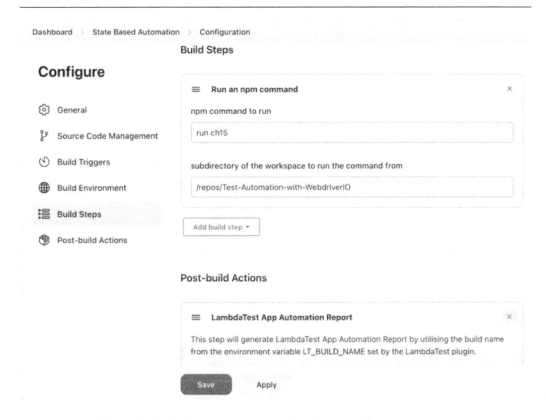

Figure 15.15 – Setting up custom state-based test runs for manual testers

To run the build, we need the name of the test and the path to the project directory.

Parameterizing

In the job configuration, we will add a parameter that we will pass into our automation framework from Jenkins named JOURNEY. This will become a system variable that our framework expects and parses to determine the path to take for hosting or attending a Halloween party. In addition, we have a choice parameter, which allows us to pass dev or prod to the Env system variable. This changes which URL will be the landing page for this test:

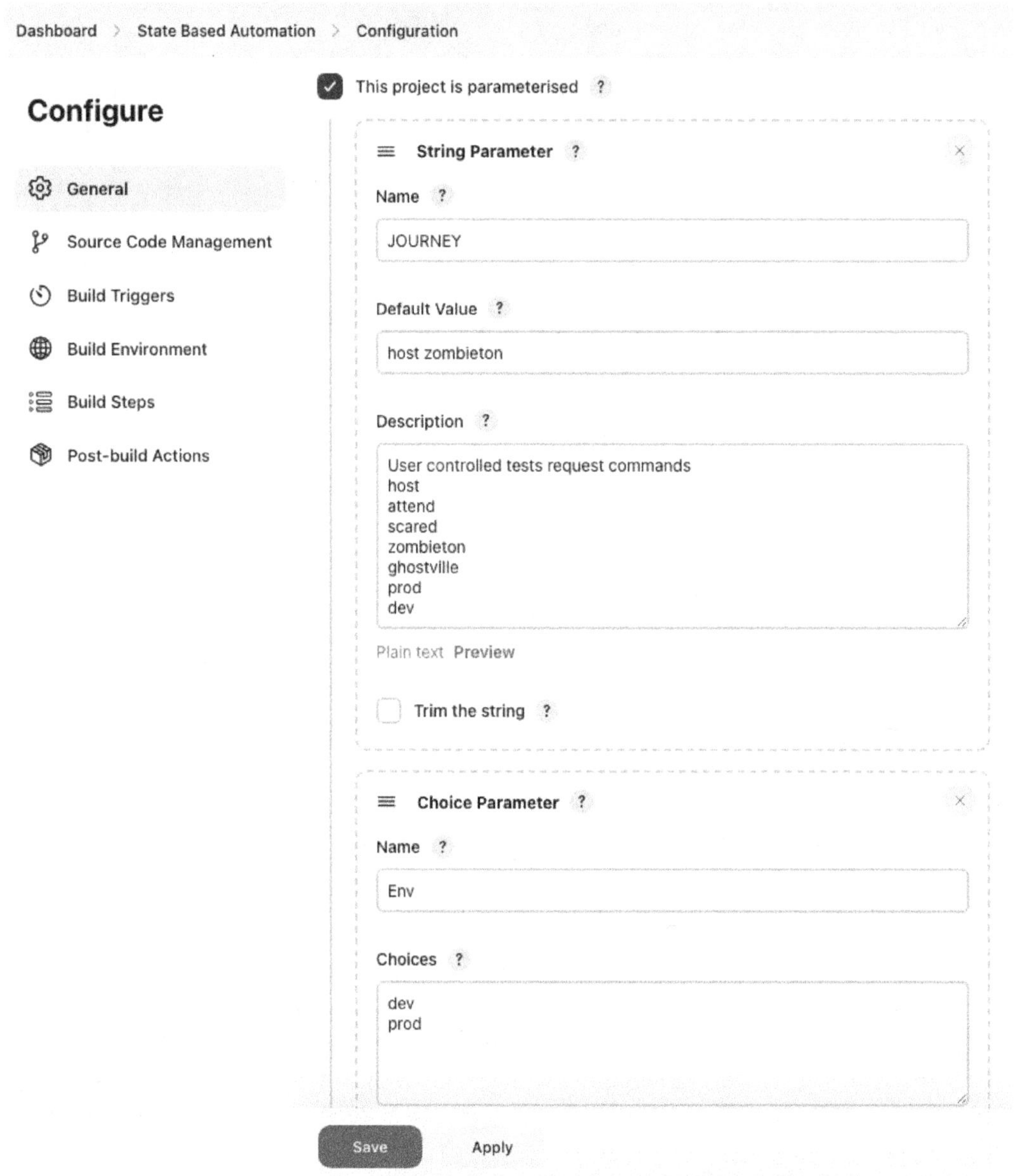

Dashboard > State Based Automation > Configuration

Configure

☑ This project is parameterised ?

- ⚙ General
- ⅃ Source Code Management
- ⏱ Build Triggers
- ⊕ Build Environment
- ≔ Build Steps
- ▦ Post-build Actions

≡ **String Parameter** ?   ✕

Name ?

    JOURNEY

Default Value ?

    host zombieton

Description ?

    User controlled tests request commands
    host
    attend
    scared
    zombieton
    ghostville
    prod
    dev

Plain text Preview

☐ Trim the string ?

≡ **Choice Parameter** ?   ✕

Name ?

    Env

Choices ?

    dev
    prod

Save   Apply

Figure 15.16 – Setting up a custom state-based journey test for manual testers

Next, we will have a slimmed-down version of the state-driven automation tests that we built in the previous chapter:

```
import LoginPage from "../pageObjects/login.page";
// Host or Attend a party in Ghostville or Zombieton
import stateDrivenUtils from "../utilities/stateDriven.utils";
describe("Ch15: State-drive Automation from Jenkins", () => {
    it("should loop around until the final or first page is found",
async () => {
        // Get the test data from the JOURNEY environment variable
        let env = process.env.ENV || "prod";
        await LoginPage.open(env);
        let testData = process.env.JOURNEY || ""; // Get test data
from JOURNEY environment variable set by Jenkins
        stateDrivenUtils.partyPath(testData); // Attend path through
the party
    });
});
```

Note that even if the tester clears the journey to an empty field, the test will still run using the happy path of hosting a party in Zombieton by default:

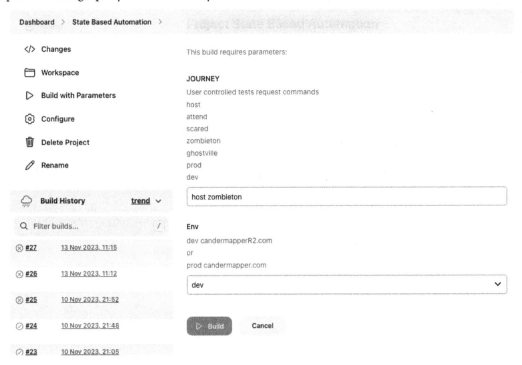

Figure 15.17 – Building a test with parameters using journey decision point suggestions

Our manual testers can now open Jenkins and launch this test with parameters. They can pick what kinds of paths they want to take as well as change the environments to run against from the **Env** dropdown.

Once this test case completes, we will see the results on our LambdaTest dashboard:

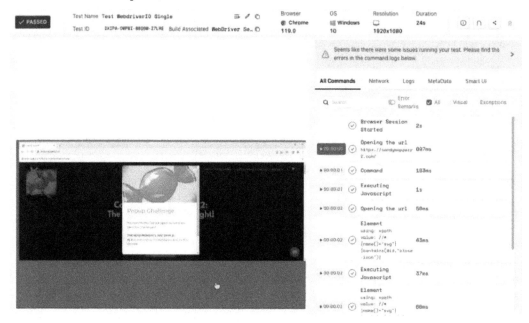

Figure 15.18 – LambdaTest results screen

By leveraging a cloud-based automation build platform, we get a lot of advantages. First, we don't need to administer the underlying OS configurations. Second, we don't need to keep track of the versions of the browsers. Finally, we get a nice video recording of the test execution, which is far superior to the individual screen captures.

All this mystical magic is accomplished with the LambdaTest config file we described in *Chapter 13*.

Add the LambdaTest Credentials here:

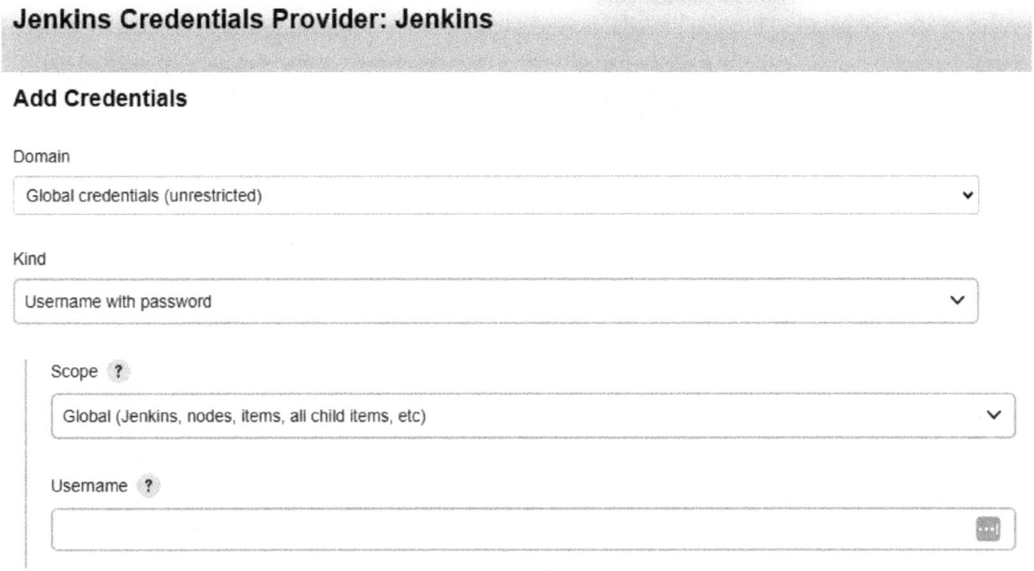

Jenkins Credentials Provider: Jenkins

Add Credentials

Domain

Global credentials (unrestricted)   ⌄

Kind

Username with password   ⌄

Scope ?

Global (Jenkins, nodes, items, all child items, etc)   ⌄

Username ?

[⊞]

Figure 15.19 – Adding the LambdaTest credentials

Now, let's see how reporting works in Slack.

Reporting in Slack from Jenkins

One of the final problems of being a superhero is being super vigilant. The problem with running a large suite of tests unattended is that we must remember to check back in occasionally to see if they have been completed. Setting a reminder can break our concentration on other work. We might be so wrapped up with other tasks that we might not get back to the results until several hours after the task has been completed. To be efficient, we could send alert messages to our email inbox, but they might get ignored if our inbox gets blasted with incoming messages. A better solution is to send updates to a team messaging platform such as Slack. This is a three-step process – that is, adding a Plugin for Jenkins, adding an app in Slack, and adding a Jenkins post-build step. The first step is to install the necessary add-ons in both Slack and Jenkins to indicate the Slack channel where messages will appear.

Adding the Slack notifications plugin to Jenkins

Navigate to **Manage Jenkins | Plugins | Available**. Then, search for and install the **Slack Notification** plugin:

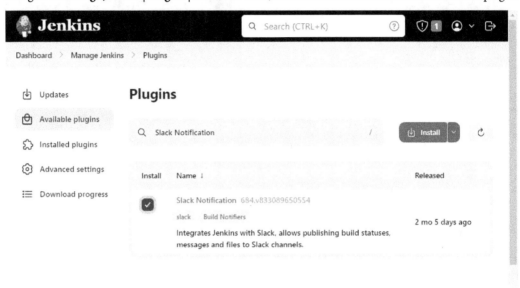

Figure 15.20 – Searching for the Slack Notification plugin

Once the plugin has been installed, restart Jenkins and log in. The **Slack Notification** plugin will now appear in the **Installed Plugins** tab. Our next step is to set up Slack integration.

Adding the Jenkins CI app to Slack

For this, we must add the Slack Jenkins CI application. Browse **Apps** and search for and add **Jenkins CI**:

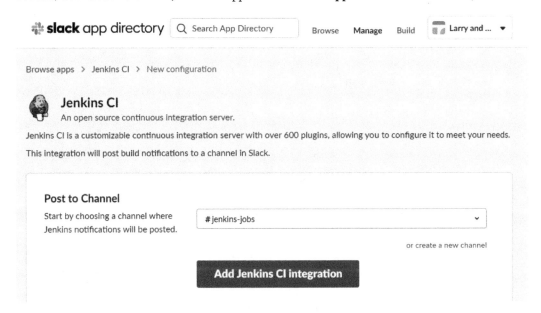

Figure 15.21 – The Jenkins CI plugin for Slack, which will receive messages from Jenkins

This app will ask you to create a Slack channel or select an existing one. In this example, we will create a jenkins-jobs channel for notifications to appear.

Our final step is to get the token to allow these two products to communicate. Navigate to the Slack app directory and add the Jenkins CI integration:

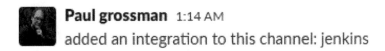

Figure 15.22 – A notification in the Slack channel confirming that the integration was completed

With the integration added, click the **Jenkins** link in the message to get the token.

This token is available from the Jenkins dashboard under **Manage Jenkins | Manage Plugins**, under the **Available** tab:

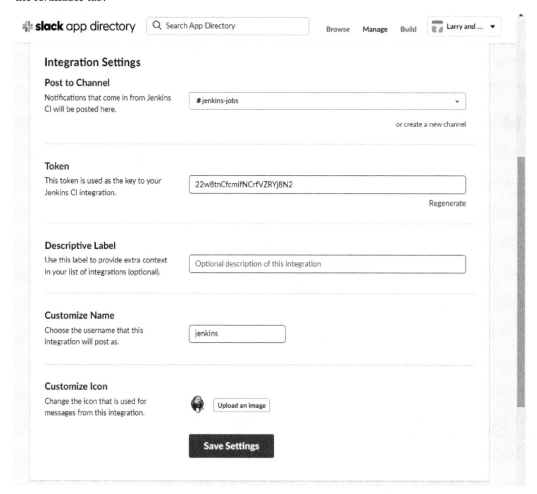

Figure 15.23 – Slack settings

Copy the token and workspace into the Jenkins app's settings and click **Save Settings**.

Next, return to Slack. Enter the workspace on the **Dashboard | System** page.

Then, add the credentials and some secret text. Enter the secret. The ID is optional. Finally, click **Test Connection**:

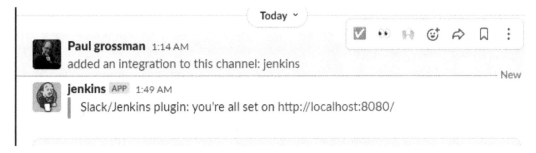

Figure 15.24 – A sample message will appear in Slack

Our connections are now complete and have been tested. Our final step is to get Jenkins to send informative messages back to Slack.

Adding the post-build Slack action

In the **Post-build Actions** area of our job, select **Slack Notifications**:

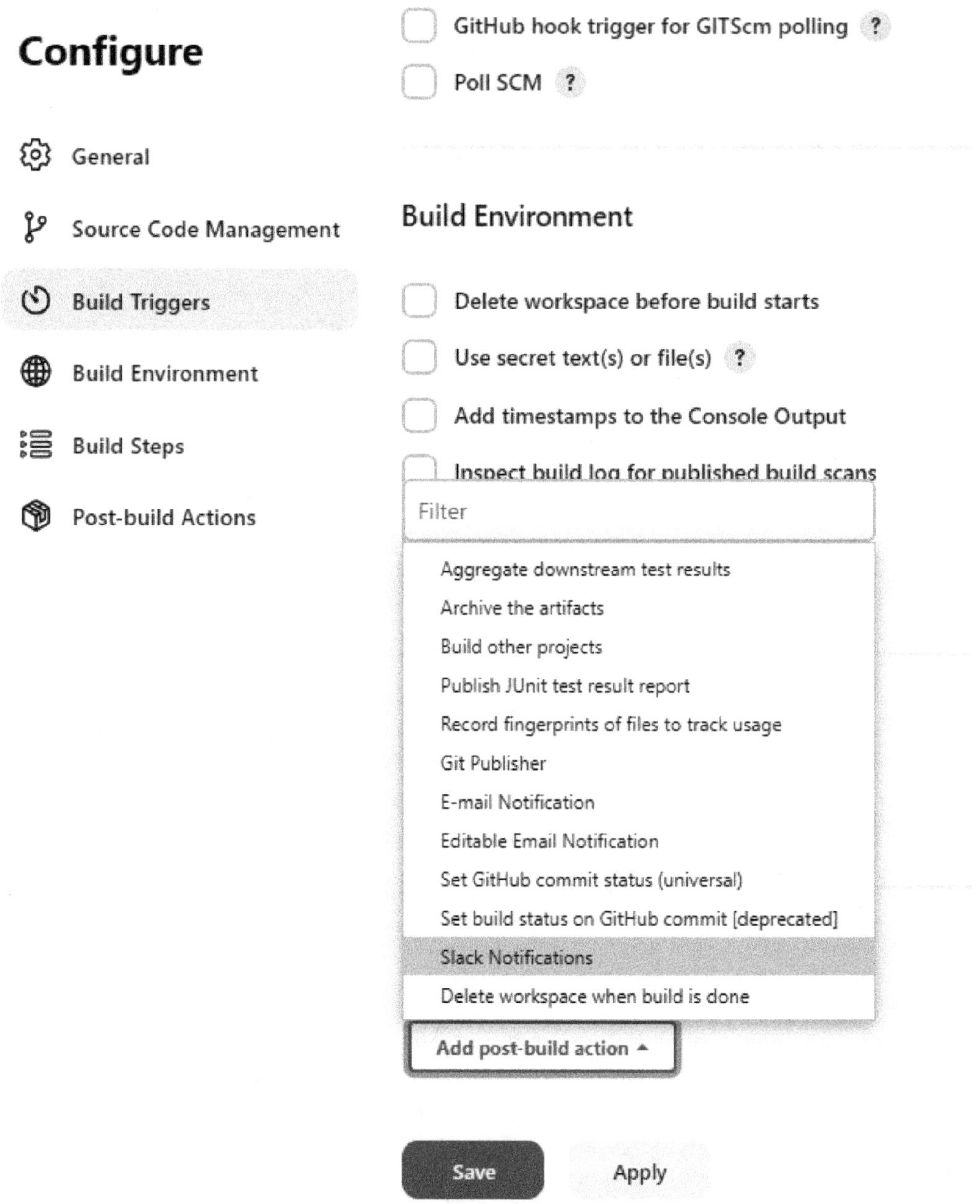

Configure

⬡ GitHub hook trigger for GITScm polling   ?

⬡ Poll SCM   ?

⚙ General

⑂ Source Code Management

⏱ Build Triggers

🌐 Build Environment

▤ Build Steps

📦 Post-build Actions

Build Environment

⬡ Delete workspace before build starts

⬡ Use secret text(s) or file(s)   ?

⬡ Add timestamps to the Console Output

⬡ Inspect build log for published build scans

Filter

Aggregate downstream test results
Archive the artifacts
Build other projects
Publish JUnit test result report
Record fingerprints of files to track usage
Git Publisher
E-mail Notification
Editable Email Notification
Set GitHub commit status (universal)
Set build status on GitHub commit [deprecated]
Slack Notifications
Delete workspace when build is done

Add post-build action ▲

Save   Apply

Figure 15.25 – Selecting Slack Notifications

Checkmark **Notify Success** and **Notify Every Failure**. Then, click **Save**:

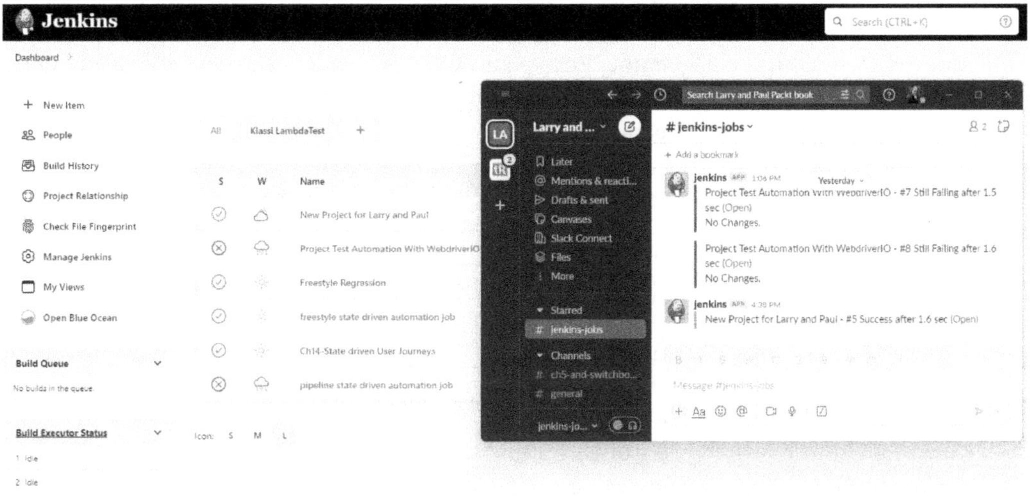

Figure 15.26 – Completed jobs with pass and fail states in Jenkins reported to Slack

Once a build is completed, updates are automatically sent to the designated Slack channel. This minimizes the delay between the job's completion and the start of the result analysis. In turn, this efficiency optimizes the use of time for all automation team members.

On-demand and scheduled suite runs

We try to have our tests run as often as possible. Sometimes, this can impact our environment, which then blocks the manual test team from doing their work.

Other times, this process is quiet and uneventful. There was a project manager who once asked if we could run automated test suites more often than just at the end of the sprint release cycle. I happily showed our histogram from our Allure reports and assured everyone the tests ran on a nightly cadence. We reviewed those results every morning for unexpected failures and state changes. As we wrote new tests and maintained others, we also noted that nearly every test was executed multiple times a day to ensure they impacted each other.

Types of debugging runs with Jenkins

We need to have a test that checks the reliability of the automation framework functions that we've written throughout this book. I used to refer to this as a unit test of the framework functionality. However, this caused confusion with the application developer team. They heard the term *unit* and assumed I was proposing to take on the unit testing in their code, a job that is always their responsibility. So, to avoid further confusion, we will refer to one test as the framework Sanity test.

The most common types of jobs are **Sanity**, **Smoke**, and **Regression**:

- The **Sanity test** is the most basic test of the framework. It is technically an integration test. It performs the browser launch, testing `SetValueAdv()` by entering credentials pulled from the Secrets storage into input field elements and exercising `ClickAdv()` by clicking the **Login** button. It should execute a limited page navigation that can test the other functionality, including `pageSync()` and selecting from a list with `SelectAdv()`. It must include at least one validation with `AssertAdv()`.

  This should not be a lengthy end-to-end test, but it could be the initial steps of one. While this is a job that could be run after every new framework commit, the test itself should also be included with every suite. If it were to fail, it would indicate that something basic has broken that needs to be investigated immediately.

- **Smoke** tests comprise a collection of tests that cover roughly 10% of the entire suite.

- **Regression** is the remaining 90% of the tests in the suite, excluding the Smoke tests.

However, there are other categories of tests that we generally set up to run nightly or weekly.

Additional suite categories

Let's look at the additional suite categories:

- **Build Verification Suite**: A subset of tests that have had defects written against them in the past. Often, this is 1/10th of the Smoke suite.

- **API Suite**: A quick way to validate API calls with payloads, validating responses and response codes. Again, this is a small quick set of tests that have no GUI interaction.

- **Long test suite**: Some tests just take an extended amount of time to complete. Let them have fun on their own, allowing the Smoke and Regression tests to finish sooner.

- **Single Test Suite**: This allows the user to request a custom subset of all tests combined. This might be Product Returns, Searches, and Saving Shopping Carts. This allows the test team to focus on only one area without having to search through multiple BVS, Smoke, and Regression runs. It can also run tests by test case name if it includes a Jira number.

- **Fail**: A list of tests that are marked as having failed recently and removed from the other suites. This suite can be a quick way to see if a single fix has resolved multiple failing tests.

Linking Allure reports to a Jenkins run

In your Jenkins job configuration, under **Post-Build Actions**, add a **Publish Allure Report** action.

Configure the **Report Version** and **Report Directory** fields appropriately. **Report Directory** should point to the directory where your Allure report files are generated.

CI/CD pipeline

CI/CD stands for **continuous integration and continuous deployment** (or **continuous delivery**). It is a set of practices and tools that are used in software development to automate the process of building, testing, and deploying software changes. CI is where the developer does frequent code merges to the central repository rather than waiting long periods before merging their code. This approach helps them identify integration issues early on and ensures that the code base is always in a functional state.

Continuous deployment (or continuous delivery) extends the concept of CI by automating the process of deploying software changes to production environments. The goal is to have a reliable and automated pipeline that takes code changes from the repository, builds it, tests it, and deploys it to the production environments without manual intervention.

The CI/CD process typically involves the following steps:

1. **Code integration**: Developers commit their changes to a version control system (such as Git) frequently.

2. **Build and test**: The CI/CD system automatically builds the application and runs various automated tests to ensure the changes are functioning as expected.

3. **Automated deployment**: Once the build and tests pass successfully, the CI/CD system automatically deploys it to a staging or production environment (that is, to cloud platforms, containerized environments, and so on).

4. **Continuous monitoring**: Once deployed, the CI/CD system can monitor the application's performance and log any errors or issues.

What is continuous testing?

Continuous testing is the practice of executing automated tests throughout the software development life cycle to provide fast and frequent feedback on the quality of the code.

Traditionally, testing was often considered a separate phase that occurred at the end of the development cycle. However, with the adoption of Agile and DevOps practices, there has been a shift toward integrating testing into every stage of the development process.

Continuous testing involves the following five key aspects:

*   **Automated testing**: Continuous testing relies on automated tests to be inclusive of unit tests, integration tests, and functional tests. These tests are scripted and executed automatically whenever changes are made to the code base and are there to ensure that software functionalities work as intended and help catch bugs early on.

*   **Early and frequent testing**: Continuous testing emphasizes that we test early and often. Once code changes are merged into the repository, tests are triggered to verify the integrity of the changes.

- **Test environments**: Continuous testing involves multiple testing environments, including local development, testing, and staging environments. These environments are used to run tests in a realistic setup, mimicking the production environment as closely as possible.

- **Test data management**: This is all about effectively managing test data. This data should be able to cover a wide range of scenarios and user cases. The test data should also be easily provisioned and reset to ensure reliable and repeatable test executions.

- **Continuous feedback**: This is all about providing immediate feedback on the quality of the code changes. Test results are generated automatically, highlighting any failures or issues. This feedback helps developers deal with failures/issues quickly, ensuring the code base remains stable and reliable.

Now that we have an idea of what CI is and how to go about it, we need to take a look at our pipelines for executing our test suites.

What does a CI/CD pipeline look like?

A CI/CD pipeline is a set of automated steps and tools that enable the CI, testing, and deployment of software changes. While the specific implementation of a CI/CD pipeline can vary depending on the project and organization, the following subsections give a general overview of what a CI/CD pipeline may look like.

Code repository

The pipeline starts with a code repository, typically using a version control system such as Git. Automation engineers commit their code changes to a GitHub or GitLab repository. This might include adding or maintaining existing test cases or enhancing the automation framework features.

CI

CI is a software development practice where developers regularly merge their code changes into a central repository, preferably multiple times a day. After merging, automated builds and tests are run to catch bugs early and ensure that the new changes are compatible with the existing code base. The primary goals of CI are to improve code quality, detect issues early, and facilitate rapid, reliable releases. CI is often integrated with other DevOps practices and tools, such as CD, to streamline the development life cycle from coding to deployment. Tools such as Jenkins are commonly used to orchestrate the CI process:

- **Code compilation**: When changes are committed, the CI system pulls the latest code from the repository and compiles it into executable code.

- **Automated testing**: The CI system runs a suite of automated tests, including unit tests, integration tests, and other types of tests, to verify the correctness and functionality of the code changes.

- **Code quality checks**: The CI system may perform code quality checks, such as code linting or static code analysis, to ensure adherence to coding standards and best practices.

- **Test reports and notifications**: The CI system generates test reports and sends notifications to the development team.

Artifact generation

Artifact generation involves creating digital or physical objects, data, or content through automated or computer-assisted processes. If the code passes the tests and quality checks, the CI system generates build artifacts, such as compiled binaries, libraries, or container images. These artifacts are the result of a successful compilation and testing process, including Allure reports and screen captures.

Deployment

If the build and tests pass successfully, the CI/CD system automatically deploys the changes to a staging or production environment. This step may involve deploying to cloud platforms, containerized environments, or other infrastructure configurations.

- **Staging environment**: The artifacts are deployed to a staging environment, which closely resembles the production environment

- **Additional testing**: More comprehensive tests, such as performance testing, security testing, or user acceptance testing, may be performed in the staging environment

- **Approval process**: Depending on the organization's policies, there may be an approval process or manual review before deploying to the production environment

CD

CD extends the concept of CI by automating the process of deploying software changes to production environments. With CD, the goal is to have a reliable and automated pipeline that takes code changes from the repository, builds them, runs tests, and deploys them to production environments without manual intervention:

- **Production environment**: If the staging tests and approvals are successful, the artifacts are deployed to the production environment automatically or manually, depending on the organization's deployment strategy

- **Post-deployment testing**: Additional monitoring and testing (business verification) may take place in the production environment to ensure the new changes are functioning as expected

- **Continuous monitoring**: The CI/CD pipeline often includes monitoring tools that track the application's performance, logs, and metrics

Continuous feedback

Continuous testing provides immediate feedback on the quality of the code changes. Test results are generated automatically, highlighting any failures or issues. This feedback loop helps developers quickly identify and fix problems, ensuring the code base remains stable and reliable:

- **Notifications and reports**: Throughout the pipeline, notifications, reports, and logs are generated and made available to the development team and stakeholders, providing visibility into the progress, test results, and deployment status
- **Iterative development**: The CI/CD pipeline facilitates an iterative development process, where developers can quickly receive feedback on their code changes and make necessary adjustments, ensuring continuous improvement

Jenkins for CI/CD

Jenkins is an excellent tool for setting up a CI/CD pipeline, allowing you to automate various stages of your testing life cycle. In a dynamic testing environment, especially when working with WebdriverIO, a well-configured CI/CD pipeline can significantly boost the efficiency of the testing process.

Jenkins can be configured to automatically trigger test suites post a code push, which ensures that the test suite is always in sync with the latest code base, reducing the potential for issues slipping through and getting into production.

Jenkins allows for parallel execution of tests, which significantly reduces the test execution time. This is a must-have feature for any testing framework that aims to maintain agility and speed in today's fast-paced development environments.

Docker helps in creating a standardized environment for testing, which is critical for ensuring the reliability of your test results. Having a consistent environment means your tests will be more reliable and less prone to errors caused by environmental inconsistencies.

Docker containers provide an isolated environment for your tests, which is a creative solution to avoiding conflicts between different dependencies and system configurations. It sidesteps the infamous "it works on my machine" problem, ensuring the test automation framework is robust and reliable.

Summary

By implementing CI/CD, development teams can streamline their software development processes, reduce manual errors, and ensure faster and more reliable delivery of new features and bug fixes. It promotes collaboration among team members, improves code quality, and enables rapid and frequent releases.

By incorporating continuous testing into the development process, teams can identify and address issues early, reduce the risk of defects reaching production, and ensure the software meets quality standards. It promotes a culture of quality throughout the development team and supports faster and more reliable software delivery.

It's important to note that the specific tools, technologies, and steps involved in a CI/CD pipeline can vary depending on the project requirements, technology stack, and organization's preferences. The pipeline can be customized and expanded to include additional stages, such as security scanning, performance optimization, or even automated rollbacks in case of issues.

Overall, Jenkins and LambdaTest simplify the process of setting up and managing CI/CD pipelines, enabling teams to deliver software faster, more reliably, and with greater confidence in the quality of their code changes.

Appendix
The Ultimate Guide to TypeScript Error Messages, Causes, and Solutions

This Appendix covers all the issues the authors encountered while writing this book, including (but not limited to) installation, configuration, and runtime errors. Each problem is followed by one or more causes, each with a solution. Problems with the same solution are grouped together. A good way to use this Appendix is to search for a small segment of the error detail copied from the terminal window, such as check if port.

Problem: Install default WDIO settings by passing "--yes" parameter still asks configuration questions

Cause: Missing - - parameter at the command prompt:

```
> npm init wdio . --yes
```

Solution: Use - - to pass the parameter to wdio:

```
> npm init wdio . -- --yes
```

Problem: Missing script "wdio"

Cause: Missing `scripts:` section or missing `wdio` script in `Package.json`.

Solution: Add `wdio` to the `scripts:` section in the `Package.json` file:

```
"scripts": {
    "wdio": "wdio run test/wdio.conf.ts"
},
```

Problem: "node : The term 'node' is not recognized as the name of a cmdlet, function, script file, or operable program. Check the spelling of the name, or if a path was included, verify that the path is correct and try again."

Cause: Node has not been installed.

Solution: Install Node.

Problem: 'wdio' is not recognized as an internal or external command"

Cause #1: The console is not at the correct file path folder.

Cause #2: The supporting packages have not been installed.

Solution: At the command prompt, navigate to the project folder and type `npm i`:

```
> npm i packageName
> yarn add packageName
```

Problems:

- Browser launches and immediately closes
- "This version of ChromeDriver has not been tested with Chrome version"
- "Must use import to load ES Module" or "require() of ES modules is not supported" (no require code in the project)

Cause: Chrome automatically updated and the `chromedriver.exe` version is out of date.

Solution: Install missing packages.

```
yarn add packageName
```

Problem: The \node_modules folder is not created when installed in a new WDIO project folder.

Problem: New project install fails with empty directory.

Problem: Tests suddenly fail to run including the \specs\ test.e2e.ts. sample test.

Cause: The project was created in a child folder where a separate WDIO project was inadvertently installed in its parent folder. The parent install created a \node_modules folder, a package.json and a wdio.conf.ts file. When the child installation is performed in the sub-folder, it will check for pre-existing shared resources in the parent folder. This will skip the creation of the \node_modules folder and potentially overwrite the parent package.json and config files. The sample \specs\ test.e2e.js may initially run in this new child folder. However, a secondary child project install can overwrite the parent \node_modules folders and config files further, potentially breaking all projects that reference the shared resources, as well as fail to complete the install process.

Solution: Avoid the shared resource model by keeping the parent folder empty: Create a new sub-folder in the parent folder. Move the \node_modules folder, package.json, wdio.conf.ts files and \test folder from the parent folder to the new child project folder. From GitHub, restore the last known working package.json and wdio.conf.ts files from the parent folder to the child folder where the tests no longer run. Rebuild with yarn install to create the missing \node_modules folder. The tests should now run. New project installations in child sub-folders should complete to success as well.

Problem: "WARN webdriver: Request encountered a stale element - terminating request"

Problem: "TypeError: elem[prop] is not a function"

Problem: Statements execute out of order

Cause: Missing await command:

```
setValueAdv(this.fldUsername, "username")
```

Solution: Add the await comand

```
await setValueAdv(await this.fldUsername, "username")
```

Problem: "ERROR @wdio/runner: Error: describe expects a function argument; received [object AsyncFunction]"

Cause: async is in the describe() block:

```
describe("async here causes troubles", async () => {
```

Solution: Remove async from the describe() block:

```
describe("no more troubles", () => {
```

Problem: "Unsupported engine"

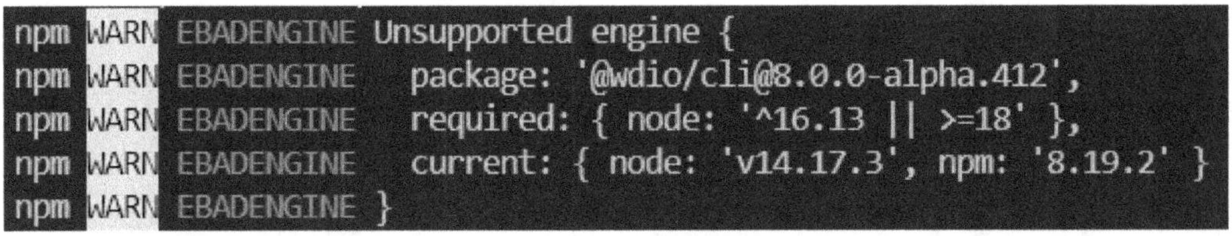

```
npm WARN EBADENGINE Unsupported engine {
npm WARN EBADENGINE   package: '@wdio/cli@8.0.0-alpha.412',
npm WARN EBADENGINE   required: { node: '^16.13 || >=18' },
npm WARN EBADENGINE   current: { node: 'v14.17.3', npm: '8.19.2' }
npm WARN EBADENGINE }
```

Figure A.1 – Results npm package manager indicating required and current node/npm versions

```
yarn install v1.22.17
[1/5] 🔍  Validating package.json...
error wdio@1.0.0: The engine "node" is incompatible with this modu
le. Expected version "=14". Got "21.1.0"
error Found incompatible module.
info Visit https://yarnpkg.com/en/docs/cli/install for documentati
on about this command.
→ Test-Automation-with-WebdriverIO git:(chapter-14-larryg) ×
```

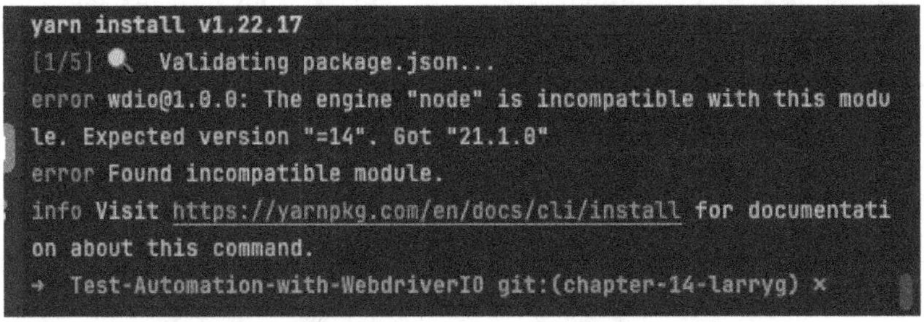

Figure A.2 – Results yarn package manager indicating expected
and out of date current node/npm versions

Cause: The current version of Node does not match the required version.

Solution: Update Node to the correct version. In this example, Node version 14 is not supported by the WDIO package and must be updated to 16.13, 18.x, or higher:

```
> nvm use 18
```

Problem: JavaScript Debug Terminal skips breakpoints

Cause: Related to unused or cached `import` statements paths

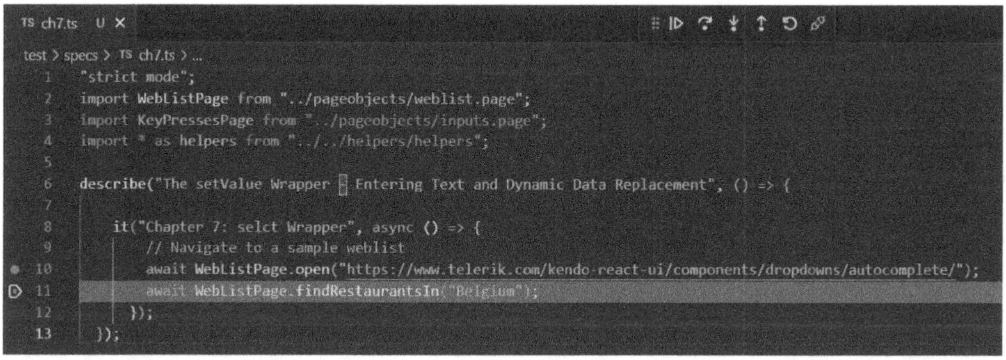

Figure A.3 –Removing the unused Helpers import stopped the breakpoint from skipping

Solution #1: Remove unused imports.

Cause #2: Missing async and await statements in the imported resources

Solution #2: Add async and await statements

Cause #3: Cached Import path case changed from "pageobjects" to "pageObjects"

Solution #3: Restart VSCode

Problem: Browser launches and locks up

Cause: Incompatibility with Node version 16.0.0.

Solution: Upgrade to Node version 18:

```
> nvm install 18
```

Problem: "SevereServiceError: Couldn't start Chromedriver: timeout. Please check if port [<PortNumber>] is in use"

Cause: Prior `chromedriver` failure has locked the port.

Solution: Kill the `chromedriver` session.

This is how to do it using the Windows CMD shell:

```
> Taskkill /IM chromedriver.exe /F
```

This is how to do it using macOS: `lsof -i :<PortNumber>` : `kill -9 <PID>`

Problem: MODULE_NOT_FOUND

Cause #1: Node path is incorrect or missing from the `Path` environmental variable.

Solution: Add the node path to the system variables.

Cause #2: Packages installed from Command Prompt without Local Admin rights

Solution: Install from PowerShell with Admin rights (Windows only):

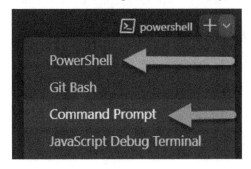

Figure A.4 –Different types of shells from the VS Code Terminal window

Get the node path type as shown in the following code and subsequent figure:

```
npm config get prefix
```

```
TERMINAL    PROBLEMS    OUTPUT    DEBUG CONSOLE

PS D:\repos\wdio> npm config get prefix
C:\Users\qtpmgrossman\AppData\Roaming\npm
PS D:\repos\wdio>
```

Figure A.5 –How to get the path to the node program manager

Add the path to the `path` system variable (Windows only):

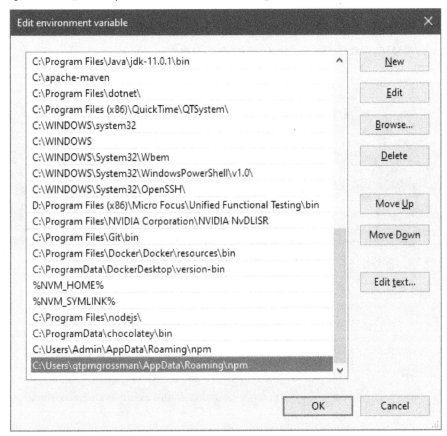

Figure A.6 –Checking the npm path is in the Windows environment variable

Do not forget to restart Visual Studio Code!

Problem: Error: Could not execute "run" due to missing configuration, file "C:\repos\wdio\test\wdio.conf.ts" not found! Would you like to create one?

This error is shown here:

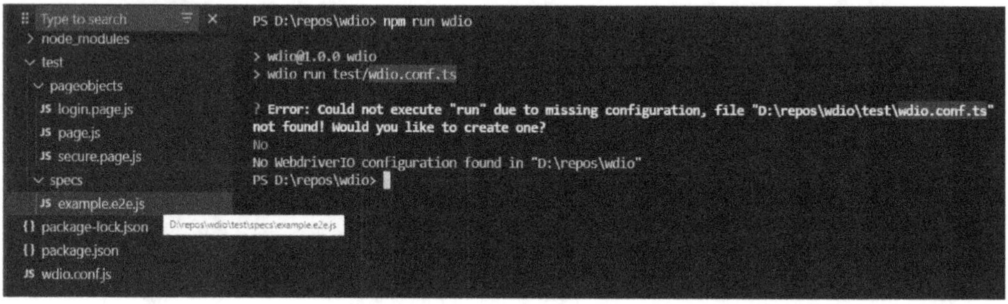

Figure A.7 –TypeScript and JavaScript projects store the wdio.config files in different folders

Cause #1: The wdio.conf.js path is incorrect under scripts in the package.json file.

Solution: Check whether tests are being launched with incorrect paths or extensions:

```
npx wdio run test/wdio.conf.ts
npx wdio run wdio.conf.ts
```

Cause #2: The script is incorrect in the package.json file. In this example, semicolons will generate the error, but double ampersands will not:

```
"allure":
  "wdio run test/wdio.conf.ts; allure generate report -clean; allure open"
```

Solution: Replaced semi-colon with double ampersands

```
"allure":
  "wdio run test/wdio.conf.ts && allure generate report --clean && allure open"
```

Problem: "report does not exist" when running an Allure report

Cause #1: Allure command missing the allure-results path.

Solution: Add the result path.

```
> allure generate report allure-results
```

Cause #2: Allure is not configured in the `package.json` and/or `wdio.conf.ts` files.

Solution: Add Allure to `package` and `wdio.conf.ts`.

Add a report shortcut to the `package.json` file:

```
"report": "wdio run test/wdio.conf.ts && allure generate report
allure-results --clean && allure open"
```

Configure Allure to `reporters`:

```
reporters: ['spec',['allure', {
        outputDir: 'allure-results',
        disableWebdriverStepsReporting: true,
        disableWebdriverScreenshotsReporting: true,
}]],
```

Problem: "[P]lugin "allure" reporter, neither as wdio scoped package "@wdio/allure-reporter" nor as community package "wdio-allure-reporter". Please make sure you have it installed!"

Cause: Allure configuration without first adding the Allure plugin.

Solution: Install Allure:

```
npm install @wdio/allure-reporter --save-dev
yarn add @wdio/allure-reporter
```

Problem: TypeError: Cannot read properties of undefined (reading 'open')

Cause: Failed TypeScript installation. This occurs when you try to access a property or a method on a variable that stores an undefined value.

Solution: Add missing package

```
yarn add package-name
```

Problem: Cannot read properties of undefined (reading 'setWindowSize')

Cause: The `browser` reference in `webdriverio` changed to `Browser` when migrating from CommonJS to ESNext.

Solution: In `wdio.conf.ts`, replace the following:

```
import { browser } from "webdriverio";
```

Problem: A service failed in the 'onPrepare' hookSevereServiceError: Couldn't start Chromedriver: timeout. Please check if port 9515 is in use!

Cause: A JavaScript Debug Shell is stopped at a breakpoint blocking a run from another shell from using the port.

Solution: Stop the running debug shell with Ctrl+C.

Problem: "Cannot find name 'describe'" and underlined in red

Problem: "Cannot find name 'it'"

Problem: "Cannot find name 'expect'. Do you need to install type definitions for a test runner?" but the test still runs.

Cause: The Jasmine type definition is missing or incorrect.

Solution #1: In the `tsconfig.json` file, change `jasmine` to `jasmine-framework` and restart the IDE:

```
"compilerOptions": {
        "types": [
            "@wdio/jasmine-framework"
```

Solution #2: Add the Jasmine type definition to the package and `jasmine` to the compiler options | types in the `tsconfig.json` file:

```
> yarn add @types/jasmine jasmine
```

Cause #2: ESLint or TypeScript Debugger is out of date or disabled.

Solution: Activate or update **Extensions**.

Cause #3: Framework is not installed correctly.

Solution: Reinstall Jasmine, Mocha, or Jest.

Problem: "An import path can only end with a '.ts' extension when 'allowImportingTsExtensions' is enabled. ts(5097)"

Cause: The `tsconfig.json` file must be instructed to allow the importing of files with the `.ts` extension.

Solution: Modify the `tsconfig.json` file:

```
{"compilerOptions":{

"allowImportingTsExtensions": true

"noEmit": true,
...
}}
```

Problem: browser.debug() generates "Failed to read descriptor from node connection: A device attached to the system is not functioning."

Cause: Benign issue.

Solution: Change `logLevel` from `info` to `warn`.

Problem: Element implicitly has an 'any' type because type 'typeof globalThis' has no index signature

Cause: Implicit any type

Solution: Declare the variable type of `: any`.

Problem: Cannot find type definition file for 'jasmine'

Cause: `File type missing`

Solution #1: Install the Node types by running the following commands in the terminal:

```
> yarn add @types/node
> yarn add @types/jasmine
```

Delete the `node-modules` folder and `yarn.lock` and rerun as follows:

```
> yarn install
```

Problem: "Execution of 0 workers" No tests get executed.

Cause: Issue with `capabilities:` in `wdio.config.ts`.

Solution: Make sure capabilities are correctly set:

```
capabilities: [{
    maxInstances: 5
```

Problems: Cannot find name 'browser' and Cannot find name '$'

Cause: The browser and the $ shortcut not added to the class.

Solution: Add browser and $ objects to the class

```
import {browser, $} from wdio/globals
```

Problem: Property 'toBeExisting' does not exist on type

Cause #1: `@wdio/globals` is missing or not listed first in `tsconfig.json` (WDIO version 8+):

```
"types": [
"@wdio/globals",
"jasmine",
        "node",
        "@wdio/jasmine-framework",
        "expect-webdriverio"
    ],
```

Solution #1: Replace @wdio/sync with @wdio/types.

Cause #2: Missing parenthesis:

```
const ASB = switchboardFactory // No Parenthesis
ASB.set("DEBUG", true) // Throws error
```

Solution #2: Add parenthesis:

```
const ASB = switchboardFactory() // No error
ASB.set("DEBUG", true) // No error
```

Problem: ERR! [Error: EACCES: permission denied (Mac OSX)

Cause: npm does not have access rights.

Solution: Give user access rights with these commands:

```
> sudo chown -R $USER /usr/local
```

Problem: ERROR @wdio/selenium-standalone-service: Error: not found: java

Cause: WDIO was installed with selenium-standalone-service but the Java SDK is not installed.

Solution: Install the Java SDK's latest version and restart the shell.

Problem: "ECONNREFUSED 127.0.0.1:9515" a service failed in the 'onPrepare' hook tcp-port-used

Cause #1: This can occur when connecting to a localhost that is not running.

Solution #1: Close the Bash shell and restart.

Solution #2: Try the ZSH shell instead.

Possible cause #2: Secure client connection has disconnected.

Solution: Reconnect to the client application.

Possible cause #3: Out-of-date dependencies.

Solution: Update the dependencies:

```
> npm update
> yarn upgrade
```

Problem: Error: Cannot find module 'C:\Program Files\ nodejs\node_modules\npm\bin\npm-cli.js'

Cause: The `import` statement is missing a file extension:

Solution: Add import statement

```
import loginPage from '../pageobjects/login.page'
```

Problem: "Note: Package.json must be actual JSON, not just JavaScript"

Cause: There is an extra comma (,) at the end of the item list.

Solution: Remove the extra comma at the end of the list.

Problem: Protocol error (Runtime.callFunctionOn) target closed

Cause: Missing `await`. Browser closed during element interaction.

Solution: Add `await` to calls to `async` methods.

Problem: "unexpected token" in tsconfig.json

Cause: Mismatched curly brackets. The entire file may be marked as invalid in VS Code (macOS).

Solution: Fix mismatched brackets and save the file.

Problem: "TypeError: elem[prop] is not a function"

Cause: Mistyped custom method, as in this example:

```
browser .addCommand("clickAdv", async function () {...}
await this.Submit.clickadv(); //Lowercase 'a' in clickAdv
```

Solution: Fix the mistyped method name:

```
await this.Submit.clickAdv();
```

Problem: "ServerServiceError in "onPrepare" Cannot find package 'chromedriver'

Cause: Both `chromedriver` and `wdio-chromedriver-service` are installed.

Solution: Remove the `chromedriver` service from the `package.json` file,

`"chromedriver": "^x.x.x"`, and the `wdio.conf.ts` file:

```
"services": ["chromedriver"]
```

Problem: Property '{functionName}' does not exist on type '({functionType<{argName>}) => void'

Here is an example:

```
Property 'toBeExisting' does not exist on type
'FunctionMatchers<any>'.ts
```

Cause: The expect library is not imported from a source.

Solution: Add import statement

```
import {expect} from 'expect-webdriverio';
```

Problem "Property 'addCommand' does not exist on type 'Browser'." (macOS)

Cause: Benign VS Code error. The code may still work.

Solution: None. If the code works, it can be ignored with the `// @ts-ignore` directive.

Problem: ConfigParser: pattern ./test/specs/**/*.ts did not match any file.

Cause: The `tsconfig` or `wdio.config` files exist in the `/test` folder.

Solution: Move the `tsconfig` and `wdio.config` files to the project root working directory where the `package.json` file resides.

If calling `wdio` from npm, the pattern is relative to the directory from which `package.json` resides.

Make sure that `tsNodeOpts` has the correct `project` path:

```
tsNodeOpts: {
        transpileOnly: true,
        project: './specs/**/*.ts'
    }
```

Problem: Error: Timeout - Async function did not complete within 10000ms (set by jasmine.DEFAULT_TIMEOUT_INTERVAL)

Cause: `wdio.conf.ts` contains `jasmineNodeOpts`.

Solution: Change to `jasmineOpts`.

Problem: Error: Error: Couldn't find page handle

Cause: Jasmine timed out the test

Solution: Set the Jasmine default timeout interval to higher than 10,000:

```
defaultTimeoutInterval: 9_999_999,
```

Problem: This expression is not callable. Type 'void' has no call signatures.ts Are you missing a semicolon?

Cause: Unknown

Solution: Add a semicolon:

```
console.log(`timeout = ${Math.ceil(timeout / 60_000)} min.`);
```

Problem: "File is not a module"

Cause: Missing `export` keyword in the module file:

```
function log(message: any) {…}
```

Solution: Add the `export` keyword:

```
export function log(message: any) {…}
```

Problem: "Couldn't find page handle"

Cause: Browser closed.

Solution: Possibly missing `await` when calling an `async()` method.

Problem: "Error: {pageName} is not defined"

Cause: Loaded page where `class` and `export default new` do not match.

Example: `Error:  SecurePage is not defined`

```
class TyposPage extends Page{
      public get typoText () {
      return $(`//p[contains(text(),'random')]`);
   }
export default new SecurePage();
```

`Solution: change the class and export name to match.`

```
class SecurePage extends Page{
      public get typoText () {
      return $(`//p[contains(text(),'random')]`);
   }
export default new SecurePage();
```

Problem: Argument of type 'ChainablePromiseElement<Element>' is not assignable to parameter of type 'Element'.

Cause: Missing second `await`:

```
await helpers.clickAdv (this.btnTypos);
```

Solution: Add `await` for `Element`:

```
await helpers.clickAdv (await this.btnTypos);
```

Problem: Unable to delete or modify files or folders in the WebdriverIO project

Cause: The project was created with Admin rights, which the user account has not been granted.

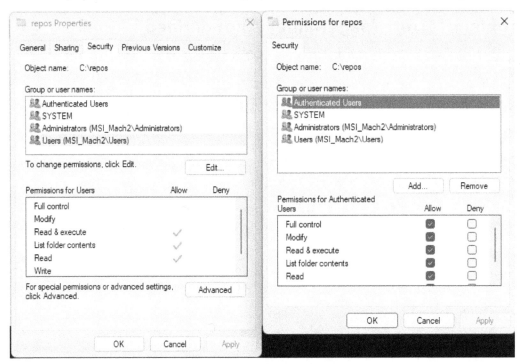

Figure A.8 –Permissions for repos

Solution: Give the user account full control of the file and folders (Windows only).

Problem: EJSONPARSE Unexpected token in JSON while parsing Failed to parse JSON data

Cause: Probably an errant final comma in the `package.json` file.

Solution: Check the `json` file for good formatting.

Problem: A long string of gibberish garbage characters is added to the wdio.config.ts file when running in JavaScript Debug Terminal in Windows

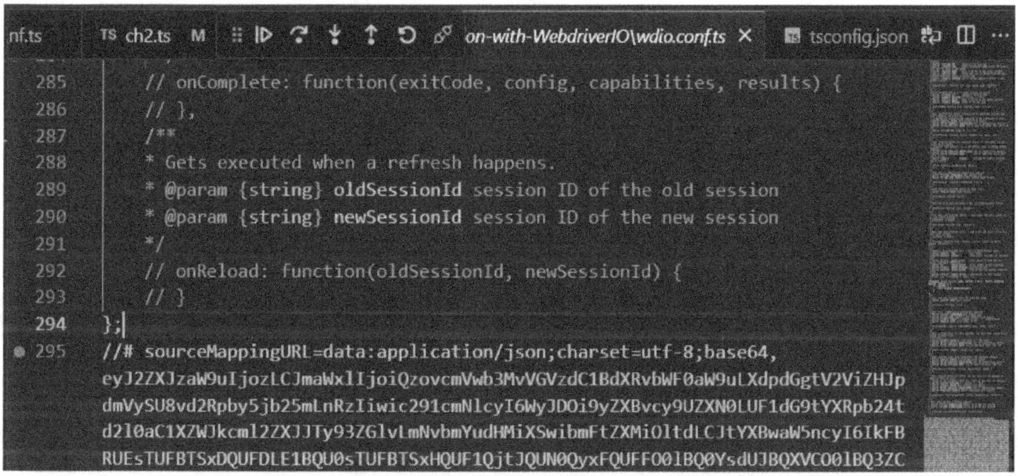

Figure A.9 – Gibberish string of characters

Cause: Global log function declared after use in wdio.config.ts file.

Solution: Move any global functions declarations to the top of the wdio.config.ts file before calls any initial calls.

Caution for Windows: Beware of limitations of long file paths:

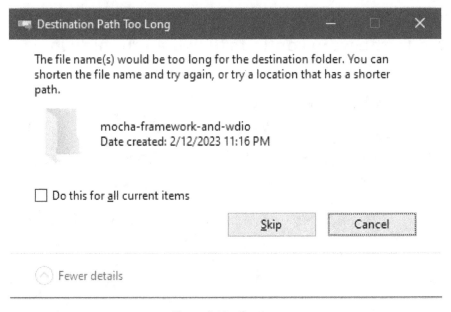

Figure A.10 – Caution

Cause: Deep path to the project:

```
C:\users\darkartswizard\git\github\repos\webdriverio-book-project\
test\wdio.conf.ts
```

Solution: Follow the **KISS** example and **Keep It Simple**:

```
C:\repos\wdio\test\wdio.conf.ts
```

Yarn and Node Package Manager (npm), Node Version Manager (nvm), and Node Package Executor (npx) Shell command cheat sheet

This is how to install yarn and Node.js:

```
> brew install yarn
```

What is the path to Node.js?

```
> npm config get prefix
> yarn global dir
```

This is how to install a new Node version:

```
> nvm install node version.number
```

This is how to change to a different Node version:

```
> nvm use version.number
```

What versions of Node are installed?

```
> nvm list
```

What Node.js, npm, and nvm versions are currently active?

```
> node -v
> npm -v
> nvm version
```

What versions of Node are available? npm has an undocumented show command:

```
> npm show node versions
```

What versions of the WebdriverIO package are available?

```
> npm show webdriverio versions
```

What versions of the Jasmine package are available?

```
> npm show jasmine versions
```

What Node packages are installed and what is extraneous or invalid?

```
> cd path-to-project
> npm list
```

This is how to remove extraneous node packages:

```
> npm prune
> yarn install
```

What node packages are installed at the global level?

```
> npm list -g --depth=0
```

This is how to initialize WebdriverIO:

```
> cd path/to/project
> npm wdio .
> yarn wdio init
```

This is how to explicitly execute all `wdio` tests:

```
> npx wdio run test/wdio.conf.ts
> yarn wdio wdio.conf.ts
```

This is how to implicitly execute a script from the `package.json` file:

```
> npm run wdio
> yarn wdio
```

This is how to explicitly execute one `wdio` TypeScript test:

```
> npx wdio run ./wdio.conf.js --spec example.e2e.ts
> yarn wdio wdio.conf.ts --spec example.e2e.ts
```

Reference links

The successful development of this book owes much to the invaluable contributions of several key resources. These provided the foundational knowledge, insightful perspectives, and essential data required to craft a comprehensive and insightful work that serves as a valuable addition to the field. Their role in the book's creation is indeed pivotal, reflecting the collaborative effort that brought this project to fruition:

- WebdriverIO:

  `https://webdriver.io/`

- yarn:

  `https://classic.yarnpkg.com/en/`

- npm:

  `https://www.npmjs.com/`

- node:

  `https://nodejs.org/en`

- nvm:

  `https://github.com/nvm-sh/nvm/blob/master/README.md`

- Allure:

  `https://allurereport.org/`

- Jenkins:

  `https://www.jenkins.io/download/`

- Lambdatest:

  `https://www.lambdatest.com/`

- Circle CI:

  `https://circleci.com/`

- klassi-js:

  `https://github.com/klassijs/klassi-js`

- SelectorsHub: `https://selectorshub.com/`

- Testing sites:

  - `https://candymapper.com/`
  - `https://candymapperr2.com/`
  - `https://the-internet.herokuapp.com/`
  - `https://www.telerik.com/kendo-react-ui`

- VS Code:

  `https://code.visualstudio.com/`

- IntelliJ/Aqua:

  `https://www.jetbrains.com/`

- Belarc Advisor:

  `https://www.belarc.com/`

Epilogue

The authors extend their warmest wishes to you, the reader, on your transformative journey from being a mere mortal to ascending the ranks as a superhuman automation engineer. We trust that you have not only acquired technical know-how from this book but also relished the exploration of the vibrant world of automation engineering.

The philosophical underpinnings of many ideas presented here can be traced back to the genius of Albert Einstein. His wisdom serves as a constant muse, motivating us to embrace the experimental spirit. Einstein famously advised that one shouldn't fear failure, for every failed experiment is but one step closer to success. His ethos has colored the pages of this book, encouraging you to continually test, adapt, and innovate in your work.

As you move forward on your professional journey, may you embrace the joy of "fooling around and finding out" – that is, of tinkering, experimenting, and sometimes failing – in order to make the unexpected discoveries that lead to true mastery. Our hope is that you will find great joy and a sense of achievement in this ongoing exploration, thereby perpetually enriching your career and personal development.

Here's to your journey of becoming not just proficient but truly extraordinary in the ever-evolving field of automation engineering. Cheers!

"Go Be Productive!" – Paul M. Grossman

"Adapt and thrive, for change is life's true constant" – Larry C. Goddard

Index

Packtpub.com

Subscribe to our online digital library for full access to over 7,000 books and videos, as well as industry leading tools to help you plan your personal development and advance your career. For more information, please visit our website.

Why subscribe?

- Spend less time learning and more time coding with practical eBooks and Videos from over 4,000 industry professionals

- Improve your learning with Skill Plans built especially for you

- Get a free eBook or video every month

- Fully searchable for easy access to vital information

- Copy and paste, print, and bookmark content

Did you know that Packt offers eBook versions of every book published, with PDF and ePub files available? You can upgrade to the eBook version at packtpub.com and as a print book customer, you are entitled to a discount on the eBook copy. Get in touch with us at customercare@packtpub.com for more details.

At www.packtpub.com, you can also read a collection of free technical articles, sign up for a range of free newsletters, and receive exclusive discounts and offers on Packt books and eBooks.

Other Books You May Enjoy

If you enjoyed this book, you may be interested in these other books by Packt:

Test Automation Engineering Handbook

Manikandan Sambamurthy

ISBN: 978-1-80461-549-2

- Gain a solid understanding of test automation
- Understand how automation fits into a test strategy
- Explore essential design patterns for test automation
- Design and implement highly reliable automated tests
- Understand issues and pitfalls when executing test automation
- Discover the commonly used test automation tools/frameworks

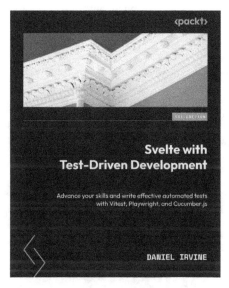

Svelte with Test-Driven Development

Daniel Irvine

ISBN: 978-1-83763-833-8

- Create clear and concise Vitest unit tests helping the implementation of Svelte components
- Use Playwright and Cucumber.js to develop end-to-end tests that simulate user interactions and test the functionality of your application
- Leverage component mocks to isolate and test individual components
- Write unit tests for a range of Svelte framework features
- Explore effective refactoring techniques to keep your Svelte application code and test suites clean
- Build high-quality Svelte applications that are well-tested, performant, and resilient to changes

Packt is searching for authors like you

If you're interested in becoming an author for Packt, please visit `authors.packtpub.com` and apply today. We have worked with thousands of developers and tech professionals, just like you, to help them share their insight with the global tech community. You can make a general application, apply for a specific hot topic that we are recruiting an author for, or submit your own idea.

Share Your Thoughts

Now you've finished *Enhanced Test Automation with WebdriverIO*, we'd love to hear your thoughts! Scan the QR code below to go straight to the Amazon review page for this book and share your feedback or leave a review on the site that you purchased it from.

`https://packt.link/r/1837630186`

Your review is important to us and the tech community and will help us make sure we're delivering excellent quality content.

Download a free PDF copy of this book

Thanks for purchasing this book!

Do you like to read on the go but are unable to carry your print books everywhere? Is your eBook purchase not compatible with the device of your choice?

Don't worry, now with every Packt book you get a DRM-free PDF version of that book at no cost.

Read anywhere, any place, on any device. Search, copy, and paste code from your favorite technical books directly into your application.

The perks don't stop there, you can get exclusive access to discounts, newsletters, and great free content in your inbox daily

Follow these simple steps to get the benefits:

1. Scan the QR code or visit the link below

https://packt.link/free-ebook/978-1-83763-018-9

2. Submit your proof of purchase
3. That's it! We'll send your free PDF and other benefits to your email directly

www.ingramcontent.com/pod-product-compliance
Lightning Source LLC
LaVergne TN
LVHW080113070326
832902LV00015B/2552